Advance Praise

"A much-needed dose of science, evidence and lived experience, *Dr. Junkie* is the antidote to an epidemic of self-defeating prohibition logic."

— David Poses, *The Weight of Air*

Dr. Junkie

Dr. Junkie

*One Man's Story of Addiction and Crime
That Will Challenge Everything You Know
About the War on Drugs*

Benjamin S. Boyce, PhD.

Apprentice
House Press
Loyola University Maryland

First Edition

Casebound ISBN: 978-1-62720-389-0
Paperback ISBN: 978-1-62720-390-6
Ebook ISBN: 978-1-62720-391-3

Printed in the United States of America

Design by Tyler Zorn
Edited by Nicholas Bosi
Promotion by Erin Hurley

Published by Apprentice House Press

Apprentice House Press
Loyola University Maryland
4501 N. Charles Street
Baltimore, MD 21210
410.617.5265
www.ApprenticeHouse.com
info@ApprenticeHouse.com

For Melissa, and everyone else destroyed by the War on Drugs

Contents

Dr. Junkie, What's in a Name?

When I was a kid, I took stuff apart. Toys, utensils, power tools, furniture, you name it; if I didn't understand exactly how it worked, the screws came out. Birthday presents often lasted less than a week. I nearly burned down the house more than once trying to understand fire. At seven, my mom discovered I had disassembled the family toilet. At ten, I worked a set of bolts out of the doors of a middle school where mom taught after-school baton classes, and the custodian couldn't lock up until we brought them back. That pick-it-apart mentality defined my youth.

I have always been intrigued by systems I don't understand. That's because I have what was once called Asperger Syndrome, but is now grouped in with "autism spectrum disorder" (ASD). Everyone experiences it differently, but one of the main symptoms is an inability to ignore things that bother us. Where others might be content with a hum in the audio or a click in the other room (or with not understanding a system like a toilet), people on the autism spectrum often struggle to tune those little things out. They drive us up the wall until we fix them.

I was undiagnosed until my mid-twenties, but once the label was applied, it provided a valuable tool for making sense of my world. Perhaps more importantly, it helped explain what had happened to me, why I had become addicted to mainlining heroin and cocaine, and why I landed on the streets, and eventually in prison, despite having what I thought was a good childhood.

Asperger's would come to bear on my experience with drugs in two distinct ways. First, the underworld drug market is a complex system, hidden from public eyes yet somehow thriving in plain sight. You can't just ask your teacher how much a kilogram of blow costs. Because of the mystery, it is also romantic. Once I learned that chemicals which would alter my consciousness existed, I wanted to understand how those chemicals worked, and how the illegal market which supplied them worked.

Second, the drugs which I was drawn to silenced that cacophony of noise upstairs. They left me calm and focused. They allowed me to channel my energy into projects which had often been overwhelming in the past. Back then I didn't know I was an Aspie—a kid with Asperger Syndrome, and without the diagnosis, I was left with the label of weirdo, rebel, and later in life, criminal. As you will see within the pages of this book, labels define us in ways that both valorize and degrade. They help us to understand what is going on inside our brains and bodies, liberating us with the knowledge that we are not responsible for the way we are wired up. Labels can cage us, both metaphorically and literally, like my label of convicted felon. Or they can open doors, like my label of PhD did for me later in my life, or like the label of autism spectrum did for me in therapy.

Throughout my life I have been given many labels. Some came with privileges and responsibilities. Others came with the baggage of cultural shame. Of all the labels which have been branded onto my name, two have been more powerful than any others in shaping my experiences. One of those labels, junkie, was used to put me in my place, at the bottom of the social hierarchy. The other, doctor, opened doors of opportunity I had never imagined. Both titles were the result of forces entirely outside of my control. Both were thrust upon me as if I had earned them on some sort of equal playing field. Both are inescapable.

I hope this book helps you find your label. And I hope it helps you avoid becoming trapped by it. The goal of life is to get better at living it every day, and that means learning new information about ourselves and the world around us. It is time to get to work.

One final note regarding labels before our journey begins. I am not a neuroscientist, a psychiatrist, or a medical doctor, and even though I will venture into the outer realms of these (and other) fields of study, I will deliberately attempt to stay in my lane, so to speak. However, I *am* a Doctor of Communication. That means I specialize in linking isolated areas of research by providing a brief overview of the ways they are related. My goal is to point out the connections and invite you to learn more, not to fully explicate any theory or evidence which appears within this text. To that end, I will remain shallow and brief in my scientific descriptions. If you want to know more about the data I introduce, follow the footnotes. The professionals I reference are much better at explaining the processes I am outlining, so I will leave the specifics to them.

We have our own work to do.

Introduction

Why War?

"Life as we find it is too hard for us; it entails too much pain, too many disappointments, impossible tasks. We cannot do without palliative remedies." —Sigmund Freud[1]

In the United States, someone is arrested for a drug crime every twenty seconds.[2]

The Centers for Disease Control (CDC) claims that someone else dies from a drug overdose every six minutes.[3]

We can talk about rehab, sober living and 12-step programs all day long, but they don't do addicted people any good if we die or go to prison before we are ready to reduce or halt our drug use. Too many drug users have been buried before they had a chance to consider a different life. They are the victims of the War on Drugs, and, sadly, their deaths were preventable.

Common ground is a great place to start, and it is not hard to find. Those of us who wish to legalize drugs have a lot in common with anti-drug warriors. We *all* want to:

1. Prevent death (from overdose and infection).
2. Reduce disease.
3. Reduce crime.

4. Eliminate underworld drug dealers.
5. Minimize drug use (especially risky use, like injection of street drugs).
6. Save taxpayer money—on prisons, hospitals, police, funerals and treatment.

Despite our common ground, anti-drug warriors and decriminalization proponents remain at odds, each accusing the other of being part of the problem, the reason for the arrests and the cause of death and disease. As our graveyards and prisons fill with prisoners of war, we continue to waste our time bickering over questions that do not matter. The blame is irrelevant during the emergency. Now is the time to fix the problem. Later we can argue over whose fault it was.

In a culture of prohibition, drug users resort to some of the most dangerous and irresponsible behavior imaginable. We ingest polluted drugs purchased on the street from people we do not know. We use our drugs carelessly because there are no instructions or warnings on the packaging. Sometimes there isn't even any packaging. When our drugs run out, we resort to taking whatever we can find to prevent detox, or to medicate our symptoms, even if it causes us physical harm. We don't do these things because they are enjoyable. We do them because the War on Drugs leaves us with no other choice.

We will not be stopped. But if we survive those chapters of our lives when we feel compelled to use drugs in risky ways, we usually grow out of it, and along the way we find better coping mechanisms.[4] We must survive to recover. Dead bodies and caged citizens do not success stories make.

As it stands, shame and stigma have assured little public attention is paid to the plight of addicted people and drug users in the United States. We tough love them out of our houses and communities, then turn away from their suffering. A century into a War on Drugs that has never been devoted to user safety, the lives and wellbeing of addicted people are less valuable than ever before.

As the war wages on, the body-count grows. More than 64,000 deaths have been blamed on drug overdoses every year since 2016.[5] In 2019, that number jumped to nearly 72,000 deaths. And *then* COVID-19 hit. As of this writing, the CDC estimates more than 96,000 drug users died from preventable overdoses during the last year.[6] The government uses these data to defend an irrational, never-ending war against the very people they claim are dying because of the war. The CDC overdose numbers are exaggerated due to inaccurate data collection techniques which I will unpack in Chapter Four, but they still represent a huge problem, and overdose casualties aren't the only victims in this war.

Nearly half of all new federal inmates are headed to prison for drug convictions.[7] Thousands of people are killed or injured every year in accidents related to drug production. Illegal meth labs and basement batches of fentanyl are incentivized by inflated drug prices and lack of access to safe supplies, endangering both manufacturers and their neighbors, whose homes become battlefields.[8] Drug-related crimes continue to claim and maim countless lives every year. And drug users face a host of preventable diseases and injuries because of unclean needles, dangerous additives, fake drugs and infected products.[9] The casualties, victims, refugees and prisoners of war continue to pile up, while the benefits of this ongoing conflict are more difficult than ever to identify.

It gets worse, because US citizens are paying out of both pockets.

While upwards of $180 billion is dumped into our prison-industrial complex every year, we continue to spend another $100 billion on illegal (and untaxed) narcotics.[10] We are dropping loads of cash into a machine designed to prevent us from doing what we clearly love doing: getting high. As our approach makes clear, our real goal is not safety or harm reduction; our real goal is incarceration and permanent social exclusion.[11] We do not help drug users in the United States. We torture them until they die. And since the process lines the pockets of wage workers and private investors, all the more reason to lock them up and throw away the key.

Despite accounting for less than 5% of global population, the United States is the site of more than 25% of the world's reported drug overdose deaths.[12] We are also home to 25% of the world's prisoners.[13] These two statistics are connected. We are a culture in denial, waging an irrational war against the human need for intoxication, and ignoring the bodies left in the wake, either dead or in jail.

It is late, but not too late. The body count will slow the moment we legalize drugs and begin to *love* drug users and addicted people. This is my radical idea, and the goal of this book.

Let's stop killing addicted people and ruining the lives of those who use drugs.

Chapter 1

Supply

"Imagine if the government chased sick people
with diabetes, put a tax on insulin and drove
it into the black market, told doctors they
couldn't treat them...then sent them to jail.
Yet we do practically the same thing every day
in the week to sick people hooked on drugs."
—Billie Holiday[14]

Poison

April something, 2004.

The morning begins with detox. It always does. The pangs
of physical withdrawal act like an alarm clock for addicted people. *Ding.*

My supply is exhausted; nothing remains except a tray full
of burnt spoons and dull hypodermic syringes. Even though I
know it won't help with the detox, I lick a few of the spoons
anyway, smiling as the bitter taste hits my tongue: heroin. But
my joy is fleeting, replaced by the stomach burn and skin itch
of heavy opiate withdrawal. I'm dope sick already, and it's barely
daybreak.

The house is a mess. A few of the hypodermics from the night before are muddy-red, still filled with a mixture of blood and heroin. Intravenous users with tiny veins sometimes struggle to hit one, and to keep the needle in once they do. The razor-sharp tip can poke right through the backside of the vein. Each near-hit allows a bit of blood to flow back into the needle before—*oops, too far*—then back to stabbing. If the search continues for too long, the blood in the needle will begin to clot, plugging up the works and ruining the injection.

If we miss the vein and inject anyway, we risk a nasty infection, but not from the heroin. Our abscesses come from the products added to street drugs by dealers trying to increase their profits.[15] My tiny-veined girlfriend ruined two needles full of dope the previous night before finally finding the sweet spot. I normally set aside enough to get high in the morning, but my extra stash is now dissolved in blood, rotting on the coffee table.

But all is not lost. While the small hole at the end of each needle is clogged, the syringes still contain liquid. With the tangs of detox already scratching at the back of my skull, I get to work.

Blood that has been sitting at room temperature for hours is sort of like chicken noodle soup: some of it is liquid, some of it is chunky, and some of it is a brothy-mixture. Trying to separate solid from liquid, I empty what I can into a spoon and begin to draw the thick mess up into an empty needle through a makeshift screen, a piece of cotton torn from the end of a cigarette filter and rolled into a ball. I hold my breath as nothing happens at first, then the new syringe begins to fill.

I inherited my father's cardiovascular system, bulgy veins and all. On the rare occasion when he would come to church along with the rest of the family, I would soothe my hyperactivity during long sermons by pressing the veins on the back of his hand. They would squirm and bubble under his skin, much like mine do as the bloody needle finds it mark. Funny how things like that come to mind when you're working on a bad idea.

The plunger descends, two bloods become one, and for the next six hours I am free from the torment of detox. In the meantime, I have work to do. The never-ending job of an addicted drug user in the United States is to stay well. The half-life of heroin is half-an-hour.[16] Every thirty minutes half of the drugs in my system will be metabolized into morphine. Another hour or two and the morphine will begin exiting my system.[17] Ticktock and its back to detox.

THAT'S WHERE FRANK comes into the story. We would often meet in public places, like parks or gas stations. He usually showed up riding passenger in an unfamiliar car, or pedaling along on an ancient ten-speed bicycle someone had traded him for a hit years ago.

Frank was my heroin dealer.

A pack of heroin, usually around 1/20th of a gram, was twenty dollars. I needed two or three every day to avoid withdrawal symptoms, and five or six to have a good time. If I didn't have any, I was sick as a dog, but that seldom happened anymore. There was always some way to hustle up a pack or two. If I was desperate enough, I would just steal a stereo out of a car and sell it to the nearest pawn shop.

Today I was meeting Frank at a local gas station. The deal was set up on short notice. I made a call and repeated just a few rehearsed words:

Sup? Three? Where?

The "three" referred to three packs of heroin, each delivered in a neatly folded envelope-shaped package the size of a postage stamp. The quantity of heroin varied, as did the potency, color, aroma, flavor and consistency. Sometimes it was pure white. Sometimes it was grey. Sometimes it was chalky, and other times it was a fine powder. Occasionally a single pack would send me to the moon, and other times it took a few more than normal to really get me high. There was no way to know which packs were potent and which were weak without using them.

Right on time, Frank rode past on his bicycle, motioning for me to follow without bothering to look my direction. We crossed the street to an apartment complex, and I parked near the exit, waiting for the transaction to begin. The dance was typical. Selling heroin will get you locked up for decades, and Frank already had a long criminal record. That meant he had to be hypervigilant, always on the lookout for cops or curious neighborhood watchers.

After a few loops around the parking lot, Frank rode over to my driver's window and grabbed my cash: $60. He gave it a quick look, pocketed it, and then reached down the front of his pants—way down, under his crotch—and pulled out a small plastic baggie containing three packs.

I could smell the shit on them as he handed them through the window. I took them anyway.

Imagine your pharmacist pulling a few pills out of their pants and offering them to you for sale. Your pharmacist would lose their license. The pharmacy would be fined or shut down. And you would never dream of paying for the pills with a smile and a thank-you. The War on Drugs forces millions of addicted people to purchase unsanitary drugs from unregulated dealers in unsafe markets at inflated prices. We inject poisons, blood and shit into our veins because the government refuses to regulate the products we consume. With nowhere else to turn, and the clock always ticking toward detox, we are left at the mercy of our dealers, who are often just as desperate as we are.

FOR A LONG time, I had no idea how Frank decided how much heroin to put into each pack, or why some were weak and others strong. One day I found myself at a dope house with him, waiting for *his* dealer to arrive from a far-away city called Detroit. Once the drop was made, he immediately got to work; he must have forgotten I was still there. So I sat silently, watching, listening, smelling and taking mental notes. You never know when a new hustle will come in handy.

Packs are a simple numbers game: purchase, cut, separate, distribute.

Frank dumped what looked like half-a-bar of bath soap onto the counter—around an ounce of heroin—and began to crush the chunks into fine powder using a crooked butter knife and an ancient credit card. A bottle of baby formula was upended, and equal parts formula-to-heroin were piled up next to each other, then methodically raked back and forth to produce a consistent blend. Within minutes, all that remained was a single pile of tan powder and a lovely-smelling mist floating across the room.

The heroin was now twice its original size, half heroin and half baby formula. Frank would later tell me he used baby formula instead of other options because he liked the way it smelled when it boiled, "like milk in a cup of tea." A stack of lotto slips, free anywhere lottery tickets are sold, had already been ripped into perfect squares and folded loosely into opened envelopes. They were about to be filled with Frank's magic powder, patent pending.

The entire production was completed in less than an hour.

The heroin Frank was cutting had likely been cut more than once already. The US Drug Enforcement Administration (DEA) tests heroin and cocaine confiscated from arrestees and consistently finds that dope purchased on the streets is between 15% and 95% pure (around 34% on average for heroin and 62% for cocaine).[18] There was no way to know what ingredients had already been added to the dope before Frank bought it. The same process carried out on his countertop may have already occurred half-a-dozen times before the dope touched Frank's hands. In a culture of prohibition, like the United States, users are at the mercy of our suppliers, who are, in turn, at the mercy of their suppliers.

Frank was also addicted to opioids. His hustle was his connection. He would purchase two bags of heroin, sell one of them after cutting it with baby formula, and keep the other for personal use. So long as he sold the diluted product before his personal stash ran out, he could avoid detox by ordering another shipment. A ragtag group of desperate detoxers, myself included, ensured that was seldom a problem.

OPIOID WITHDRAWAL CAN be treated with a number of strong pharmaceuticals, including fentanyl, oxycodone, morphine, and even less-potent painkillers like codeine and tramadol. That's because these drugs all work on the same brain structures, known as G protein-coupled receptor sites.[19] The three best known of these sites of action were originally called mu receptors (named after morphine), delta receptors (named after deferens, the tissue where they were first discovered) and kappa receptors (named after the first chemicals known to act on them).[20] Most opioids act primarily on mu receptor sites, and it is here that they work to produce the euphoria and sedation which we experience as relief from pain and anxiety.[21]

These docking ports were once thought of, metaphorically, as keyholes, and the enkephalins or endorphins produced by our bodies which attach to them (or drugs, as the case may be) were thought of as perfectly shaped keys. But as Thomas Hager points out, "it's not quite like that in the body; its maybe more like trying to fit different-shaped wooden pegs into different-shaped holes. You might not be able to put a big square peg into a round hole, but you could loosely fit in a small, square peg."[22] That's why so many opioids produce somewhat similar effects, yet each has its own pharmacological personality, its own shape. A hit of fentanyl, for example, would send me to the moon just as rapidly as a shot of heroin, even when I was highly dependent. Codeine, on the other hand, lost its kick but still took the edge off the worst withdrawal had to throw at me. I would have preferred heroin every time. But in the underworld of illegal drug sales, I often had to take what was available.

What was available was usually unlabeled powder or sticky tar-balls, diluted and polluted on kitchen countertops across the country.[23] It was strong one month and weak the next, cut with baby formula today then talcum powder tomorrow. There was no way to know for sure what I was getting, aside from crossing my fingers and using it. And once I made that terrifying jump, it became easier each time.

As I will discuss in Chapter Two, this lifestyle, which many addicted people find themselves forced into, increases our risk of struggling with substance use disorder, the medical term for addiction.[24] Humans are wired-up to develop addictions to chemicals that show-up in varied doses, at different times of the day, and in different environments. If you want to minimize your chances of becoming addicted to *any* behavior or substance, you should take the *same* dose of the *same* drug at the *same* time in the *same* place using the *same* method of consumption, every day.[25] Swapping chemicals, dosing at different times throughout the day, and changing the potency and/or methods of consumption can all increase the likelihood of addiction and dependency (which are not the same thing).[26] Unfortunately, all of these behaviors are maximized in a culture of prohibition. We couldn't design a system better suited to increase the likelihood and severity of addictions if we tried.

The word addiction is as misunderstood as any other loaded term in our culture. It rolls off the tongue like patriotism, sin, or God, evoking the uncertainty that comes with words which different people define in totally different ways. For the purposes of this book, I will leave it to the experts. *The Diagnostic and Statistical Manual of Mental Disorders (DSM-5)*, which your doctor likely uses to diagnose patients, explains, "The essential feature of a substance use disorder is a cluster of cognitive, behavioral, and physiological symptoms indicating that the individual continues using the substance despite significant substance-related problems."[27] The National Institute on Drug Abuse defines addiction as "characterized by drug craving, seeking, and use that persists even in the face of devastating life consequences."[28] And one of my favorite authors in the field of addiction research, Maia Szalavitz, describes it as "a coping style that becomes maladaptive when the behavior persists despite ongoing negative consequences."[29] In other words, addiction is characterized by the continuation of a behavior (gambling, social media, taking drugs, etc.) despite life-impacting disruptions caused by that behavior. The more severe the life disruptions, the more severe the addiction.[30]

Without the negative life consequences, the behavior isn't an addiction at all. And that's probably more common than you think. More than 80% of all current users of alcohol, heroin, cocaine, methamphetamine, marijuana, or any other drug, do *not* meet the criteria for substance use disorder for one simple reason: our continued behavior has a positive (or neutral) net impact on our lives.[31] If a behavior such as taking a drug or gambling increases your overall quality of life, and if it causes few negative consequences, then it is not an addiction. If a behavior is directly related to negative life consequences (health issues, lost jobs, accidents, etc.), yet you keep doing it anyway, then it is an addiction.

The United States is a country that has always loved drugs. No nation in human history has spent as much time and money on intoxicating substances as we do today.[32] We consume far more cocaine than any other country, and a full 80% of the world's opioids.[33] Whether antidepressants, coffee, sugar, booze, weed, or the so-called hard stuff, most of us are well-acquainted with at least one chemical which we use to better our lives. In addition, there are plenty of behaviors which we use to scratch that itch of boredom or vice, things like church, exercise, gambling, social media, porn, sex or even work. These activities bring us joy, and when we are stuck in the muck of a bad day (or a bad month) we know they are right there waiting for us, promising that same joy if we can set aside a few minutes to partake. Most people who use drugs or enjoy exciting hobbies don't turn fully toward those things and give up on the rest of life. Normally we keep going to work, we regulate our intake to avoid overmedication, or we wait until after we drive to have that drink or smoke that joint. We tend to keep our drug use in its place most of the time. It isn't until things get out of control that the term addiction is appropriate.[34]

Physical dependency is also not enough to classify one's drug use as substance use disorder (addiction).[35] Think about your own life and how you might become uncomfortable or less productive if certain enjoyable activities were no longer available; you are dependent on them to be your best self. More than half of us would detox tomorrow if we stopped drinking coffee.[36] More than 12% of us take antidepressants which should not be discontinued without consulting a doctor, since most cause some sort of dependency.[37] As many as one in eight US citizens are dependent on alcohol.[38] When COVID-19 shut down recreational organizations in 2020, many quickly realized they were somewhat dependent on church, school, book club or the casino. Our lives become less enjoyable and productive when these things suddenly disappear. We may not be addicted to these vices, but we are, to some degree, dependent on them.

Some drugs, like cocaine and methamphetamine, don't cause traditional physical dependency at all. Yet few would use that fact to argue such drugs are never addictive.[39] Dependency and addiction are separate conditions. And while dependency might *drive* addiction at times, it is not synonymous *with* addiction. In fact, sometimes dependency and its accompanying features are a good thing.[40] More on that later.

Life is full of disappointments and failures. Our hobbies and recreational activities make it worth living when things get bad. Throughout our cultural history in the United States, finding the perfect mix of work and play has long been a goal of entrepreneurial capitalists.[41] Drugs are an important piece of that puzzle.

Throughout this book, I will hold to the current definition of addiction as only diagnosable in cases where a behavior leads directly to negative consequences, yet we keep doing it anyway.

As Szalavitz has explained it, "Whether you love a person, a drug, or an intellectual interest, if it is spurring creativity, connection and kindness, it's not an addiction—but if it's making you isolated, dull and mean, it is."[42] Tellingly, within this definition lies a clue to how we might better assist people struggling with addictions. Humans learn to repeat a behavior because it brings us comfort, or because it reduces our anxiety. That's what learning is; we go back to those things which work. But when a behavior no longer results in positive results, yet we don't *learn* to stop using it, we move into the realm of addiction. When we struggle with addiction, something appears to be out of whack with our *learning* circuits, not our morals or our self-control. More on that in Chapter Three.

POWER WORKS MOST visibly in the margins, in the nooks and crannies of a massive system too large to be fully regulated. It is in these spaces that one can easily spot the fruit of policies built to dominate and criminalize culturally stigmatized groups while avoiding the appearance of outright racism or classism. The laws might be colorblind and equitable, but their enforcement is not.

Frank lived in the margins. He had no business address, no identification and no driver's license. He never held a job, and as far as I know, he had no official place of residence. He sold drugs which were not supposed to exist in the United States— heroin, cocaine and street-produced methamphetamine mostly. And if he hustled through the day, he could scrape out enough to pay for his own habit, sometimes just barely. The government had nothing to offer him, aside from a prison cell. And the entire system is built to make him appear to be the bad guy.

The war has never managed to keep drugs off the streets because that was never the ultimate goal. It would end if it was ever won, and we would have to deescalate, which means defund. As we saw (yet again) in 2020, any attempt to defund the police will be met with guttural outcries, both public and political.[43] In addressing his opponent's reluctance to embrace his "End Poverty in California" campaign platform, Upton Sinclair once said, "It is difficult to get a man to understand something when his salary depends on his not understanding it."[44] Those who make their bread off the war machine are unlikely to act contrary to their own interests, for if the war is ever called off, they will lose their careers. The War on Drugs works to incarcerate and criminalize users and dealers, and to ensure those who use and sell drugs are forced to do desperate and dangerous things to make it through the day. The goal is to keep the prisons full and the system permanently expanding.[45]

HEROIN WASN'T THE only show in town. I also used fentanyl and oxycontin when I could afford them. The pharmaceutical stuff was around four-times more expensive than heroin on the streets. I bought my oxycontin from a stay-at-home mom who had been injured at a young age and permanently prescribed high doses. I bought my fentanyl in medical patches from a cancer patient.[46] Neither of these drugs was ever discolored or polluted. They often came straight from the pharmacy, and they were never cut with adulterants or covered in biohazards. Just like Frank, the people who sold them were users themselves, and they were desperately poor, operating in the margins to survive. The money they made from selling drugs was the only thing keeping them afloat. They *needed* me to continue buying their medication, and I *needed* them to keep selling it.

All three drugs (fentanyl, heroin and oxycontin) got me well when I was dope sick, and high when I took enough of them. They could all be crushed and snorted, smoked, or mixed with water (or another solvent) and heated to produce an injectable liquid. And all three continue to produce massive untaxed profits for your friendly neighborhood drug dealer. Yet one is stored and dispensed at a reputable pharmacy, and it can't be contaminated on a dirty countertop without the pill or patch being visibly altered. From my perspective, it was easy to see how legal, regulated drugs were far safer, while street drugs were cheaper and more exciting. That feeling of dangerous excitement that comes from navigating the illegal drug market plays a vital role in the likelihood that we will struggle with addiction.[47]

If I could have avoided all of my dealers by talking to a doctor and receiving daily doses of heroin or oxycontin, I would have opted out of the underworld market altogether. As counterintuitive as it might sound, I also would have been much more likely to stop using of my own accord at some point.[48] But since my pain was more than just physical, it is unlikely I could have found a doctor who would prescribe me opiates; they might well have been risking their career to do so.[49] Our system is designed to ensure that any health care worker who treats a drug user with compassion and common sense won't be in business for very long. They might even be arrested.

So it was back to Frank for me, or to my convalescing friends when my money was right.

It doesn't have to be this way. In fact, it wasn't always this way. In the United States, drugs like cocaine and heroin were once legal and easy to find. Even after they were outlawed, doctors were allowed, and to some degree required, to write prescriptions for addicted people who wished to maintain their addictions with safe supplies.[50] These patients never had to lie about their desire to stop using or their daily consumption patterns. They were encouraged to tell the truth without fear of being cut off. And they could do so indefinitely. Had I been alive prior to the twentieth century, I could have received daily doses of cocaine or heroin prescribed by my doctor for the rest of my life if that's what I wanted to do.[51]

Those days are gone, replaced by shit-stained heroin baggies and blood-filled syringes. The idea of safe supply has become a luxury many cannot afford. The result is a permanently expanding prison system fueled by a never-ending War on Drugs, and a massive body count which continues to grow at increasing rates.

Pure

Humans have always used drugs, and some of us have always struggled with addiction and overdose. We have been trying to get our friends and family members (and ourselves) to stop using drugs with little success ever since we evolved into *homo sapiens*, possibly earlier.[52] And for more than a century, the state has attempted to force those of us who live in the "Land of the Free" to do what our friends and family members never could—*stop using or else!*[53] Yet everything from stigmatization and imprisonment to fear-based lies and death have been unsuccessful in turning humans away from drugs. We will not be denied our narcotics.

Prior to 1877, there was no such thing as the War on Drugs. It wasn't until 1914 that the federal government, following the lead of many states, passed its first laws restricting access to certain chemicals.[54] Before that, thanks in large part to the physical and emotional trauma brought home after the US Civil War, drugs like heroin and cocaine were sold over the counter, without a prescription, and few cared if their neighbors or family members used them.[55]

Since drugs were legal, they were regulated. If one pharmacy sold you a bad product or treated you poorly, you could take your business elsewhere and inform the authorities. More on this pre-prohibition market in Chapter Two. For now, it's enough to recognize that regulation and free-market capitalism make it difficult for dealers to sell polluted products. It's obvious when you think about the drugs we currently regulate and sell. Coffee, sugar, nicotine, pharmaceuticals and alcohol are seldom cut or contaminated in our contemporary markets, and when they are, there are legal and efficient ways to both warn consumers of dangers and make customers whole.[56]

Perhaps the most twisted aspect of the current dealer/user relationship is in the codependence which naturally evolves. Dealers are incentivized to sell polluted products, to keep users hooked, and to price gouge. The dealer *needs* the user to continue using, preferably in permanently increasing doses. His livelihood depends on it. Addicted people, on the other hand, *need* our dealers to continue selling, preferably in larger (and therefore cheaper) quantities. Our well-being depends on it. There is no space in this cycle for treatment or personal growth.

Doctors and medical professionals, who have been cut out of addiction treatment for nearly a century, would encourage users to not only use less, but also to use the safest method of ingestion and the safest pharmaceutical product for their needs. And unlike the street dealers of today, they could do so without worrying about their salaries taking a hit. Doctors get paid whether you leave their office with an anti-biotic or an oxycodone, or even empty-handed.

FRANK WAS NOT a bad guy. He was neither the first nor the last cog in the machine of illegal drug sales, and he was every bit as desperate and trapped as I was. He got his drugs from someone who was far down the production line, and after he sold them to me, I, too would often make a fast buck by flipping a pack, sometimes to others who were going to do the same. The chain of possession is so long it is untraceable.

In fact, in a culture of prohibition, *all* drug users are drug dealers.

The War on Drugs forces the price of illegal chemicals through the roof. As a result, even small quantities of narcotics which might cost pennies to produce are hundreds or even thousands of times more valuable on the streets. With that inflated value comes inflated crime rates, since you can't call the police if someone sticks you up and steals your dope.

Naturally, those lacking accumulated wealth are tempted to engage in illegal activity aimed at making a quick buck, while the rich are buffered from this aspect of the war. They might be arrested and charged with possessing drugs, but they are unlikely to be charged with crimes of desperation, such as those for which I was convicted: petty theft, larceny, retail fraud, drug dealing and identity theft. These are the go-to, quick buck hustles for an addicted person nearing detox. The wealthy are also less likely to be caught selling drugs because they don't need to hustle to support their habit. So long as you have a fat bank account, your addiction will play out much differently than that of the poor person who lives across town. Drugs don't make people commit crimes. Laws restricting drugs make people commit crimes.

Drug users do not get high and then suddenly find ourselves struggling with compulsive urges to rip off our neighbors or assault strangers. The drugs don't make us dream-up plots and schemes to ruin your day. We steal for the same reason that Jean Van Jean stole: we are hungry.[57] In *Les Misérables* it was bread, a basic commodity which had become so expensive that those in need could not afford it, in large part because of laws and policies enacted by the state. Today it is heroin, cocaine, methamphetamine, and other drugs which cost pennies to produce but, due to government restrictions, are both polluted and overpriced on the streets.[58] We steal to get by, not to get rich.

Consider the bloody dope I was shooting up earlier in this chapter. It costs around a thousand dollars to produce a kilogram of pure, uncut heroin, or around a-dollar-per-gram.[59] A pure gram of heroin is enough to get most any addicted person through a day, if not longer. But on the streets of the United States, that same gram costs upwards of $300 (sometimes more) and it might be cut with enough cornstarch or baby formula to look like more than a dozen grams, so it might actually fetch thousands of dollars. At every step of the process, from production to injection, hands are touching and cutting the product, adding their own poisons and scraping out a profit, Frank after Frank.

If drugs were legal and regulated, a gram of heroin or cocaine would cost a few bucks, much of which would go into taxpayer coffers, or the pockets of private business owners. That capital could then be put to work taking care of those whose lives have been most negatively impacted by the War on Drugs. Given the $100 billion US citizens spent on illegal drugs last year alone, that cash could pay for things like housing, treatment, medical care, and even grants for indigent users to pay for their drugs.[60]

You may be scratching your head—*is this guy suggesting the government give people cocaine, methamphetamine and heroin?*

Yes, but not because I want people to use more of these substances. Rather, because I know that we can't stop people from using, and I want to keep them alive so they can do boring things, like pay taxes, build careers, raise kids and get on with their lives. I have no desire to pay for a prison in which to house them for stealing or for dealing to their friends so they can pay for their drugs. I would rather just give them their drugs and cut the dealers out the equation altogether. This plan is the only one I know of that immediately leaves all illegal drug dealers unemployed, because they won't be able to sell their polluted, overpriced dope if it is cheaper and safer just up the block.

While we are at it, I also don't want to pay to have addicted people arrested and prosecuted. I don't want to pay for the army of tanks and soldiers who are responsible for arresting them. I don't want to pay for their funerals or their emergency medical care anymore. I prefer they remain alive and healthy, and I *would* be willing to pay for that. The easiest way to accomplish these goals is to simply give drug users their drugs, and then stick around. Once professional relationships are built, users will know exactly where to go if they ever want treatment or therapy. As it stands, these services, which most addicted people desperately need, are difficult to access without insurance.

This radical idea of decriminalizing and regulating all drugs is not as bizarre as it might sound.

ACROSS THE GLOBE the list of grievances against the War on Drugs has reached a tipping point, and in many areas politicians with nothing to lose have legalized or decriminalized all drugs in moves of desperation. Many of them were surprised when legalization resulted in a massive *reduction* in overdose death, intravenous drug use, diseases related to addiction, and discarded needles in public spaces, like parks and sidewalks.[61] The results have been so astounding that virtually nobody in these areas wants to go back to the way it was before.[62] Portugal, Columbia, Canada, Spain, France, Germany, Ireland,

Switzerland, and the Netherlands have all taken legal action to reduce or eliminate the criminal penalties associated with drug use.[63] And the results have been encouraging, to say the least. Meanwhile, places like the Philippines and the United States have ramped up the war each year, and they have seen nothing for their violent efforts aside from predictable increases in both drug use and overdose.[64]

When drugs are cheap, legal and easy to find, drug users experience a host of odd reactions. Most notably, we often reduce our use, or quit using outright.[65] I describe the results of these social experiments in detail in Chapter Four, but it is easy to understand why this happens. We all know that empathy and love tend to have the effect of bringing people out of their metaphoric shells, but we have long refused to extend this courtesy to our addicted friends and neighbors. Instead, we have wielded the sword of so-called "tough love," pushing users out of our lives and issuing ultimatums that force them to their proverbial "rock bottom."

It is at this so-called "rock bottom" that we addicted people find ourselves behaving terribly, resorting to desperate measures and making critical mistakes, sometimes at the cost of our lives. We discard our drug paraphernalia irresponsibly, leaving pipes and needles in public spaces to avoid arrest. We share equipment, leading to infections and diseases. We poison ourselves with drugs we know are polluted with unsafe chemicals, all while supporting an underworld of crime and violence. Meanwhile, we are always running from the police, who are paid to hunt us down and lock us up.

When cops cannot arrest citizens for having drugs or needles in their pocket, users quit discarding them in local parks and public spaces. When addicted people can get cheap, uncut drugs from clinics, we immediately quit visiting our under-world dealers, who are then forced to find alternative jobs when nobody wants their watered-down dope. The War on Drugs dries up as soon as empathy enters the conversation. The warriors know this. That is why they are so adamant about securing and maintaining cultural legitimacy with a constant echo-chamber of Drug War propaganda, from news to com-mercials to Hollywood cautionary tales. They have convinced many of us that the War on Drugs is something we cannot do without. Yet some drugs have already been removed from the list of enemy combatants, and despite their legality, society has not come crashing down. Just the opposite actually.

Alcohol bootleggers are rare in the United States, even though alcohol is relatively easy to brew. They have a hard time selling their unregulated products in a culture where corporate brewers have century-old reputations to maintain and govern-ment authorities to deal with if they sell consumers bad beer. Growing up in Southwest Michigan, I was often offered home-brewed moonshine, and I sometimes accepted, until a funky batch left me sick for two days. From that point forward I got my liquor from the liquor store. I haven't bought a bad batch since.

This is the most damaging aspect of the War on Drugs, and it is so obvious it hurts. We have been trying to get people to stop using drugs for more than a century, and we have failed. We knew it when the 21st Amendment passed and (re)legalized booze. We knew it in the 1970s when President Nixon doubled down on the War on Drugs, and in the 1980s when President Reagan did the same. Yet we have consistently responded to our frustration at failing to rid the world (or at least our country) of a natural human condition by dumping more money and more guns into the mix. And the results have been as consistent as our approach: little to no reduction in the supply of illegal drugs on our streets, along with an uptick in both addiction and overdose. We have made sure that using drugs is as dangerous as it can possibly be, and that people are more likely than ever to use them anyway.

We can never stop people from using drugs, but we can redirect them. The US could reduce disease contracted from contaminated street drugs by giving users pharmaceuticals instead of street heroin. We could normalize the process of speaking with a doctor every time we want drugs, at which point we might be offered both safer alternatives and various forms of treatment. It sounds counterintuitive, but only because most of us have been indoctrinated with the idea that drug-use is immoral, unethical, and somehow preventable, and that doctors should never prescribe drugs to users for enjoyment or recreation. We have forced addicted people to the streets for treatment of a sort of learning disorder, and we are tricking ourselves into believing that if we just do it long enough, maybe another century or so, we might finally make drugs and those who use them disappear.[66] It is a costly trick we are playing on ourselves, in both money and lives.

Chapter 2

The Price

"The problem with heroin addicts isn't so
much the heroin. It's the lack of heroin. That's
where the stealing, lying and hustling come
in. When junkies have free access to their
drugs, they act like regular people. Better than
regular people really. They share, they cooper-
ate, they look out for each other." –unnamed
heroin user[67]

Expensive

Cocaine had always been a blast, but never more than once
I started injecting it. I stumbled onto the drug the same way
users stumble onto most drugs, at the dope house when I was
purchasing my regular supply. Without licensing requirements
and safety regulations, people who sell narcotics often pick up
an extra batch of this or that, then peddle it to their consumers,
like candy bars in the grocer's checkout aisle. When we take
more than one street drug at a time, the chance of suffering
complications increases, but our dealers are not trained to talk
to us about these risks.[68]

What you experience when you snort cocaine is the come-down of what you experience when you mainline the drug. Injecting cocaine is riding Hunter Thompson's Edge every time.[69] A chill shoots through the vein you hit, flows up to your heart, then up to your neck. The bitter flavor of cocaine hits your tongue hard enough that you would swear you had just dumped a bag of the stuff into your mouth. But before you can really think about how much you are salivating, everything goes dark in your outer-most field of vision, and a tunnel forms. Sometimes it closes entirely for a few seconds.

Your heartbeat appears in your ears, and the world vanishes in a hot rush. For the briefest of free falls, nothing exists except your booming pulse:

Wah-wah. Wah-wah. Wah-wah. Wah-wah.

Your heart feels like it might explode out of your chest, and your brain feels like it is plugged into a wall outlet, but if you can get past the terror, it is a glorious brush with death. I don't suggest anyone do it. There are better ways to get to that place, if indeed you really wish to go.[70]

Within a minute or two after injection, everything will slow down, and from there it is just like snorting cocaine: edgy, anxious, twitchy and paranoid. The action is so short-lived that users often shoot up more and more. We binge for days or even weeks, tuning out the rest of the world. And that's where the problems begin.

As we now know, stimulant drugs like cocaine and meth-amphetamine are best thought of as drugs of desire because they increase the pleasure we derive from doing things like writing, riding go-karts, or talking to strangers about things that are not their business, things that make us say, "oh no…I didn't say *that* last night, did I?"[71] They make these activities more fun by increasing our desire to do them. Drugs like opioids, on the other hand, are drugs of satisfaction. Where cocaine makes you want to go do something satisfying, heroin provides the satisfaction of having done it already.[72] These descriptions are meant to act as generalizations, and everyone who uses drugs will have a somewhat unique experience, but opioids tend to act as drugs of satisfaction and stimulants tend to act as a drugs of desire. [73]

This is part of the reason why heroin will usually satiate even those who are deep into an addiction, whereas cocaine will still affect us, but when used for days on end, it no longer provides the kick it once did.[74] As we all know, unsatisfied desire is only fun until it becomes obvious it will never be satisfied. Anyone who has made it more than a few hours into a righteous cocaine or meth binge knows the feeling of chasing something you will never reach yet feeling compelled to keep chasing it anyway.

When I would take methamphetamine, for example, I would stay up for days or even weeks on end, desperately trying to reach the ultimate buzz I knew I would never quite achieve. Each hit of methamphetamine ramps up the desire circuits in the brains, so it keeps the party going (headed nowhere). But seldom do you find someone who has been up for ten-days-straight shooting heroin, because with one hit you head directly to satisfaction. Drugs of desire don't provide satisfaction so much as they make us long for satisfaction. They make us feel like we are headed somewhere exciting, although we never reach our destination.

ANOTHER WAY TO think about these two classes of drugs forces us to put on our evolutionary-biologist-hats, and to peer back in time to an era when humans were only just humans, slowly being crafted by our environment into creatures perfectly suited to it. Evolution can get complicated, but for our purposes I will stick with a simple definition: evolution is the process by which small differences in our bodies leave some of us more or less suited to survive when everyone else (or most everyone else) dies.[75] Over the course of tens of millions of years, these small changes add up, and species slowly evolve based on environmental demands.[76] Within that simple theory are answers to many of life's most confounding questions. As Theodosius Dobzhansky has suggested, "Nothing in biology makes sense except in light of evolution."[77]

The power of the theory largely credited to Charles Darwin is in the simple fact that your offspring will share some of your traits, but only if they are born. If you die before you can reproduce, well then you won't have any offspring. In nature, this process, called natural selection, usually shows up when a mass extinction event occurs, and a large population of some species of plant or animal dies off.[78] Those who live through the catastrophe are likely to have shared some difference which allowed them to survive when their neighbors died, from starvation, from radiation exposure, from dehydration, or from any other cause. The trigger event is different with every disaster, but the resulting scenario plays out in a reliable way. Only those who are alive can reproduce, and their children often have the same characteristics as their parents, including whatever it was that allowed them to survive when others perished.

It isn't always as catastrophic as starvation or radiation. As we became an ever-more complicated species, all sorts of traits began to pop up which made us either more likely to survive, and therefore to be around to reproduce, or more likely to die, along with our posterity (who would never exist). It could have been anything. Imagine you were born with huge feet and your tribe lived on a mountain. You might survive an attack from predators because you can navigate the rocky hillside, whereas your neighbor with puny feet might fall to their death, and we are right back to who can and who cannot reproduce. Dead people cannot make babies.

Some of these traits are temporary, and they wash out of the population in due time. Imagine a flood comes through the area and dumps some sort of toxic chemical on the soil, leading to a year or two of bad crops which kill some people, while others manage to survive because of an ability to tolerate the toxins. Or perhaps a new virus sweeps through a population and kills many, while others appear to be largely resistant to the worst effects. The characteristics which allowed some to survive would be important for a short time, so they would increase in the surviving population, because parents have babies who share their characteristics, while dead people do not. But those specific traits might not be so important that they stick around for centuries, because chances are no more toxic floods are coming and that virus has run its course.[79] If an immune person wound up with one or two great-grandchildren who were born without immunity, that might not matter, so long as the contaminant is no longer an issue. If those children survive into adulthood, they might have kids of their own who are born without resistance. In these examples, the traits which allowed for survival would likely remain local and temporary, not important enough to spread throughout the entire human population.[80]

Other traits are global and enduring, specifically, those which are so valuable to survival that they spread all the way through a population. One of those traits is the reason we humans are susceptible to addiction at all. It was so successful at helping those who had it survive when others died that it made its way through our entire gene pool; everyone has it.

Human beings are programed from conception to hunt and to feast.[81] Now days it isn't always a literal hunt for an animal, but we all have a drive to achieve something, to get something, to earn something, to prove something: to hunt. And once we achieve, get, earn, or prove it, we have a desire to revel in the glow that will certainly follow: to feast. The two are separate but connected, dependent upon one another. And as Freud taught us, the updated environments in which we live might reduce our *need* to hunt, but they cannot reduce our *desire* to hunt, because we are still the stuff of natural selection handed down to us from our ancestors.[82] Now days we direct those urges and drives toward new and updated activities, things which manage to scratch the same itch in our contemporary cultural setting, where hunting is seldom required and often frowned upon when done for sport. Freud referred to this process of urge-diversion as sublimation, and he believed it plays a huge part in our identity formation.[83] The things we enjoy and the ways we manage to work those things into our lives are, largely, an adaptation to our internalized desire to hunt and then feast.

Of course, sometimes it is a literal hunt, perhaps the best metaphor for understanding the phenomenon because our minds can take us there even if we have never actually been on a hunt. Just thinking about it makes my pulse quicken, and I have no desire to hunt. I simply have something built in that knows intuitively what *hunt* is. And once I get my prey or reach my goal, I have something built in that knows intuitively what *feast* is. They are both pleasant, yet also distinct.

The two states of mind work together. You can easily imagine how one might feel robbed if a hunt was not followed by a feast, because that means the hunt was unsuccessful. You might also think of the different things going on in our bodies during the two states of mind, how our chemical soup of neurotransmitters and hormones is tweaked to aid in accomplishing the two related activities of hunting and feasting. When we are hunting, we remain wide-eyed, fully engaged, heart pounding, dopamine flowing, preoccupied with making the perfect move at just the right second to catch our "prey."[84] When we are feasting, on the other hand, we are calm, satiated, happy, unreserved, relaxed and satisfied, having obtained the object of our desire.[85] This circular process feeds our human need to learn from experience, as each hunt provides new memories of success or failure which inform our future decisions. Hunting and feasting are how we discover new ways of being in the world. They are how we learn about our surroundings in real time, whether we are using drugs or not.

Stimulants, like cocaine and methamphetamine, are drugs of desire, which means they mimic the experience of the hunt.[86] These drugs ramp us up, get us excited and engaged, and we ramble on about unprovable theories, or we scrawl notebooks full of nonsense because we don't have a good target for all of that desire. Worse, there is no goalpost, no prey which can be captured to end the hunt. There is no point during a cocaine session when one realizes, "okay, here is the place I was looking for. I am done now." That is part of the allure these drugs possess; they keep you in the thrill of the moment. That is also one of the greatest dangers associated with amphetamines or cocaine; they keep us stimulated and engaged, trapped in a never-ending hunt with no real target.

BEFORE I GO ANY further, I want to make clear that I am not suggesting people abstain from drugs of the hunt, like methamphetamine or cocaine. I know plenty of people who use that drive to direct their focus, to finish a project in which their interest is waning, or to polish their work without becoming distracted. And they aren't making it up. When taken in controlled, responsible doses, methamphetamine improves cognitive performance, visuospatial perception (our ability to locate objects in 3D space), sustained attention and response speed, and many of these effect persist even when the drug is taken in large doses for extended periods.[87] The long-reported anecdotal evidence of cocaine's creativity-inspiring effects has now been scientifically verified, which comes as no surprise to anyone who has used it to overcome writers block or a project stall out.[88]

These drugs have a slightly different effect on me, largely because of my neuroatypicality (Asperger's), which leaves me over-wired and easily distractable, unable to focus on much of anything when I consume stimulants in high doses. But every so often, when I am struggling to do just that—to let go of my hyper focus on one issue and just enjoy the experience of the hunt, a line of cocaine works wonders to get me there without the hassle of mindful meditation or a two-hour therapy session. Those things are important too, but sometimes there just aren't enough hours in the day. Drugs of the hunt are not good or bad. Neither are drugs of the feast. They are just substances which we should be allowed to utilize for the betterment of our lives.

Back to the hunt and feast. When one becomes addicted to cocaine (especially intravenous injection), one can get stuck in repetitive, exhausting loops that feel as if they will never end.[89] And a hunt that never comes to an end is extremely unsatisfying. Eventually you just want to throw down your weapon and head home disappointed. But you can't do that with cocaine, because the dose has to run its course, and unlike the hunt in the wild, which, when successful, ends in the climax of feast, cocaine ends in a slow descent into unsatisfied boredom.[90]

The half-life of cocaine is around an hour and a half, and even longer if one also consumes alcohol at the same time.[91] It can be hard to sleep and impossible to concentrate on much of anything, and although it doesn't seem to bother some users all that much, it drives many of us up the wall, so much that we decide to keep using cocaine to avoid it.[92] This state of anxious-yet-bored arousal which presents when cocaine begins wearing off isn't what we normally think of as physical withdrawal, but avoiding that restless feeling is a big part of the reason why cocaine users binge. We aren't selfish and hedonistic; we are trying to avoid the boredom of an eight-hour detox.

Drugs of satisfaction, like heroin and benzodiazepines, are the flip side of that coin. These are drugs of the feast. They mimic the calm, happy, already-did-it feeling of having captured your prey and finished the day's work. That's why people act so different while under the influence of these two categories of drugs.

Unlike drugs of desire (drugs that mimic the thrill of the hunt), drugs of satisfaction, like opioids, always worked for me, even when I was at my most unhealthy point of addiction. When my anxiety was bad, they were an effective short-term solution, so long as I could dose freely throughout the day. When I used heroin, oxycontin or fentanyl, I was confident and courageous. And that makes sense. I felt like I had accomplished something complicated, and I was riding on the endorphin rush of self-confidence which follows such a feat. In my brain, that's exactly what was happening.[93]

Here's the problem. I was also clinically depressed, and in my case, depression meant a lack of desire to do, well, anything. I didn't get excited when I thought about books, go karts, a nice meal or a sexual encounter, and it only got worse when I contemplated talking to someone about my problems. My heroin use had increased, sure, but the drug was still getting the job done, as long as I could manage to dose multiple times throughout the day. Aside from a few expensive trips to the bathroom every few hours and long sleeves when my track marks were bad, nothing really changed. I was functional, and my anxiety was bearable, so life was good. I am simplifying the situation, of course, but my point is drugs of satisfaction never interrupted my life; they actually improved things when I used them at reasonable levels, and when I could afford them.

Then I stumbled onto mainlining cocaine. I say stumbled because I didn't even know you could shoot up cocaine until I saw someone else at the dope house do it. Once I started using it that way, it was boring (not to mention expensive) to snort it, so I continued to use it intravenously. There was no pre-use discussion, no education as to what the drug would do to me, and no advice about how to minimize danger. I was handed a needle filled with cloudy dope and given the nod. From there my path was a predictable one. The roller coaster ride and the cocaine-mouth effects that come with injection are an acquired taste, and I quickly developed a thirst for the stuff.

Boredom and some extra cash would lead me to purchase cocaine, and with the lifestyle I was living throughout much of my addiction, including hustles, petty theft and fraud, it was not unusual to wind up with a nice payout every few days. The hunt cycle would begin. I would take a shot, note the explosion on my tongue, then ride the ringer: the clanging of my heartbeat in my ears. The initial punch was followed by a slightly-longer jolt of energy and excitement. It was indeed like being in the middle of a hunt, chasing and sliding my way through the woods behind my prey, and that state of mind was often quite a flip from the depression and anxiety I would be struggling with prior to using.

During the rush, I would make frantic plans to head out and do something the second I wasn't too high to stand up. And then I would come down, lose interest in the plans I had made, and decide to shoot up more cocaine instead. The hunt was stalled, but not over. I always knew another shot would put off detox and fire the hunt back up, if only for a few moments. A few days would pass, and the coke would either stop working or run out, leaving me right back where I started, exhausted to boot. With no doctor or therapist to be found, I would head back to the streets and to the dope spot. That's where I was welcome, any time of day or night. Those were my people.

I didn't use drugs because I was a bad person who wanted to do bad things. I used them because something was wonky—anxiety, depression and Asperger's in my case, and the drugs worked well to treat some of the symptoms I was experiencing. But they also worked to exacerbate some of my other conditions, and purchasing them on the streets added a whole extra layer of problems. Plus, the constant missing piece throughout this story is medical professionals who value the health and well-being of their patients. I needed therapy in combination with drugs. That is the only thing that changed between then and now; I began to value my mental and emotional wellbeing, and to get the help I needed to unpack my psychological baggage.

While cocaine might work great as a short-term treatment for depression, the high blood pressure and anxiety persist long after the pleasure-fueled confidence subsides.[94] It is not a very effective drug for treating these conditions simply because it is so short-acting and high-intensity. And when we use the wrong drugs, or when we use the right drugs in the wrong way, our issues often get worse following a temporary improvement. Without medical professionals involved, we go back to the dope house for the only solution we can find, and once we enter the war zone of illegal drug use, we begin to experience all sorts of additional life problems.

THE BIGGEST ISSUE for poor people who are addicted to drugs is cash. Addiction is expensive. Cocaine on the streets of a Midwest town costs around a hundred dollars per teener, or one-six*teen*th of an ounce. That's just under two grams. Drug users and dealers have an entire vocabulary, a coded form of speech that minimizes illegal statements and identifies us as part of the in-group. Teeners, stems, rigs and packs are contemporary code-words to get into today's speakeasy.

The amount of dope we purchase at any one time, teener to kilo, is important. There is some magic street math involved. If you double your teener purchase and buy an eight ball—that's one-*eighth* of an ounce, or three and a half grams, you can get a deal at $150. As the quantity goes up, the price goes down. A half-ounce (14 grams) can usually be purchased for around $500; an ounce for less than a thousand.[95]

The bulk discount became my lifeline. When things got bad, I could hustle through a day or two by fronting an eight ball, "borrowing" it from Frank with the promise to pay him later, then selling enough of it to break even while keeping a few doses for myself. But that also meant *I* was a drug dealer. At times, according to the laws in my home state of Michigan, I was even a drug *trafficker*. The added anxiety didn't help anything.

Our current cultural beliefs about addiction assure us that drug users and drug dealers are different groups of people. We are told that addicted people have a disease, and that they should be pitied, offered treatment and viewed in an empathetic light. If all goes well, they might even be returned to a social position of conformity: *clean and sobor for 30 days*, as the script goes. Our wrath, per public opinion, ought to be saved for the despised drug dealer, "the despicable dope-pedaling vulture who preys on the weakness of his fellow man," as the architect of the War on Drugs (Harry Anslinger) was known to repeat.[96]

But when our journey into the underworld of addiction began in Chapter One, we quickly realized that *all* drug users are drug dealers. Whenever the substances we use are illegal, purchasing large quantities results in massive discounts. While a single dose might cost twenty dollars, ten doses cost just $100 ($10 each). We are incentivized to purchase our dope in bulk, and to support our habits by supplying our friends and fellow users.

To understand why drugs work like this, we need to start at the beginning of the process. Let's take a look at where drugs begin.

COCAINE IS PRODUCED relatively close to home. If you are doing blow in the United States, chances are it probably came from one of three South American countries: Bolivia, Columbia or Peru.[97] The white powder that many US residents call cocaine is actually a highly processed product: cocaine hydrochloride. Crack is processed a bit differently, but it is essentially the same drug (chemically).[98] It is simply prepared in a fashion that allows it to be heated to a higher temperature without burning up. This means that it can be smoked, lit on fire and vaporized to enter the body through the lungs. It hits harder and faster because of the way it is used, not because of the chemicals it contains. Cocaine is cocaine, regardless of how you consume it.[99]

Cocaine comes from the coca plant, *erythroxylum coca*, a small bush indigenous to the Andes mountains region, where locals have been cultivating it for centuries.[100] The alkaloids contained in the coca leaves have medicinal properties, and chewing the leaves is a cultural tradition that goes back centuries.[101] But the average coca leaf is less than 1% cocaine alkaloid, nowhere near enough to get you high in the sense that we typically think about cocaine.[102]

Local farmers known as *cocaleros* grow small gardens, sometimes less than an acre to avoid the attention of government forces who might destroy their crops.[103] State sponsored programs to replace coca with legal produce have failed for one simple reason which remains the central driving force of the War on Drugs: cash. Farmers who struggle to make ends meet cannot afford to sell bananas or coffee when coca is worth more money. And coca is always worth more money, because the market is designed to ensure plenty of space at the bottom for price increases. Coca farmers are the worst paid of anyone in the cocaine supply chain.[104]

A few times every year, farmers strip the leaves from their bushes and dry them in the sun. The dried leaves are worth between $3 to $12US per kilogram.[105] It takes just over 200 kilograms (around 500 pounds) of coca leaves to produce just one kilogram of cocaine hydrochloride. Those raw leaves will fetch the farmer as little as $600US.[106]

The recipe for cocaine is currently under revision, and a quick look at another drug might help explain why.

Consider the recent social movement in the United States surrounding cannabis, which was effectively illegal in all fifty states until 2012.[107] In the 1990s, the average potency of cannabis in the US was less than four percent tetrahydrocannabinolic acid, better known as THCa.[108] By 2014, the potency had increased to twelve percent, as growers selectively bred the plant for profitability.[109] But in states like Colorado and Washington, where growers could operate without fear of arrest, THCa levels shot up to nearly thirty percent in some strains of cannabis (higher than that if you believe the labels on dispensary products).[110] In the same way that dogs were domesticated from wild breeds in a relatively short period of evolutionary time, and broccoli, kale, cabbage and cauliflower from the same wild-growing weed, drugs are being selectively bred to maximize potency.[111] It's called artificial selection, and it is just like natural selection (evolution), except that humans get to decide which traits are selected for survival. In this case, a high content of cocaine alkaloids means a plant is more likely to survive, and to be planted by farmers looking to maximize their profits.

This process has already happened with coca. If you compare wild varieties of the bush, which contain less than .01% cocaine alkaloid, to domestic varieties, which are already a hundred times more potent, it is clear that selective farming has reduced the amount of coca leaf necessary to produce a batch of cocaine.[112] This process will likely continue, causing the production price to decrease as plant potency increases. On the heels of a hundred years of war, cocaine is getting *cheaper* to produce.

Back to the production process. The raw leaves are no good to investors. They are too bulky for easy transport. Best to reduce the product to a notebook-sized block of cocaine powder. A few chemicals will be necessary, as well as some labor. The resulting kilogram of cocaine will have cost less than $1,000US to produce, and it could easily fit inside a briefcase.[113] There are tens of thousands of individual doses in a single kilogram.

The production process is unregulated and illegal, carried out somewhere in the jungles of Bolivia or in the back yard of a Peruvian farmer. Chemicals such as chlorine, kerosene, cement, sulfuric acid, sodium carbonate, hydrochloric acid and acetone are combined with the chopped leaves to extract the cocaine alkaloids.[114] The leftovers are frequently discarded in local ecosystems and waterways.[115] Sadly, most cocaine purchased in the US is manufactured in this manner. The War on Drugs ensures such damage to wildlife and local communities will continue for the foreseeable future.

The leaves are now a kilogram of cocaine hydrochloride which required just $1,000US to produce, and it can be sold for $2,200US in any major Columbian, Peruvian or Bolivian city.[116] From there, it will likely be smuggled out of the country by entrepreneurs headed to the United States. It increases in value as it worms its way towards the US Heartland. At each stop it grows larger and less pure, as sellers maximize their profits by diluting their product.

We can keep the math short and sweet. Once our kilogram hits the Southern United States, it is worth between $19,000 -$27,000 wholesale.[117] Drive it up north and you can fetch upwards of $30,000, still selling it in bulk.[118] At every step of the process dealers must flip their product as quickly as possible. Decades of our lives are at stake if we are caught trafficking.

The producers and farmers barely scrape out a living.[119] The traffickers make a quick buck by moving product from one location to another. Then the midlevel investors work their magic of multiplication. A main supplier who purchases a kilogram for $30,000 ($30US per gram) might choose to "cut" the drugs, like Frank did with his heroin, turning one kilogram into two (or three, or four) with just a few hours work, adding substances such as powdered milk, baking soda, sucrose, starch, crushed pills, and laundry detergent.[120]

Remember, the DEA's confiscated drugs typically test between 15% and 95% pure (around 62% for cocaine and 34% on for heroin, on average).[121] According to the John Hopkins Center, street drugs are even less predictable than that, ranging from 3%-99% pure.[122] In San Diego, where dope might be expected to be relatively unadulterated given proximity to the Southern Border, street level cocaine tested at around 56% in 2015, and street level heroin tested at around 35%.[123] Our drugs are hardly drugs, yet a gram of "cocaine" on the streets can fetch upwards of $100, even after it has been cut.[124]

The story of heroin is the same. A producer will spend as little as a thousand bucks per kilogram to turn raw opium into heroin hydrochloride.[125] The dope can then be sold in Afghanistan for around $2,4000 per-kilogram, then smuggled into the United States, where it is worth upwards of $70,000 per-kilogram, wholesale. Once it hits the resale market, it can cost up to $300 per-gram on the street (netting $300,000 per kilogram).[126] It, too, has been endlessly cut, but with heroin, the process of diluting the drugs is far more dangerous. With cocaine, dealers use products like Novocain, toothache powder, caffeine or ephedrine to mimic the drug's appearance and effects.[127] Lucky for users, most of the substances used to cut cocaine are not psychoactive, and those which are tend to be less potent than the cocaine they are used to supplement.

With heroin, the cutting process is far more dangerous. Fentanyl(s) and other synthetic opioids, some of which are hundreds of times more potent than street heroin, can be purchased for cheaper prices than heroin and used as cutting agents.[128] The unfortunate consequence, as evidenced by the so-called "opioid epidemic," is that users inadvertently overdose on what they think is normal heroin because they are actually using a drug dozens (or hundreds) of times more potent.[129]

This new market of synthetic opioids is expanding for two reasons. First, the Iron Law of prohibition says that whenever a substance is illegal, the most potent form will become the most common form.[130] Before alcohol prohibition in the United States took effect, the majority of drinkers preferred beer, but afterward they switched to strong spirits.[131] When sports fans want to smuggle booze into an event, they opt for mini shooters instead of bulky cans of (warm) beer. When drug dealers want to move as many doses as they can in a confined area, like the trunk of a car or the cargo area of a plane, they select drugs that can be diluted *after* they reach their destination. They can carry more doses-per-load that way, and smuggling is all about profit.

The second reason for the fentanyl(s) trend has to do with medical uses of opioids. Chemists have been attempting to reduce the time these drugs remain active in the body so they can be administered during outpatient surgery. The goal is to allow doctors to effectively test a patient's level of pain prior to discharge.[132] That combination of powerful and short acting is, ironically, both beneficial and dangerous. Fentanyl is estimated to be a hundred times stronger than morphine.[133] Carfentinal, just one of many updated fentanyl molecules, is estimated to be

100 times stronger than fentanyl.[134] In fact, carfentinal is too strong for most doctors to consider using it on humans. But that doesn't prevent it from making its way into the illegal drug supply. When it is cut into street drugs, the results can be disastrous.[135] I use the term fentanyl(s) because there are multiple forms of these drugs seeping into our heroin supply, a problem which will likely continue for the foreseeable future.

IMAGINE YOU ORDER a light beer, or a glass of wine, and when it shows up it looks and tastes exactly like you expected. But it turns out the bartender accidently swapped out your 4% beer or wine with a new product which is 99.9% alcohol, yet tastes exactly like normal beer or wine. You might take a sip and find it refreshing, then take a larger swig, and maybe even another. If you were drinking normal beer or wine, you would be fine, hardly even buzzed. But if you were drinking something dozens or even hundreds of times stronger, like fentanyl(s) are to heroin, you would already be in big trouble, and once the booze hits your bloodstream, you would probably be headed to the hospital with an overdose. You didn't even use irresponsibly; you only took a few sips. But you consumed a mislabeled, polluted product, and suffered predictable results.

Synthetic drugs are the new frontier of the drug war. They are difficult to detect and often simple to make at home from precursors available at your local grocer and recipes available online.[136] The advent and popularization of 3D molecular printing ensures these drugs will become more popular in coming years; some doctors are already printing drugs in-office.[137] Methamphetamine labs were the first visible wave of this homegrown drug movement in the 1990s, but they were not the last. Currently, the majority of non-pharmaceutical fentanyl(s) purchased on the street are manufactured in small labs in China, then shipped to the United States illegally.[138] As the crackdowns continue, we can expect these labs to make their way stateside in short order, eliminating a step in the process.

Right now, cocaine and heroin are more valuable than gold on the streets of the United States.[139] Right now all of the profits wind up in the pockets of desperate users and underworld drug dealers. And all we have to do if we want it to end is legalize and regulate all drugs.

Cheap

There is a United States that many do not know exists. In this country, drug users are not criminalized and stigmatized. There is a cultural understanding here that the majority of those who use intoxicants never develop addictions, and that even those who do are capable of managing their own affairs.[140] In this Land of the Free, supply is not restricted, and users are never forced to seek out illegal dealers in underworld markets. Instead, edible opium and tinctures, cannabis oils, and cocaine solutions can be purchased at convenience stores without a prescription.[141]

For those who do find themselves struggling with addiction, the treatment in this country is never prison, and addicted people seldom experience shame or social exclusion. Here, the Supreme Court has ruled that when a doctor "gives an addict moderate amounts of the drugs for self-administration in order to relieve conditions incident to addiction," they are just doing their job.[142] Medical care providers give people cocaine and heroin in this country, and they stick around to help them when issues upset their lives. Even when laws restricting access to some drugs begin to pop up, morphine clinics provide a way for addicted people to get their drugs without engaging under-world market.[143]

Contrary to what you might think, most drug users in this country do not end up unemployed, homeless, unhealthy or dead from overdose. Here, three out of four people actively addicted to opiates or cocaine maintain steady jobs, *even when they are using*.[144] A full 22% of self-described "addicts" in this United States are wealthy, while only 6% are poor.[145] There are countless stories of people who take doses of heavy opiates every day, some beginning as early as 12 years old, and they still live productive, fulfilling lives.[146] Addiction here is neither a death sentence nor a debilitating condition; it is just something that happens from time to time, a hassle which is easily remedied, once the doctors and therapists are brought on board.

The reason you have never heard of this United States is because it no longer exists.

The country described above, where drug users and addicted people could live fulfilling lives without fear of arrest and prosecution, has been replaced by a police state where addicted people are shamed by our families and pushed out of our social support groups by faulty notions of tough love. We are hunted down by police who have been co-opted as soldiers in the War on Drugs, then stigmatized by society at large as criminals and sinners. We are offered the label "diseased" as our only alternative to that of "outlaw," and then treated as if the courts had never heard of the disease model. Prosecutors would never lock someone up for drug-related crimes if they really considered addiction to be a disease. Meanwhile we are told that all of this is the fault of the drugs themselves, even as the system continues to extract its pound of flesh as payment for what it claims to consider a medical condition.[147]

Despite what most of us have been told since we were kids, the drugs we consume are not the cause of most of our drug-related problems.[148] It is the environment in which we use these substances that is responsible for the lion's share of damage done.[149] Heroin and cocaine do not cause skin infections or abscesses, but contaminated drugs purchased from unregulated street-level dealers and injected from dirty equipment often do.[150] Getting high on methamphetamine or crack does not naturally land one in prison; it is the laws society upholds and enforces against certain citizens which confine us to cages.[151] Hepatitis and HIV don't come from the drugs that users inject. These diseases plague addicted communities because of our cultural refusal to provide access to legal, clean supplies and paraphernalia.[152] Addicted people are not killing themselves. They are under attack. The US government has decided they ought to be wiped off the face of the Earth.

Prior to drug prohibition, things were different. Heroin and cocaine were legal for non-medical use without a prescription until 1914, and cannabis wasn't effectively outlawed at the federal level until 1937, with the passage of the Marihuana Tax Act, a law with anti-Mexican racism cleverly built into its name.[153] Before these instrumental pieces of legislation, there was no federal War on Drugs, no criminalization of drug use, no burgeoning prison population serving time for possession. There were no cultural campaigns of misinformation fooling us all into believing awful things about drugs and those who use them. Sure, the stereotypes surrounding drug use existed, but they were whispered in hushed corners and hinted at during Sunday brunches. The typical attitude regarding drugs and addiction was live and let live, and at most, drug addiction was seen as a personal vice, similar to alcoholism today.[154]

The products available at the time are fascinating and sometimes unbelievable from our position, a century into a war which has prevented many of us from learning about our cultural history. A brief trip down memory lane might provide some perspective on just how far we have come. The menu is extensive.

Lloyd Manufacturing once sold cocaine pain relief drops, which they advertised with an image of two children playing alongside the caption, "Instantaneous Cure!"[155] Mrs. Winslow's Soothing Syrup was a morphine-based product marketed to parents as a treatment "for children teething."[156] And the contemporary favorite of fear-mongering, anti-drug campaigners, heroin, was sold over the counter by Bayer as a cough suppressant from 1898-1910.[157] For a buck and a half, anyone in the country could order a carrying case from Sears-Roebuck which contained two needles, a syringe, and two vials of heroin.[158] While Sigmund Freud was studying the medicinal properties of cocaine by consuming daily, self-administered doses, Coca-Cola was using the same chemical as an ingredient in its original formula.[159] Throughout the early twentieth century, drug users in the United States could easily and affordably obtain their drugs, they were generally active and employed, and they seldom caused problems for society.[160]

A century later, much has changed. These products are no longer available on store shelves, so we seek them out in unregulated markets. Unless we are extremely wealthy, drugs like cocaine and heroin leave addicted people financially devastated because of the massive markups required to support the web of underworld dealers. The full-time jobs and family connections we had a century ago are gone, replaced with mandatory drug tests and intervention-style tough love when people suspect we might be using. Our social support comes from other struggling users who are shamed into lying to their family and friends at the risk of being tough loved into solitude. Society's stubborn refusal to acknowledge obvious evidence has left us in a bad place. We are doing far worse now than we were a century ago, but drug users have not changed; it is the culture in which we consume our drugs that has been updated in an effort to destroy us. We now live in what Tim Rhodes has called a "Risk Environment" designed to *ensure* drug users encounter dangerous situations and resort to illegal behavior.[161]

We can learn from our history. We can work the double magic of getting addicted people off the streets and eliminating nearly all illegal drug sales, and we can do so virtually overnight, all while reducing the crime associated with both. But first we have to undo the work of a century of state-sponsored brainwashing. First, we have to learn the truth about drugs and the war against them. We must exchange our current system of shame and torture for one that emphasizes love and compassion. This is the real work of ending the War on Drugs.

OURS WAS A clever brainwashing, not the type you notice right away, and so incredibly soothing that it has become a national anthem of sort: *drugs are dangerous and we must war against them.* There is a fragile serenity that arrives on scene, both personally and culturally, when an unpreventable threat is met with force. When COVID-19 began locking people in their homes in 2020, many responded by buying every roll of toilet paper in their immediate vicinity, even though they knew it wouldn't keep them any safer. Humans lose our calm demeanor when we experience loss of control. We do whatever we can to reestablish the illusion as quickly as possible, even if that means purchasing worthless rolls of tissue. But first, before we will act like thoughtless fools, you have to convince us that a threat exists. The recipe for successful illusion has evolved throughout the decades.

The short story is that the War on Drugs began when the US population was growing at an unsustainable pace. Between 1860-1910, it nearly tripled, from 31 million to nearly 93 million.[162] During this time, as in all capitalist societies, business-owners set up shop and peddled their goods to consumers, competing for the customer's buck. One of the most popular services offered was medicine, a field that, like many in the early twentieth century, was fracturing as science challenged tradition. There was no shortage of business, since immigrants arriving from far-away places brought with them immune systems unfamiliar with local germs, and germs unfamiliar with local immune systems. As the population exploded, medicine became a popular field.

The local practitioners who had been passing along potions and spells for centuries did not know much about morphine or cocaine, the fruits of a budding field of science later referred to as Western Medicine. The reductions and pills pharmacists on main street began selling were not on the menu at the local medicine-woman's home. And you couldn't buy the medicine-woman's potions off the pharmacist's shelf, at least not at first. But there were a few differences between the two forms of medical care that could be exploited to establish a monopoly. That's exactly what happened.[163]

The medicine woman had generations of experience. While her remedies may have proven ineffective at times, she was unlikely to prescribe you something that would result in your death.[164] The same could not be said for the pharmacists of the era, some of whom dispensed arsenic as medicine, used lead needles in early versions of hypodermic syringes, practiced bloodletting (controlled bleeding) as panacea treatment, and even injected mercury as a cure for some ailments.[165]

When people got sick, they had two options. They could go to the local medicine-woman, who might give them roots to chew and say a prayer to her god.[166] Or they could go to the pharmacist, who might give them a cure or some poison, depending on the shop. Neither could corner the market for obvious reasons; they were both quacks by contemporary standards.

But one of these groups owned businesses and paid taxes, and their coin bought them the right to make the rules, to lobby, to vote, and most importantly, to define what medicine was and who should be allowed to practice it. The ingredients for prohibition were present. All that remained was for someone to present them with the proper language. That language evolved throughout the early 1900s, after the American Medical Association established its legitimacy, as well as its early goal of ensuring nonwhite people were largely restricted from practicing medicine throughout the era.[167]

By 1877, the United States had been disabused of any illusions that Post-Civil War Reconstruction would prove effective. The old system of race-based slavery, called White Supremacy, had been updated to a new, nicer-looking system called Whiteness, but the end result was the same.[168] White folks held nearly all of the political power, wealth and land in the country, and they therefore made all of the rules.[169] Being humans, the rules they made tended to normalize and protect their way of life, and in so doing, they constructed barriers to the success of others who looked, worshiped or spoke differently than they did.

Jim Crow was part of this new, nicer-looking system called Whiteness. During slavery, black folks had been treated as less than human, relegated to the status of property. During Jim Crow, in an effort to feign social progress, nonwhite people were treated as less-than white. They could give their coin to some white business owners, but they were denied access to many of the mechanisms of privilege which already existed, from infrastructure to Constitutional rights.[170] Jim Crow laws worked, in part, by restricting access to public locations, places like grocery stores, parks, churches, restaurants, voting booths, and pharmacies. Among the rights restricted to all nonwhite people long after slavery supposedly ended in the United States was the right to purchase the same drugs white people could purchase any time they wished.[171] But this prohibition wasn't written into law, at least not at first. It was a marginal rule, unspoken and therefore ripe with power. Since nonwhite people could not enter the pharmacy in most towns, they were restricted from using drugs without anyone needing to write it in law.

This is just one of the many ways that white folks waged psychological warfare on black folks long after slavery ended. When my white great-great-grandmother pulled a muscle, she could take opium or cannabis tincture purchased at the local drug store. When her black neighbors pulled a muscle, they were forced to tough it out. The same pain that was inflicted via the whip during slavery was psychologically inflicted via Jim Crow laws restricting drug access to nonwhite consumers. And it was all in the margins, beneath the law, unwritten and hard to spot. Power is always most visible in the borderlands, in the spaces where we seldom look, and it operates in ways that allow those who wield it to avoid responsibility for their actions.[172] Power is also stubborn; as Frederick Douglas said,

"Power concedes nothing without a demand."[173] The practice of refusing to give black patients the same drugs prescribed to white patients for the same conditions persists to this day.[174] In the United States, black pain is taken less seriously than white pain by medical care providers, and it always has been.[175]

EARLY INTO THE 1900s, the unwritten restrictions regarding nonwhites and drugs lost their effectiveness when companies began offering delivery services through the mail.[176] The heroin-filled syringes and cocaine toothpowders that were once the sole property of white folks suddenly became available to everybody, including nonwhite consumers.[177] It was in this historical moment that political powers harnessed the racial animus which is a persistent feature of the United States, and which desperately needed a release valve amidst the failed attempts at Reconstruction.

As Civil War veterans died of old age, the stereotypes surrounding the drugs which they had been using were suddenly up for debate. What if politicians could convince white folks that cocaine-wine wasn't easing grandpa's discomfort, but was instead corrupting the minds of recently freed black folks? What if the pharmaceutical drug manufacturers could convince voters that cannabis wasn't relieving mother's menstrual cramps, but was instead causing Mexican immigrants to plot against white women? Politicians made their names utilizing white fear of cultural Others to instigate a war against drugs and those who use them. They did so by constructing it as a war against poor people and people of color.[178]

Sure, negative stereotypes about drug users existed prior to the 1900s, but they were held back by the (white) majority's comprehension of who was addicted. So long as it was one of their own, the fear was tamped down; nobody cared if grandpop took a swig to ease his aching back. But once those personal connections passed, the stigma, which had existed all along, could grow, stoked by the winds of power-hungry politicians looking to make a name for themselves.

It isn't hard to diagnose the racism from our vantage point, but it would have been even easier to spot back then, that is, if you had wanted to spot it. Cannabis tincture was for sale across the country when the original Drug Enforcement Administration (The Federal Bureau of Narcotics) began railing against something called marihuana.[179] Those speaking out against this supposedly new drug emphasized the heavy H in the spelling, and it even made its way into the final bill, called the Marihuana Tax Act of 1937.[180] That H was aimed at Mexican immigrants, who were experiencing their own brand of US racism.

The US government played up that fear by telling stories, eagerly printed by the press, in which "marihuana" made people criminally insane, murderous even.[181] Some people from Mexico brought with them the cultural practice of smoking cannabis, whereas white folks tended to drink it in tinctures and patent medicines. That difference allowed the government and news organizations to single out Mexican people without mentioning them; they simply claimed smoking marihuana causes people to lose their minds and attack anyone nearby, including white people.[182] These messages were so powerful that they echoed through time. A century later, Donald Trump began his successful run for US President by reminding a crowd of supporters that people coming here from Mexico are, "…bringing drugs. They're bringing crime. They're rapists."[183] Fear is a powerful motivator. The War on Drugs was a hit.

The same recipe of racism plus fear mongering was used to outlaw other drugs as well. Opium was originally criminalized by associating it with Chinese immigrants who brought with them the cultural practice of smoking, whereas whites in the United States typically consumed our opium via tincture, orally, and our heroin or morphine via injection.[184] So the government began by outlawing so-called opium dens under the accusation that Chinese immigrants using the drug would lose their minds and enact violence on white people, particularly white women.[185] In the early days of the War on Drugs, politicians didn't even try to hide their racism, so it should come as no surprise that it fueled so many pieces of legislation throughout that era.[186] Yet some officials managed to press the bounds of acceptability even in that atmosphere.

The architect of the War on Drugs, a man named Harry Anslinger, was so openly racist that his reputation came to proceed him early into his political career.[187] When Harry was appointed head of the newly created Federal Bureau of Narcotics in 1930, his days were already numbered. His department was created to track down illegal drug and alcohol dealers, but national alcohol prohibition was already a disaster, and the 21st Amendment would be ratified just a few years later, re-legalizing booze nationwide. The country was moving, as a whole, away from drug prohibition, and when Harry's budget was reduced by more than half a million dollars shortly after he took office, it only frustrated him further.[188]

Anslinger had taken the job with ambitions of notoriety, hoping to make history as the man credited with ridding the world of drugs.[189] But with booze no longer illegal, and marijuana not yet outlawed, it seemed he might be relegated to the footnotes of history. His legacy would be laughable; cocaine and heroin prosecution weren't enough to rationalize his department's existence. So he got to work doing what he was best at, stoking up white fear of nonwhite people and gaining political support with red meat racism.[190] It was he who engineered the hard H marihuana legislation, without which his legacy might have been lost to the dustbin of failed political movements.[191] And he didn't stop there.

Cocaine, too, was misrepresented, associated with black folks, specifically black men with the creation of the stereotype "Cocaine Crazed Negroes."[192] Numerous newspapers, including the *New York Times*, used that term in headlines to spread the lie that black men who used cocaine would act violently towards white people, especially white women, developing super-human strength and immunity to bullets.[193] These stories were often provided by Harry and his department, and with the government's stamp of approval mitigating any possible libel claims, newspapers ran the scandalous articles, working to one-up each other. Perhaps Harry's biggest success was his ability to manipulate the system by tricking the media into doing the work for him. He provided high-definition photographs and salacious stories which made it appear that drugs, including marijuana, were a huge problem, and he invited newspapers to use the content free of charge.[194]

The circulation of these stories through respectable media outlets had very real effects. According to numerous versions of the story, the lie that cocaine use would make black men bulletproof led some police departments in Southern towns to exchange their .32 caliber guns for others which fired larger bullets.[195] The myth that black men who use drugs become super-human killers who must be confronted with state-sponsored violence persists to this day, although the list of drugs we pretend causes such nonsense has expanded to include things like PCP and methamphetamine.[196] The political practice of leaning into pre-existing racist stereotypes is not original. It is one of the oldest and most successful tricks in the US political playbook.

THE WAR ON Drugs has always been a war on poor people and people of color. Little has changed in how we enforce drug laws, despite woke-sounding politicians who claim to have empathy for drug users. But a lot has changed in the world since the War on Drugs began, especially the ease and speed with which we can transfer and access information. The lies sewn into the Drug War are no longer iron clad, and most of us know something isn't right with the brain-as-a-fried-egg model.[197] The claims that drugs cause brain damage and chromosome deformity have long since been debunked, and many of the original lies are now as laughable as *Reefer Madness*.[198] We also know that the idea of legalizing and regulating drugs isn't as absurd as we might once have thought, since every country to do so has seen tremendous success from a harm reduction perspective, a term which I will discuss in depth later on, but which means exactly what it sounds like.[199] Ending the War on Drugs would seem to be an obvious choice, and one that is long overdue. Yet the war wages on. What gives?

Malcolm Gladwell's book *The Tipping Point* describes the process through which some phenomena reach a level where they become self-sustaining.[200] You can think of how some companies have managed to survive updates in technology or policy which forced their competition out of business by relying on brand recognition, or by dipping into reserves of cash accumulated over years of successful operations. Once you get a project up and running, it is easier to keep it running than it is to stop and begin anew. The tipping point is that sweet spot when a project, a movement, a system, or an organization becomes self-sustaining, and as such, much more difficult to destroy.

Coca-Cola is a great example. When John Pemberton originally unveiled his crowning achievement, originally called Pemberton's French Wine Coca, it contained large doses of both cocaine and alcohol.[201] But a year after his wine hit the market, his home state of Georgia began passing alcohol prohibition laws a full 30 years before the federal government.[202] This should come as no surprise given Georgia's location in the Heart of the South and the ease of producing alcohol in small, homemade batches. It was one of the first drugs white people couldn't keep away from nonwhite people, so Georgia outlawed it, making it legal to arrest (and according to the 13th Amendment, to enslave) anyone who broke the law.[203]

Again, power worked in the margins, in hard-to-spot yet easy-to-notice ways. You can imagine how simple it would be for an officer to simply ignore white folks who were drinking, while nonwhite people could be singled out and arrested, the real point of the War on Drugs from the start. Many ex-slaves wound up back on the same plantations where their families had been imprisoned, and they were again forced to work as legal slaves under the criminality clause of the 13th Amendment.[204] As always, the appearance of racial progress in the United States was largely a facade.[205]

Back to Pemberton's pet project, the cocaine-lace wine he sold which was slowly outlawed, one chemical at a time. Pemberton survived the upheaval because he had already amassed a group of loyal customers and a bankroll to buffer the switchover. His new product, Coca-Cola, was originally advertised during the temperance movement as an alternative to the sinful vice of alcohol, even though it still contained substantial amounts of cocaine.[206] Coca-Cola later dropped the cocaine from its ingredients years before federal prohibition would have forced their hand, and they survived this cultural update as well. They had reached the tipping point; they had amassed enough cash and earned the loyalty of enough customers to keep them afloat when their competition failed.

Meanwhile, Pemberton continued to find new drugs to replace those outlawed by the government. In the end he settled on caffeine, which itself was almost banned by power-hungry politicians who would have us smuggling coffee beans if they had their way.[207] The case against caffeine went all the way to the Supreme Court, and it nearly ended in the drug being outlawed. We have, unfortunately, long passed the tipping point in the War on Drugs. It is a self-sustaining, permanently expanding, perpetually failing monster, gobbling billions in taxpayer dollars which it uses to attempt the impossible over and over, yielding predictable results.

THIS IS WHERE the conversation gets difficult, because many of us have a stake in this war's continuation, even if we don't realize it. If we stop locking people up for drugs tomorrow, and if we provide safe, legal, cheap drugs to users, we will witness a rapid transformation in our cultural landscape, resulting in many law-abiding people losing their jobs. The tipping point works both ways. The massive lay-offs and the domino effect of lost wages which are certain to follow the war's end might well cause an economic catastrophe if we don't prepare.

Prisons will empty, slowly but surely, as more than 1.5 million annual arrest for drug crimes will no longer occur, along with countless others for crimes committed to get drugs.[208] The revolving door of criminal justice will jam up, as those who usually replace paroled cons will not materialize because we won't be committing "crimes." They won't have to, even if they are desperate for drugs, because those drugs will be cheap and accessible; they might even be free. The massive lay-off of correctional officers will begin shortly after legalization takes effect. Their services simply won't be needed. The same will happen on the streets; law enforcement budgets will dry up and officers will be sent packing because they will not have criminals to arrest once our condition is treated like the learning disorder it is.[209]

Mortuaries will lose business, certainly not the 96,000 deaths per year which the CDC falsely blames on drug overdoses, but some, to be sure.[210] Ambulance services, private security, rehab facilities, private prison stock, food service, inmate-produced products, handcuffs and other equipment, officer training programs, new jail construction, contracts with jail suppliers; all of these markets will suffer losses when we legalize or decriminalize drugs. This has, sadly, turned into a conversation about whose lives and livelihoods matter most: drug users who we label as having a disease but treat like criminals, or law-abiding citizens who have dedicated themselves to what they were told are prideworthy careers.[211]

But what kind of ridiculous choice is this? How on earth did we find ourselves here, where such a debate is not only normal, but unavoidable? Why aren't we talking about how we might reassign ex-warriors to cultural positions where they still find satisfaction and meaning once their services as soldiers are no longer required? We can get ahead of this avalanche and minimize the impact, but not if we keep ignoring the path we are on.

The way we build our society says much about whose lives matter and whose do not. The War on Drugs is coming to an end, one way or another. We can watch hosts of careers evaporate into the smog of cultural obsolescence, or we can get to work building a new economy to replace the one which is about to be decimated. The longer we wait, the harder it will be. But there are ways to minimize the damage.

Chapter 3: The Spot

"Sherlock Holmes took his bottle from the corner of the mantel-piece and his hypodermic syringe from its neat morocco case. With his long, white, nervous fingers he adjusted the delicate needle, and rolled back his left shirt-cuff. For some little time his eyes rested thoughtfully upon the sinewy forearm and wrist all dotted and scarred with innumerable puncture-marks. Finally he thrust the sharp point home, pressed down the tiny piston, and sank back into the velvet-lined arm-chair with a long sigh of satisfaction." –Arthur Conan Doyle[212]

The Dope Spot

The lights were always low at Frank's favorite dope spot, the house with blue walls. He paid the renters a pack or two of heroin every day to use their apartment for a few hours, and during that time he would usually sell dozens more packs to locals like me, poor thieves and beggars who were day-to-day hustling to get our next fix. He wasn't there at the same time every day, but if you stuck around long enough, he was bound to show up.

That's what crack houses are: bored, broke drug users waiting around for their next fix to arrive.

Mixing cocaine and heroin is pretty common in the drug world. Given current understandings of the thrill of the hunt and the thrill of the feast, that makes sense. These drugs complement one another, just like their associated states of hunting and feasting in nature. This two-part cocktail is known as a speedball, and it holds special status as the stereotypical rock bottom of addiction in Hollywood spectacles and gritty autobiographies alike. But it turns out that shooting these two drugs up together from the same needle is tricky, and sometimes impossible.

Heroin and other heavy opiates usually require heat before a user can inject them, and sometimes they have to be prepped with acids just to create an injectable liquid. Powder cocaine and methamphetamine, on the other hand, can both be dissolved without heat, so users just add water, then shoot. And crack (along with some pharmaceutical pills) has to be dissolved with an acid, then mixed with heroin which has already been boiled in water. You can't just mix your speedball up and then cook, because stimulants purchased on the streets can't be heated without risking a reaction in the cutting agents—you might accidently bake the chemicals into a paste which is too thick to inject.[213]

People do use heroin and cocaine (or heroin and methamphetamine) at the same time, but most of us alternate between them, shooting them up in separate needles. While it is technically possible to use an actual speed ball and inject both drugs at the same time from one needle, the process is much more complicated than simply shooting the drugs up one at a time, so most users don't bother. Plus, the drugs kick in separately anyway, the cocaine or (meth)amphetamine first, then the heroin second.[214] So even when we manage the trick of injecting them from a single rig, there isn't some special buzz unique to the mixture. It just saves us a shot later on.

As we saw in Chapters One and Two, the illegality of these drugs allows dealers to sell them for grossly inflated prices. Some of us turn to theft in our desperation for a fix. When I was at the height of my addiction to cocaine, heroin and fentanyl, I lived each day $20 at a time, scraping, begging and scamming my way to that magic mark, and then running to Frank for a pack. The dope would get me just well enough to hit the streets for a few more hours. It became a lifestyle because it was all consuming. There was no time left in the day after I had spent it all hustling to survive.

As time went on, those days of extra cash resulting in adding cocaine to my diet became more and more frequent. I also took other drugs when cocaine or heroin were in short supply. Hunter Thompson once wrote, "once you get locked into a serious drug collection, the tendency is to push it as far as you can go."[215] No joke.

ONCE OUR CULTURAL acceptance of tough love allowed my friends and family to push me away, I hit the streets, and things got predictably worse. I landed with other addicted people in the same boat, and we often wound up sharing criminal charges as well as paraphernalia. The social circles that form in drug-using communities are some of the strongest bonds of our lives. We are all we got. And that becomes a problem when we are desperate, because instead of supporting one another through life goals and positive achievements, we support one another into committing felonies and winding up in prison, or into trying new drugs or new methods for consuming them without doing our homework first.

These relationships become even more important once our social circles cut us off completely. We become self-fulfilling prophecies, tough-loved straight to the streets, then put in desperate positions where we make decisions we would never dream of making if our people had our backs. Humans are social creatures, especially when we are struggling with something heavy, like addiction. It's no surprise that when non-addicted people burn bridges with their drug-using friends, those friends seek out new networks which often result in the very fate we have all been promised awaits anyone who tries some drugs even once: jail, institutions or death.[216] In the heat of addiction, our morals are sometimes compromised, because desperation makes people do things they might not otherwise do. Its more than just criminal activity. We make all sorts of bad decisions.

There were times when I hit the dope house so sick that I couldn't wait to shoot up, so I would use the semi-public bathroom, not far from the image that just popped into your mind. Using your dope in a public space, like the living room, means sharing it, and when we are on a budget, that's not always something we can afford to do. But there is a war going on in the streets, so shooting up indoors is always safer than shooting up outside, where we might be discovered by the police.

It was the same bathroom in every dope spot, arranged differently but stained with the same filth of apathy. The ceiling was always splattered with blood from needles which became clogged. The toilet was always broken and stained, but people kept using it anyway. And the smell was so bad that you had to move fast to avoid retching.

The trick was to draw water directly from the running spigot. If the utilities were disconnected, and they often were, I had to bring my own water or use what was left in the back of the toilet. Other times it was creek water, or even beer, anything to dilute the dope so it would flow through the needle.

Our fear of arrest and our shame at the prospect of being discovered keeps us shooting up in back bedrooms or on the toilet, rushing to avoid suspicion. It's why we hide beneath bridges and behind businesses, getting high in hidden spaces where our overdoses become fatal without anyone noticing. Its why we overuse equipment and hide it in unsanitary locations: our socks and underwear, or, like Frank, inside our bodies. It's why we blow ourselves up making drugs or refining them to a different form when we can't get them any other way. And when we struggle with addiction, it's why we know better than to admit it; the risk of tough love is too great. Instead, we keep it to ourselves until it gets worse, until we become the loathed monster which the public service announcements promised we would become.

YOU MIGHT BE thinking, *not me. I would never shoot up, and certainly not in a dope house bathroom. Toilet water? Seriously?* That's how I feel, and I am the guy who was doing the things described in these stories. What gives? How could I tolerate such filth?

To understand how I wound up there, we need to put our evolutionary-biologist-hats back on and talk about the related processes of tolerance and sensitization. They both show up with substance use of any sort, and they are both decidedly inconvenient for addicted people. But just like the thrill of the hunt and the thrill of the feast, they are biological events which are completely unrelated to drugs throughout most of our lives.

Drugs always take advantage of natural processes in the human body. They are not magic chemicals that turn on secret portions of our brain or unlock feelings we otherwise never experience. They simply provide a different route to the same states of being which are achievable through numerous methods.[217] That's important, because our tendency to push people away when they use drugs is rooted in a belief that they are doing something taboo and dangerous, that they are toying with an off-limits vice sure to land them in rehab or the morgue. The reason we can become addicted to non-chemical things like sex, gambling, work, social media and unhealthy relationships has to do with the naturalness of the processes associated with addiction. Humans experience tolerance and sensitization every day.

Tolerance is exactly what it sounds like; we develop the ability to put up with something. Most of us can drink far more coffee or alcohol as adults than we could as teenagers without becoming physically sick. That's because our bodies have come to recognize these chemicals as effective, safe and expected, so our biochemistry self-adjusts to tolerate higher doses.[218] Tolerance also results in users having to consume more of a drug to achieve the same effects which were once possible with lower doses.[219]

Sensitization is the flip side of that coin; it alerts us to potential dangers with smaller doses of a drug (or a behavior) than we once had to consume to experience things like anxiety, appetite loss or itchy skin.[220] Tolerance is responsible when a heroin user who used to get high all day on two packs eventually needs three, then four, then five. Sensitization is responsible when the paranoia, anxiety and headache which used to show up on day five of a binge now show up on day two. They are two related processes which work to keep us alive by improving our expectations of the world.

Tolerance begins when we encounter something we enjoy. From an evolutionary perspective, your brain has one job which is much more important than any other: staying alive (so you can reproduce).[221] We do this by separating the things we encounter into two main categories, good, safe stuff which we can drop our guard around, and dangerous, exciting, stuff we better pay close attention to if we don't want to wind up dead. These two general categories form the basis for sensitization and tolerance.

When we find a cozy space that becomes predictable or things that makes us feel good, we develop tolerance as a way to make sure we can spend more time with those things. We adjust our expectations and even our biology to ensure that we can consume more the next time without fear of overdosing, or in the case of people or places, to ensure that we can ignore the annoying aspects of someone's personality and hang out with them a little bit longer. Your parents were probably akin to superheroes in your mind when you were a kid, but as you aged, their annoying habits probably became more and more obvious. That's because you were tolerant of them. They were vital to your childhood safety, and you learned to put up with a lot of their annoying quirks without overdosing. Your body became habituated to their presence, and it was easy to ignore negative aspects that might otherwise have annoyed you. But once we reach a certain age, that tolerance begins to wear off, and we are more easily put off by things we once found endearing.

Tolerance is how the exciting becomes ordinary, how the new becomes routine. It is the result of us learning, through repeated exposure, that a particular substance (or behavior, person, environment, etc.) does not require us to raise our guard or to become hyper vigilant. Instead, we learn to run on autopilot. We drive the same route to work and hardly remember the trip, or we wander to the fridge around the same time every evening for a glass of wine. It becomes automatic, and it feels safe and cozy when we do it. That's why we do it, and that's why we develop tolerance.

Sensitization, on the other hand, happens when we encounter a situation or substance we don't enjoy, or when an experience is exciting and, therefore, dangerous from an evolutionary perspective. The earliest example of this for many of us is trauma, when we go through something that is so unpleasant we find ourselves avoiding anything that brings that memory back up, including people and places where we risk a similar or memory-inducing event.[222] We become sensitized, so it takes less of a drug or a behavior to get us to notice negative effects, less input for us to become anxious and concerned. Those who witnessed the Boston Marathon bombing in 2013 or the World Trade Center strikes in 2001 were often jumpy and easily spooked for weeks or even years following the attacks.[223] They were sensitized to a traumatic, dangerous situation. Their bodies were prepared to recognize the same situation a little bit faster the next time it showed up, hopefully allowing a few extra seconds of time to fight or to run away.[224] Sensitization is our body protecting us from what it sees as a threat by making sure we notice it as soon as possible, sometimes before it actually exists, as often happens in the case of trauma.[225]

One of the oddest things about addiction is that it can cause people to become sensitized to certain effects of a drug at the same time as we become tolerant to other effects of the same drug.[226] But the tolerance only works in relationship to the enjoyable, safe effects. We have to consume more to achieve that medicated state of mind which was once easy to reach with much lower doses. Sensitization, on the other hand, applies only to what the body sees as negative effects of a drug, the reactions which we read as dangerous or exciting. We feel anxious or paranoid with much lower doses than it once took to get us there. Tolerance and sensitization play out simultaneously.

THE STORY WE hear over and over about addiction comes from people who tell us it is miserable, that life is unbearable, and that every day is a nightmare. But that description ignores one important piece of the drug debate, the fact that drugs work really well. There are awful parts of addiction, to be sure, and admittedly, the drugs don't always work as well as they once did, especially with excessive use. But nobody would ever become addicted to a drug or a behavior if something about it didn't work to medicate their underlying issue. As odd as it might sound, picking up drugs or gambling or some other vice can be a logical decision in certain situations. We are all humans who only have so many tools at our disposal for navigating a life that can, at times, be depressing even for those who don't struggle with the chronic condition (of depression).

Heroin works great to calm anxiety, reduce symptoms of depression and brush aside shame.[227] Cocaine is an incredible self-confidence booster, and it has been shown to enhance creativity in various ways.[228] Methamphetamine allows people who are otherwise debilitated by ADHD and other conditions (or just lack motivation) to accomplish all sorts of life goals that might otherwise remain unfinished, and when taken in appropriate doses, it has been shown to improve cognitive performance, memory and one's ability to learn.[229] Ketamine and MDMA are proving more effective than months or even years of traditional therapy in treating PTSD, depression, anxiety and trauma.[230] Marijuana has been shown to decrease anxiety, depression and feelings of being overwhelmed, plus it is one of the only drugs effective in combatting the nausea of certain cancer and HIV treatments.[231] Drugs work great. Some just happen to come with effects that can get us into trouble if we aren't prepared, or if we use them irresponsibly.

Addiction is best thought of as a learning disorder, or a developmental disorder; the terms are interchangeable.[232] That might sound odd if you have always heard that addiction is a disease, but the learning disorder model is much more common than you might think.[233] In fact, I don't know of a single theory of addiction (aside from demon possession) that doesn't, at its roots, boil down to mistakes in the process of learning.[234] It is easy to recognize when you think about how learning normally works. We consume a drug or perform a behavior in an attempt to accomplish something; perhaps we are anxious or depressed and looking for relief, or maybe we are hungry and looking for a snack. The action either works or it doesn't. If it works, we remember it, and we learn to use it again in the future, the next time we find ourselves in a similar situation. If it doesn't work, we toss it away and try something different next time; we learn to avoid it.

Sometimes, when a drug or a behavior works incredibly well and comes with few negative consequences, we find ourselves going back to it compulsively, out of sheer habit. Eventually we might not think about it at all. That's how normal learning works. We try something out, like a technique, a pill, a theory or a recipe, and if it works, we learn to keep it on our mental shelf of options for the future. No disorder so far. We find a new grocery store with cheaper prices, or a new route to work with less traffic, or a new sex partner who makes us feel good about life, and we stick with it because we enjoy feeling good. We switch to a benzodiazepine, or we start having a glass of wine before bed, and we notice our quality of sleep improves, so we continue to partake.

But when behaviors don't work, or when they stop working, we should quickly learn to avoid them. When we take a new route to work and wind up stuck in traffic for an hour, we should learn to avoid it in the future. When we try a new recipe and it tastes awful, we should learn to eat something else next time. When we change our medications and have a terrible day, we should consider going back to something that works. With addictions, we don't learn. We keep going back anyway, despite the lack of positive results, or even in the face of negative consequences. That's where the disorder comes in; something is wonky with our normal learning process.

Drugs have plenty of positive effects. If they didn't, we wouldn't use them. Drugs also have plenty of negative effects, and those also show up every time we use, from the first dose to the last. The unpleasant issues don't just pop up *after* we become addicted. They are there all along. We just have an easier time minimizing them and focusing on the positive effects, at least until sensitization begins to do its work.

Shooting cocaine was a blast, but it also came with a huge downside. I had all of the excitement and energy in the world for around ten minutes, but I couldn't do anything with it because I was jittery, fidgety, sweaty and bug-eyed from over-medication. Heroin always caused me uncomfortable constipation, and at times it dulled my senses with repeated doses, even in situations where I would have preferred they remain sharp. Methamphetamine tended to make me itchy and keep me up for days on end, even though I would have preferred to leave those effects behind and only consume the euphoria and energy-causing bits. We notice these negative effects every time we consume drugs, but they don't bother us very much at first.

As we move deeper into addiction, we find ourselves noticing the nasty effects of drugs with smaller doses, while at the same time we have to take more to get the same positive effects which were once possible with much smaller doses. Tolerance takes hold and the drugs stop working, or they stop working as well as the once did, but we keep taking them anyway, relying on our memories of the good times when the positive benefits outweighed the negative. Making matters worse, many addicted people don't have anything else in their lives that has ever worked as well as the drugs do (or did). We have never wanted anything as much as we have wanted those drugs because they make us normal and functional. They allow us to feel the same way some people get to feel every day without ever using drugs.

The learning disorder model focuses on the pivotal point in addiction when the negative effects come to outweigh the positive, yet we don't learn to avoid the behavior in question.[235] Instead, our learning doesn't work right, and we go back to the behavior or chemical even when it doesn't work, or when it causes negative consequences. This has a lot to do with the difference between wanting and liking, another natural biological process which is directly related to addiction.

LEARNING DISORDERS, LIKE addictions, often pop up in adolescence, during our so-called formative years.[236] This is another clue about what is really going on in our bodies. Have you ever seen your favorite childhood snack and bought it, thinking, *this is going to be so good*, only to find yourself incredibly disappointed when it didn't seem anything at all like what you remember? When you are a kid, things just taste better. The cheap snacks, the greasy cheeseburgers and French fries, the sticky taffy and hard-to-chew bubble gum; it's all magic in the mouth of a preteen. If you go back and try these same foods at 40, you will almost certainly find yourself wondering if the recipes have changed. Perhaps they have, but more likely you are just noticing the results of something called pruning.

Between birth and our teenage years, we actually lose around half of our neural connections to reward and pain, the two feelings which direct our decision-making more than any others.[237] When we are babies, everything either terrifies us or blows our minds (or both). Peak-a-boo is life altering for a two-month-old. But the more we experience life, the more we cut off those messages through the process of tolerance, because we realize the things which once excited or terrified us are not all that exciting or terrifying anymore. We form models of the world, and we learn to predict the outcome of situations once seen as exciting, new and novel. Likewise, things that used to amuse us to no end, like a peak-a-booing parent, no longer produce pleasure. They become normal, unexciting, expected and safe as our tolerance for them increases. Pruning is just the natural process through which we begin to record real information about the world around us as we learn what to expect from it.[238]

We become sensitized to other elements of our environment, specifically, the things which we perceive as dangerous or exciting, and it takes less of them to make us anxious or alert. It might have taken a lot of social discipline for you to notice not fitting in as a toddler, but by your adolescent and late teen years, you probably became hypersensitive to social cues, or even outright preoccupied with fitting in. These processes of sensitization and tolerance are no different than what happens with drug use.[239]

Luckily, childhood pruning happens slowly, over the course of years. But when you reach adolescence, things get tricky. Try to imagine a full half of the pleasurable thing you do suddenly failing to bring you pleasure. What if your hobbies, social clubs, television shows, games, events, religious organizations, career achievement, and even spending time with your family suddenly lost their allure, or even became unpleasant. Then take away a number of the remaining activities which still bring you pleasure, but which you have been told you are no longer allowed to derive pleasure from doing, because you are too old to watch cartoons, play with dolls or ride your bicycle all day. It is no wonder that so many of us struggle through our coming-of-age years. Our lives are torn away from us by our biology, and it feels, to some degree, as if our bodies are turning on us.[240]

This process also explains why most of us form some semblance of our adult personality at that point. We hone down things we enjoy and begin to stick to just those that bring us the most pleasure, since it takes more effort to achieve the same joy that once came from playing make-believe or putting on a sock-puppet show. Since we get less reward, and when we get it, it is less intense, we naturally skip the kid toys and coloring books in favor of big-risk, high-reward scenarios. We are trying to get back to that incredible bliss we used to experience all the time with little effort, that space of childlike amusement where everything made us happy, whereas now it feels like nothing does.[241] In the 1990s, we called it teen angst. Mine involved crashing car after car doing silly stunts and driving too fast.[242] It is a natural and unavoidable part of growing up, and like both tolerance and sensitization, it totally sucks.

It is at this point in maturation that humans are most susceptible to developing addictions.[243] But it's not because teenagers are illogical, as much as that might sometimes appear to be the case. Just the opposite actually. When our brains turn against us, robbing us of the pleasure we once received from all sorts of things nearby, we naturally look hard for activities to replace what we feel is missing. And we go big. We take drugs, we practice dangerous sex, and we drive too fast, all to scratch that itch. Many guardians make the problem worse by either ignoring it, or condemning it, pressuring their children to lie about their desires and drives, and worse, their mental health. It is normal to experience a loss of enjoyment as we grow from young children into teenagers, then on to adults. That's what growing up *is*. Maturity is the result of becoming tolerant to some things and sensitized to others, thereby learning what to expect from our environment.

THE PROCESS OF maturation also has a lot to do with dopamine, perhaps the most misunderstood neurotransmitter most of us know nothing about.[244] Dopamine is not synonymous with pleasure. In fact, dopamine tends to *decrease* slightly when we experience many forms of what we would call pleasure.[245] It also sometimes increases in response to painful stimuli, or when we lose a big bet.[246]

Just like most of our knowledge surrounding addiction and drug use, we have settled for a simplified and incorrect version of events that makes it easier to blame addicted people for problems that arise because of our environment, not the drugs we use.[247] It is easy to get angry at a drug user if you believe they are stealing more than their fair share of dopamine while you are forced to get by with your regular ration, especially if you think dopamine is synonymous with pleasure. That story fits well with our cultural shame-based framework. It gives us a way to express our disgust at the user while ignoring cultural barriers dedicated to hindering their success. And that is why we have stuck with this story, even though it is wrong.

Dopamine is not only mislabeled as the pleasure hormone, but it is also pretty uncommon in the human body. Of the 86 billion or so neurons that make up the average human brain, less than one million specialize in dopamine.[248] Worse, we tend to have no idea when those neurons are active. If we were asked to note times throughout the day when our dopamine level spiked, many of us would pick times when it actually waned.[249] As humans, we are constantly telling ourselves a simplified story about the world around us.[250] Visualizing dopamine as synonymous with pleasure is the easiest way to construct a mental image of our brains which aligns with the scraps of knowledge we have been spoon fed by anti-drug commercials and DARE officers. We know just enough to be wrong.

The story we hear most about addiction has taught us, incorrectly, that dopamine shows up after a song ends, after an orgasm, after a piece of chocolate cake and a cigarette.[251] We have learned it is released as a reward. But that's not exactly right, because dopamine isn't just responsible for pleasure. It is largely responsible for desire and motivation, like the desire you feel for a song to play, or the motivation you feel for sex, or the drive to get up and cut that piece of cake, or maybe eat the whole thing.[252]

Dopamine gets us interested and involved in an activity. It peaks during the thrill of the hunt, but it wanes as the activity concludes, during the pleasurable experience known as the thrill of the feast.[253] Dopamine is also vital for learning. It is responsible for the feeling of excitement we sometimes experience when we begin to grasp a new concept, or when we start to work out the solution to a problem before it is given to us.[254] That's how learning works, and that's why dopamine is key to proper learning. It is the driving force behind our desire to get to work.

The current data suggests humans experience two different sorts of pleasure. One of these feelings shows up when dopamine peaks, *before* the song ends, and the other shows up when dopamine wanes, *after* the song ends.[255] That isn't to say dopamine causes the first sort of pleasure, but only that it shows up along with it; as scientists constantly remind us, correlation does not necessarily mean causation.

I like to think of the brain more like a symphony than a series of solos. Dopamine is working alongside a million other processes and chemical reactions, all unfolding in real time to provide the chorus we call consciousness. The two major forms of pleasure we experience tag some of our memories as enjoyable and worth repeating, but they do so in very different ways. Since only one sort of pleasure is accompanied by a spike in dopamine, the other must come from something else entirely unrelated to the fabled neurotransmitter. Dopamine doesn't make us feel good so much as it makes us feel like we are *about to* feel good. It marks upcoming memories as exciting and important before (and while) they happen.

We can think of the two types of pleasure humans experience as learning and having learned, as solving and having solved, as building and having built, or as hunting and feasting. One is intense, involved and direct. This is your dopamine buzz that shows up when you are hunting, not eating, or building, not living in the building, or learning, but have not yet fully learned, or having sex, but not yet climaxed.[256] This is the thrill, the downhill rush on a roller coaster, the in-the-moment excitement of *I am really doing this!* It is during these moments that dopamine assists us in learning things we find interesting by making the memory of a chapter, a lecture or a vacation stand out as pleasurable, and therefore, as memorable.[257] The more pleasurable an experience is, the more memorable it will be down the road. The more memorable something becomes, the more it defines who we are as individuals.

Dopamine highlights important memories; it makes them crisp and remarkable.[258] When a stranger asks you to tell them a story about yourself, chances are a dopamine-fueled memory pops to mind before less exciting stories about watching television or cleaning the house. We define ourselves, in large part, by events which stand out as more important than others. The feeling of dopamine-fueled excitement is vital for classifying memories in order of significance, which is why running from a lion or losing a huge Roulette bet both come with a release of dopamine.[259] They are both examples of the first sort of pleasure humans experience, the dopamine fueled thrill of the hunt. And our ability to retrieve those memories rapidly was vital to our early survival as a species. An extra split second to run from a Tiger is often life or death.

The second form of pleasure we experience involves the feeling of satiation. This is the satisfaction we feel *after* finishing a project, solving a riddle, having an orgasm or riding a roller coaster. Unlike the pleasure produced during the thrill of the hunt, the pleasure of contentment (the thrill of the feast) is not accompanied by a spike in dopamine.[260] Just the opposite, actually.[261]

Like many neural chemicals and processes, dopamine has been greatly misunderstood throughout the last forty years of addiction treatment.[262] Dopamine is a neurotransmitter that causes wanting, desire and interest, resulting in a specific type of pleasure which we all experience in different ways. It shows up with the hunt, it comes with a rush, and in drugs, this is largely mimicked by stimulants like cocaine and methamphetamine.[263] Dopamine appears when we become excited, when we get pumped up and ready to make a memory. And that's important, because excitement motivates us far more than contentment. Wanting something motivates us far more than liking something.[264] The idea of a roof over my head and food in my kitchen is nice; I like it. The idea of skydiving or driving a fast car is motivating; I kind of *want* to do it right now. That wanting is the fruit of dopamine-tagged memories.

That is why dopamine is so vital to learning. Sure, we can learn things we are content with knowing, things we would *like* to learn. And we can muster the motivation to do things that we would *like* to do, such as working forty hours each week to keep that roof over our heads. But it is much easier to seek out information when it is something we *want* to know. It is easier to get up early to read a book or tackle a project when it is something we *want* to accomplish. That wanting *is* dopamine. Drugs of desire, like cocaine and methamphetamine, effect dopamine levels, thereby instigating the feeling of wanting. They activate the thrill of the hunt.[265]

AS MOST ANYONE who has struggled with addictions of any sort can attest, that dopamine spike which activates our wanting circuits shows up not only when we use, but when we perform rituals associated with use.[266] Seeing the pipe; smelling the dope; boiling the heroin; drawing the fix up into the needle—all of these things get us just as high as our drugs when it comes to the rush of dopamine. Just like running from a tiger or riding a roller coaster, these memories are elevated to such an important status that they come to define us.

Those triggers don't disappear when we stop using. We can go years without drugs, then see a house painted the same blue as an old dope spot, or catch a whiff of hand sanitizer that smells like fentanyl, and all the urges come flying back. This is yet another reason to legalize and regulate drugs. The rituals of dopamine activation are minimized when our use involves walking into a heroin clinic and getting high, a short-and-sweet process which replaces the all-encompassing lifestyle of street use. During my addiction, I spent most days preoccupied with dreaming up a hustle, coming up with cash, tracking down someone with dope, setting up a buy, commuting to the location, hiding the dope in the car, creeping back home without getting pulled over, and all of this *before* the in-house rituals of use began.

The routines associated with finding, buying and preparing my drugs became associated with my use; I got high on the entire process, not just the part where I shot up or smoked out. Mentally and emotionally, the events were inseparable. That means I spent the majority of my waking hours emersed in the cycle of want-driven, dopamine-fueled behavior directly aimed at producing and consuming cocaine and heroin (and other drugs). My addiction became a full-time job.

Remember, both sensitization and tolerance amplify anxiety and discomfort, and they both reduce the pleasure we experience when we perform certain activities. But without them we wouldn't be able to distinguish between the mundane and the unknown, between the dangerous and the safe, between comfort and discontent. They are invaluable human tools for making senses of our world. Whenever we encounter something we find exciting or dangerous, we learn to watch for it to show up next time; we become sensitized. And whenever we encounter something we find safe and comfortable, we learn to let our guard down and tolerate larger doses without becoming sick or annoyed. It isn't just drugs. It's life.

Back to my earlier example, from my own experience mainlining cocaine and heroin. The nasty effects of these drugs appeared with lower doses each time I used, because my body read them as dangerous, uncomfortable, exciting and possibly deadly. Once classified as a threat, my brain made adjustments to ensure I would notice these effects as soon as they showed up. But the positive affect which once came easily became more difficult to achieve, since my body was reading it as good, safe and comfortable. The satiation of opioids was seen as a welcome guest, so my body worked to adjust its chemistry as to hardly notice it at all, allowing for larger doses without risking overdose.

The bathroom is perhaps a better example. I would have a hard time standing in a room like that now days, but back then I could overlook the biohazards and shoot street dope into my body, risking as many infections from the bathroom as from the drugs. That's because I read the space as necessary to my survival, as key to my ability to take the drugs I needed without being apprehended. Because of that perception, which, tellingly, was largely outside of my conscious comprehension, I developed a tolerance for a situation that otherwise would have caused me to overdose on disgust and run out of that bathroom, and probably out of that house. Tolerance allows us to put up with a high dose of a substance or a situation which might otherwise cause us to overdose. Our bodies adjust automatically, so long as the behavior or substance is classified by the brain as safe and enjoyable.

In a gross twist, there was also sensitization involved. The process of shooting up was exciting, so I came to associate that filthy space with the increased heartbeat and anticipation of getting ready to slam dope. To this day, the smell of filth is still linked in my mind to memories of mainlining cocaine and heroin in bathrooms like the one at the house with blue walls. The stench of a dirty rest area or a gas station restroom always brings to mind the sights, sounds and smells of dope sizzling in a spoon, the prick of the needle, the *wah-wah* of my heartbeat appearing in my ears.

This is how rituals of use come to be associated with the intoxication of consumption. We wind up feeling the excitement of taking drugs when we seek them out, not just when we take them. And it is all a result of the War on Drugs, because nobody would shoot dope in filthy bathrooms or abandoned allies if not forced to. We could come to associate those same ritualistic feelings with drug clinics and safe injection sites— spaces where we would only go if we were planning on using already. But so long as the War on Drugs persists, our rituals will take place in unsafe spaces, and our bodies will associate all sorts of stimuli with the rush that comes from using.

The same thing happened with the drugs I was taking; tolerance and sensitization worked in unison. Cocaine binges became shorter as I started hitting the wall sooner; the drug would stop working no matter how much I injected. Like most stimulant drugs, cocaine causes an increase in the sort of pleasure associated with learning, building and hunting, but not the sort of pleasure associated with satisfaction. There was no epiphany at the end of the project, no feast at the end of the hunt, and my body began to recognize the futility of the mission just a little bit earlier every time I binged.

But drugs that mimicked the thrill of the feast always worked if I had a large enough dose. The more I relied on stimulant drugs, which mimic the pleasure of chasing a goal but never provide the satisfaction of actually achieving that goal, the more I found myself running smack into that same issue, always heading towards something that I never actually reached. Addiction to cocaine can come to feel like having sex forever without ever reaching orgasm. What a drag.

Researcher Donald Klein proposed this concept for understanding human motivation as iterations of hunting and feasting, of building and having built, of learning, and then understanding, of having sex and the satisfaction that comes after.[267] With his framework, we can think differently about the idea of using heroin and cocaine together, the mysterious, stigmatized speed ball which began this chapter. Both drugs provide a reaction meant to take the place of the other drug's shortcomings. After all, the hunt is a bust if it doesn't end in a feast, and the feast is never as good without the rituals that proceed it during the hunt.

It might sound complicated, but it is actually quite a bit simpler than the normal explanations of drug addiction being a disease of selfishness, or a sin of self-indulgence, excuses that make no sense unless you ignore the more than 80% of drug users who never struggle with addiction at all.[268] Tolerance and sensitization are vital to our understanding of the world and of ourselves. The things we feel comfortable doing and those which make us run the other direction are always and only the result of what we have been through, and ultimately, what our brains do with those memories. Drug use and addiction are no different. There are no magic chemicals involved that non-addicted people don't have in their bodies. There are no genetic differences that make us drug users freaks or weirdos. Just the opposite. We are humans, and humans learn by experience. When something works, we do it more, and when something sucks, we avoid it.

It's the same thing with dopamine; it isn't some magical happy hormone that gets hijacked in addiction. It is a vital part of learning about the world around us, including drugs and other potentially addictive behaviors. The sooner we stop differentiating between them and us, between addicted people and non-addicted people, between what's going on in my brain and what's going on in yours, the sooner we can move toward a perspective of love that will ultimately replace generations of shame. We can do better than tough love and intervention-style power moves.

Tolerance and sensitization are both irritating; users would often prefer they didn't happen at all. And to be sure, if a clever neuroscientist could engineer a drug which prevented them from happening, nobody would *ever* struggle with traditional addiction, because each hit would be like our first. But there is a really good reason for both phenomena. Evolutionarily, they made us more likely to survive once-upon-a-time, so much more likely than our neighbors who didn't have this built-in reaction that the tolerance/sensitization trait is now, like the thrill of the hunt and the thrill of the feast, a species-wide characteristic, a universal trait which everybody alive shares. We actually use it every day to make sense of our world. We become tolerant to things our brain categorizes as safe and good, because, evolutionarily, it was handy for us to be able to consume or abide more of those substance or behavior without risking overdose.

These are the sorts of things that make us happy: coffee, alcohol, and even people who we need in our lives.

We become sensitized to things that pose a threat, or things that we find exciting, and therefore potentially dangerous. This process would have been incredibly helpful 10,000 years ago, when recognizing danger earlier than your friend might prove lifesaving in the event of a predator attack or a rockslide. Once again, dead people can't have babies.

The Drug Clinic

Our current system of drug prohibition works to turn normal, law-abiding citizens into criminals if they find they benefit from a substance that is illegal for them to possess. For me it was marijuana at fifteen years old. I was caught medicating outside of my high school and arrested for disturbing the peace. Given my normal state of mind and the disruptions I often caused in classrooms when not medicated, the charge was a bit ironic. I was using weed to calm down, to focus, and to avoid disrupting the rest of the class.

I was only in jail for an hour that first time. I had enough cash to bond myself out. But that day, as a teenager not yet old enough to drive, I learned that I would always be a target of soldiers funded by taxpayers to track me down and lock me up. *I* was a bad guy!

I didn't feel like a bad guy. I only smoked pot because it had such a positive effect on my quality of life. I was extremely depressed and socially anxious throughout middle school and into high school, until shortly into my 11th grade year, when I tried marijuana and discovered a source of relief. It was the late 1990s, so research and treatment options for depression, anxiety and autism were not what they are today. My neural makeup, which I would only later come to understand as typical Asperger Syndrome, was overwhelming, and I had no idea my daily experience wasn't normal to everyone. Everything was in my field of vision all the time, and I couldn't tune any of it out.[269] Weed made it all manageable, and it wasn't just me who felt that way. Studies later confirmed that more than 85% of people on the autism spectrum report improvement in anxiety, agitation, depression and rage attacks after using cannabis products regularly for just 6-24 months.[270]

That makes sense, given how cannabinoids (the active ingredients in cannabis) work in the body. They are neither traditional drugs of the hunt, nor of the feast, although at times they work to activate both brain circuits. Weed gets us high by taking advantage of our endocannabinoid system, which is generally involved in regulating our states of emotional and biological arousal, everything from hunger to sexual excitement to depression to tissue inflammation.[271] The endocannabinoid system basically keeps the body's other systems in check; it downgrades biological responses like inflammation or pain once they are no longer needed.[272] Researchers have referred to it as a "master regulator in the body," and given its extensive list of duties, that's not an overstatement.[273] Our physical response to any situation, stressful to enjoyable, has a lot to do with our ability to effectively regulate everything in real time, a process which relies on the endocannabinoid system[274]

This also explains why smoking pot was such a valuable tool for me as I navigated adolescence. Like many, my Asperger's symptoms amounted to an over-wiring of sensations, an inability to ignore things that bothered me, and an obsession with avoiding the anxiety that came from experiencing unpredictable circumstances, especially social situations.[275] Smoking pot turned it all down by regulating my emotional reaction to my environment. It was a life saver.

But there was a big problem. Weed laws throughout the 1990s were straight up draconian. I was risking arrest every time I left the house.

To make matters worse, I grew up in a Charismatic Christian home where psychology and medication were, for the most part, considered tools of the devil designed to separate God's people from their maker. And I had absorbed those messages given to me by my church, by my culture, by my school, and by my parents. I *knew* (wrongly) that marijuana was a "gateway drug" which would undoubtably lead to harder drugs, and that using it was a selfish sin worthy of concealment to avoid punishment.

It only took a couple times using cannabis to recognize the shell I had crawled out of, a shell which I hadn't even realized was there before. I thought *everyone* felt like I felt. But once my anxiety melted into a haze of skunky smoke, I discovered a better way of being in the world, a peaceful existence I hadn't before realized was possible. It was like the eye doctor had flipped the lens I needed into the vision machine, and suddenly everything became clear. I hadn't even realized it was out of focus.

After that there was no going back. Sometimes something works so well that you don't care about consequences. At fifteen years old, I had found my panacea, and nobody could tell me otherwise. I finally felt like a normal kid, and I refused to let anyone take that away. I found out later that this experience is not unusual. Many of us find the right drug and suddenly realize we have been missing out on what the rest of the world seems to experience every day, things like happiness, clarity, anxiety-free interactions, and quality of life. Once we experience a few days without disruptions, we naturally want to keep it that way. Responsible drug use improves the quality of many more lives than it disrupts.

After I was arrested for pot, everything changed. That day, I came to understand the necessity of making a sincere and constant attempt to avoid detection if I wanted to stay out of jail. I became preoccupied with dodging the authorities. I learned how to travel lightly and discard illegal items before the police caught up with me, even if that meant throwing them out the window or eating them. I thought of every officer I saw as a threat, rightly so, which made it incredibly difficult to think of them as heroes. Cognitive dissonance is exhausting, so I simply laid down the illusion that the police were good guys. I couldn't have it both ways. They would take me to jail, ransack my car looking for evidence, and ruin my life if they had the chance. In my mind, they were the enemy. And my perspective became my reality.

In the United States, we put every kid or adult who is curious about getting high in the same position. They risk their lives buying drugs on the streets instead of from reputable dealers and medical professionals, and then they risk their freedom and their reputation by possessing whatever their substance of choice might be. We couldn't design a system better suited to turn law-abiding citizens into indignant criminals.

IT DOESN'T HAVE to be this way. Users could get their drugs from clinics run by the state, places where medical professionals encourage us to seek appropriate therapy and treatment before handing over our next dose. These clinics already exist, although they are seldom discussed and often stigmatized. Some of them even allow people to come in and use their own drugs, and they keep an eye on users in case they overdose, offering a friendly ear in the meantime. Such services have many names, but they are best known as safe use sites.[276] They have existed throughout the world for more than twenty years, and there has never been an overdose death reported at a single one of them.[277]

These facilities also exist in the United States, but they are illegal as of this writing, so they are nameless and unspoken spaces where drug users take care of one another.[278] I spent time in some of these sites back in the early 2000s, and more than once I saw someone who would likely have died if not for the intervention of others who considered themselves medical professionals. The heroes who hang out with drug users all day become underworld den mothers of a sort. They suggest safe use practices. They offer clean needles or bleach for sanitizing the ones we have. And most importantly, they keep a supply of Naloxone (brand name Narcan), a drug that can immediately reverse opioid overdose and shock users into immediate detox.[279]

Naloxone has been available since the early 1970s, but to this day many law enforcement agencies prohibit their deputies from carrying it under the faulty logic that users might overdose less often if they believe they won't be revived.[280] As gross as the bathroom in the house with blue walls might have been, it was safer to overdose there than it was to overdose outside, in a car, in an alley, in a back bedroom, or anywhere else. No one in the dope house would take me to jail or let me die. Outside those walls, both were likely.

The attitude of caring about one's fellow human is not unusual in the drug world. The few US safe use sites covered by journalists show the same results as legal sites abroad: zero overdose deaths even amidst a national uptick in overdose cases.[281] It is long past time to make these facilities official, and a few cities and states have already made moves and even passed preliminary legislation to make that happen.[282] But they have been repeatedly shot down by legislators responding to voter apprehensions that such facilities might *cause* addiction.

It is worth considering, briefly, the absurdity of such an accusation. Right now in the United States, when we think about illegal drug use, we tend to envision a dreamy world where people are always addicted, frequently they overdose, and once in a great while they overcome their personal shortcomings (only) through sobriety.[283] Our imaginations are largely resigned to Hollywood representation and news reports, because most of us don't spend much time in actual dope houses or illegal drug labs. We might instead think of Leonardo DiCaprio in *The Wolf of Wallstreet*, Robert Downing Jr. in *Less than Zero*, Tupac in *Gridlock'd*, or Zendaya Coleman in *Euphoria*. We use those representations to make sense of the War on Drugs.[284] They are, after all, the only representations most people know. And herein lies the problem.

Mainstream media echoes the public service announcements and DARE officers of the 1990s. On television we see a world were sometimes drug users have a blast, but they are out of control and should be stopped for the good of society before the inevitable disaster occurs. More often we see a world where drug users descend into immorality, physical illness and even death, all as a direct result of the drugs they are consuming.[285] But television is not reality; it is a snapshot selected for its entertainment value, a single perspective of a short moment in time, tweaked to emphasize spectacle.[286] Of course producers focus on the scary or the exciting, the sensational elements that keep viewers tuned in.[287] We don't want to watch a story about a factory-floor worker who takes his Vicodin every morning and then goes about his business; what a drag. It doesn't matter if that's the reality most drug users experience. Hollywood is a wicked lens through which to view drug use, but we don't have any other options so long as safe use sites remain illegal.

When these facilities are allowed to open, things will change. We will suddenly have a real space, a legitimate reality to consider alongside our Hollywood tripe, and there is nothing romantic or exciting about watching people shuffle in and out of a heroin clinic all day. It is excruciatingly normal; our lives are just like your lives. Safe use sites would not romanticize drug use or increase addiction. If one were already opened up the street right now, would you drop everything and start using heroin? Probably not. And even if you would, whatever you are struggling with that has you considering heroin would be better managed by medical professionals, therapists and counselors than by desperate street dealers. As a vital bonus, safe use sites force social interactions with doctors, substance abuse counselors, therapists and people who are in recovery, all important connections to have if one ever decides to reduce or halt their drug use.

Such facilities would allow people to see the real world of drug use and addiction, and in so doing, they would abolish the fantasy of romance and attraction which currently comprises our beliefs about what drug use looks like. Safe use sites make kids *less* likely to use drugs by removing the romance of the unknow. They also add a safeguard entirely absent from the current drug market, one already built into legal, regulated drug sales: buyer age verification.[288]

This is more than just conjecture. In 1976, when the Dutch government stopped prosecuting cannabis possession and allowed it to be sold in shops where other drugs are not available, they immediately noticed a reduction in the amount of people using other drugs.[289] It didn't take researchers long to make the connection; when dealers can't offer cocaine or heroin to customers who only want marijuana, less people wind up using these other drugs. When the dopamine-hunt rush is underway, and we pop into our dope spot to grab some marijuana, we are primed to say yes to anything we are offered, even if we normally wouldn't be interested. But this never happens at the beer store or the marijuana dispensary, because these shops don't have additional drugs to tempt us. Regulation and licensing requirements *reduce* drug use.

So does the logical endpoint of regulation, the safe use site. In England, Dr. John Marks prescribed heroin to patients at the Merseyside Heroin Clinic from 1982 until 1995, and during that time he noted results which mirror those of other countries who have experimented with drug regulation.[290] Those who were enrolled in his program and others like it used *less* heroin, committed *fewer* crime, and suffered *fewer* medical complications related to their use than their counterparts using street heroin.[291] These facilities also decimate the underworld market, effectively funneling cash away from drug dealers and into pharmacies and health clinics.[292] Remember, right now the United States is spending $180 Billion in every year on the prison-industrial complex, much of it earmarked for the War on Drugs. Between taxation and reductions in prosecution costs, these programs will more than pay for themselves, and some researchers estimate upwards of 50% reduction in criminal justice costs on the heels of legalization.[293]

Heroin clinics and safe use sites are beneficial on almost every level. But they do come with one consequence which many policymakers wish to avoid: they wind up reducing police budgets when crime and drug arrests dry up. Given the tremendous data set showing how successful such facilities are at saving and improving the lives of both drug users and their families, this threat to the police state is likely the only reason they are not allowed in the United States already. We are trading the life and well-being of drug users for the significant salaries of members of drug enforcement units.

FOR NOW, HEROIN clinics and safe injection sites remain illegal in the United States. But we have plenty of other drug clinics where addicted people can get legal access to drugs. The most common of these programs are known as Medication Assisted Treatment (MAT) programs, and they were vital to my success when I decided to stop using heroin in the early 2010s.

Methadone is a strong opioid, like heroin and morphine, but it possesses some unique pharmacological properties that makes it valuable for treating addiction, perhaps most notably, its half-life. Unlike heroin, morphine or fentanyl(s), which begin breaking down in the body rapidly once consumed, methadone lasts more than a day. This means that users can take their scheduled dose, usually a pill or a liquid, and remain well-lubricated, avoiding detox for 24 hours or longer.[294] Buprenorphine, brand named Suboxone, is a similar formulation of synthetic opioid, and it also allows dependent people to dose just once each day and then get on with their lives.[295] When taken in prescribed doses, it doesn't even get users high.[296]

Since heroin has a half-life of less than an hour, addicted people are on the go all the time, racing to stay ahead of detox by securing our next fix and finding a safe place to sneak away and use it. But with methadone, we need not rush anymore, because we have more than a day before detox shows up and ruins everything. It is still there, just out of sight, waiting for us to run out of dope. But it loses the power of urgency. In the meantime, many of us get therapy and begin to address deep seated issues which have led us to overuse drugs, and sometimes we find alternative, or even better methods for coping. The bandage of medication assisted treatment buys us time, and sometimes that is all we need.

MAT programs are not one-room drug dens where users pick up their fix and hit the road. They are medical facilities where drugs are dispensed by trained professionals, and where on-site therapy is required as part of all treatment plans.[297] Drug-tests are frequently administered to ensure patients are complying with program guidelines, which can prove a double-edged sword when those in charge threaten to kick people out of the program for continued heroin (or even cannabis) use.[298] When I was on methadone, a decade prior to the writing of this, I nearly lost my spot in the program for repeatedly testing positive for marijuana, and, at times, for an inability to pay nearly $150 per week. I often wonder where I would be today had I been just a day late or a dollar short. Had I been kicked out of the program, I certainly would have headed back to the streets and returned to the same vicious cycle of daily hustling to secure my next overpriced fix. I might still be stuck in the hunting/feasting loop today.

Many patients remain on methadone for years, or even indefinitely. I took it for almost half a decade before weening myself off, of my own accord and in my own time. Like most users, nobody was going to tell me when to stop using. Methadone allowed that to happen.

Since there is no perceptible buzz or high for those who use an opioid like methadone or buprenorphine daily, many of us decide to simply use it for the rest of our lives.[299] But for those who do decide to reduce or stop their intake, methadone offers an incredible advantage over cold turkey methods. Since it is labeled and dispensed by professionals, users can measure our dose to the microgram, allowing us to methodically reduce our intake in small increments, virtually unnoticeable on a day-by-day basis. Eventually we can work our way off methadone with little or no perceptible detox.

No one should *ever* be forced to endure physical withdrawal symptoms from opioids. The Drug War thrives on unnecessary suffering, which, in turn, fuels all sorts of crimes of desperation meant to secure another fix. Yet the people committing these crimes, which costs citizens billions of dollars each year, could be satiated with pennies worth of heroin, or a buck worth of methadone. And unlike 12-step programs or abstinence only treatment, long-term methadone or buprenorphine use has been shown to reduce death rates in heroin users by 50% or more.[300] We have yet again bumped into the tendency of our system to value one life over another. The United States is trading the health and wellbeing of drug users for the salaries of well-paid police officers, ensuring petty crimes which could be prevented by giving out cheap heroin will continue to negatively impact the lives of citizens.

DRUG REPLACEMENT THERAPIES are valuable in more ways that most users realize when we enter these programs. We show up because we are sick of running from detox, and it keeps catching us faster and faster. We just want the cure, or rather, the long bandage—the dose that lasts 24 hours. But when we start to follow the dosing requirements of these clinics, we get the added benefit of hotwiring our brains to decrease our potential for addiction. Our daily habits of ritualistic hustling are replaced with, well, nothing. Where we used to spend all day in the dopamine-fueled thrill of the hunt, we are now free to devote those energies anywhere we wish, and the addiction which was activated all day long is instead reduced to a five-minutes stop every morning, often accompanied by a therapy session. The buildings and areas we once associated with getting high are replaced with small, sterile rooms and therapists' offices. The role of addiction in our lives is greatly reduced by design.

To understand why, we will need to play the role of evil scientists. Say we wanted to cause someone to become addicted to drugs. How might we make sure that happens? And how might we make sure their addiction becomes as debilitating as it could possibly be?

We could just give them a bunch of heroin, cocaine or methamphetamine and stand back. According to our dominant cultural narratives about addiction and drugs, this should be sufficient, because all drugs are supposedly super-addictive and dangerous. But in the real world this probably wouldn't work, because the vast majority of people who try even the most socially stigmatized drugs, like smoking crack or slamming meth, will never struggle with addiction at any point during their lives.[301] There is a good chance that we could give our subject all the dope in the world and they would never develop an addiction, even if we waited for years.

This might run contrary to your common sense. You might *know* that drugs like heroin and cocaine are immediately addictive. But that is only because you live in a culture without adequate (or any) drug education. What we get is usually tidbits and snippets from fear-mongering public service announcements. We see cheerleaders giving up on life and throwing away their future after trying MDMA or heroin once. We see high school students melt into blobs of inactive, mindless fiends. For decades we have heard the sizzling egg and been told that this is our brain on drugs. And even though we view such commercials as funny and exaggerated, we still learn from them.[302] We assume that some of what they are telling us is true. Even when we notice the fearmongering and the exaggerations, we still feel like there must be *something* to the underlying message. I mean, it wouldn't be on TV if it was a complete lie, right?

It is no wonder most of us believe that when a rat is put into a cage with a bottle of heroin or cocaine, it will take the drugs until it dies. We have been fed this line for so long that it may as well be written into elementary school textbooks. But like much of our cultural knowledge about drugs and those who use them, it is not true.[303]

The experiment with the rats did take place, numerous times in fact, but it did not turn out like you might remember. When rats are put into cages with nothing but water and a drug like cocaine or morphine, they do indeed tend to use the drug until they become dependent, and sometimes they even overdose and die.[304] But these rats aren't dying from drug use so much as from loneliness and boredom. The follow up experiments have shown us just how damaging tough love really is.

When you fill the same cage with toys, spinning wheels for the rats to run on, and other rats so they can play and have sex, well then you have a party, and the rats find themselves largely uninterested in the drugs. They have better things to do, and most of them don't ever develop anything resembling an addiction.[305] That makes sense if you think about your own life and the vices which make it worth living. Whether it is a few drinks after work, a heavy work-out session, a gallon of coffee in the morning, your weekly Bible study, or your kinky sex life, we all have drugs that help us feel better about the world. And we all put aside those desires and urges, or we at least regulate them, for things like work, recreation, sleep and study. We keep them in their place, because there is too much socialization and wheel-running to be done. Luckily for most of us, we live in the cage full of other rats and toys, and when everything is going well in our lives, we tend to play with those toys and engage in those social relationships, leaving the cocaine and morphine in their place. We (and the rats) might still use drugs, but we seldom develop life-interrupting addictions.

On the other hand, when addicted people are forced to run around all day, preoccupied with finding a way to survive, we may as well be the rats in the toyless cages. Our lives become nothing but the drugs. It takes so much effort and time to get and use them that our rituals become our entire existence. By the time we evade detox, our energy is sapped. But when we begin to use services like methadone or buprenorphine (or heroin) clinics, what used to take hours now takes minutes, and we can spend the rest of our days doing boring stuff, like reading books, working or thinking about what we want to do with our lives. The toys in the cage suddenly become visible, the other rats let us back in, and we again have time and energy available to play with them. Tough love is toxic. It puts us in a cage with nothing but morphine, crack or meth, and in that situation, we are naturally inclined to overuse.

That's not the only advantage clinics offer over street use. The medication schedules and the exact doses also work to reduce the risk and severity of addition.[306] For all of their problems, methadone clinics are on to something.[307] It is unfortunate they are not (yet) allowed to put more drugs on the menu.

BACK TO OUR evil experiment. Let us imagine that our patient is among the less than 20% of people who might struggle with addiction at some point in their life.[308] Perhaps they suffered a recent loss in the family, or maybe they are going through some personal issues that make intoxication seem more tempting than normal. How could we increase the odds that they will struggle with a severe addiction? If we really wanted that to happen, we would design a system exactly like the one that currently exists in the United States.

To maximize addiction potential, we should provide inconsistent doses, sometimes pure, sometimes diluted, at different times on different days, ensuring a consistently inconsistent medication schedule. The current illegal drug market is a perfect model for what this would look like. Frank's magic powder is weak today and strong tomorrow, supplemented on various days with fentanyl(s) and powdered milk. This unpredictable situation leaves the user's body unable to get a good read on what to expect and how to adjust prior to getting high. Remember, tolerance and sensitization rely on environmental cues, so we would want to make those hard to spot in our experiment.[309] If we really wanted to maximize this effect, we should make sure our patient smokes fentanyl this morning, snorts oxycontin this afternoon, and shoots heroin later this evening. We would want them dosing with different drugs at different times in different ways (smoking, injection, snorting, etc.). And we would want them constantly unsure of just how high they were about to get prior to use, forcing their tolerance to go into overdrive.

Relatedly, set and setting are always important. Set is the term used to describe what is going on in your brain and body when you take a drug, and setting refers to the environment where you are using your drugs. They are both vital to tolerance and sensitization, so if we want to get our patient hooked, we should force them to get high in different locations every day. Sometimes we should let them dose at home, where they feel safe and relaxed. But mostly we should force them to get high in unsafe and unfamiliar locations, places where they are already on edge, like a filthy bathroom in a dope house.[310] The risk of both addiction and overdose goes way up when users are forced to get high out of their element, so we should make sure our patient is always looking over their back, rushing, hiding and lying about their use.

It doesn't get any better if we follow through with the experiment. We can drop our patient off in any city in the US and be certain the environment we are looking to create already exists. Addictions are driven by the terror that one's medication might be withdrawal at any moment, that detox is always right around the corner no matter what one does today.[311] So we should stigmatize and criminalize our patient for their use, shaming and punishing them at every opportunity if we really want them to dive into addiction.[312]

While drugs will always have a reliably pleasant effect, we should reduce our patient's access to alternative forms of pleasure and contentment. It would be incredibly helpful if we could get the public and the police on board, parroting lies about the dangers of drugs and the immorality of those who use them. If we nail the recipe, our patient's friends and family members might even begin to enforce "tough love," effectively cutting off support from the outside world as addiction begins to set in. Once drug users realize our loved ones see us as broken and infectious, we often come to believe those lies ourselves.[313]

We can also stoke up the terror that drives addiction if we charge our patient grossly inflated prices, beginning a slow process which will eventually leave them bankrupt. We can make that terror inescapable by making all locations carry similar restrictions regarding the use of drugs. Designated spaces where people are allowed to use a substance without legal penalties are shown to reduce overall levels of consumption while encouraging responsibility, so getting rid of them would be a must if we really wanted to maximize addiction potential.[314]

We have seen the magic of sanctioned use areas reducing overall consumption play out repeatedly in the US. Smoking areas not only reduce the spaces where people smoke, but they also reduce overall smoking rates.[315] Marks' heroin clinic in England, and others like it across the world, have consistently reported their patients are more likely to abstain from using street drugs than their counterparts in methadone treatment or 12-step programs.[316] It turns out that when you provide authorized spaces for an activity, people begin to respect the rules about abstaining in unsanctioned areas. When weed is illegal everywhere, smoking in the middle of a college campus is the same crime as smoking in one's home, or in one's car. But when there is a smoking section, we tend to self-police and use it. If we wanted to avoid that effect, we should make sure there are no sanctioned use locations, no safe consumption sites, and consistent laws restricting our patient's use no matter where they go.

We should also convince our patient that addiction is a disease, since holding that belief has, in itself, been shown to increase the likelihood and severity of relapses.[317] If we did all of these things, sadistic as they are, we could greatly increase the negative consequences of addiction simply by leaning into the natural tendencies of human nature. This description of how-to-torture aligns perfectly with our current approach to drug control in the United States. It would be difficult to design a system better than the one we currently use if we wished to increase the likelihood and severity of addictions across the board.

Our brains are wired to be more susceptible to addiction when we use inconsistent doses, or when we use at inconsistent times throughout the day. The War on Drugs ensures that will happen, because the heroin I buy today will be different than the heroin I buy tomorrow, even if it all comes from the same dealer. I might get super-stoned today because someone cut fentanyl(s) into the batch, then not-so-much tomorrow, because someone cut Vitamin B into the batch. I might dose at 8AM if I kept my stash right, or it might not be until noon if I have to hustle up enough cash for a pack. I might smoke fentanyl patches one day and shoot heroin the next, then snort an Oxycontin the third day, all based on what is available on the streets, or within my budget. Our brains learn from our environments, and the current War on Drugs trains us to expect the unexpected, to not know if a shot will be accompanied by a slight buzz or a near overdose, or if a dose will come at 8AM or noon, or whether it will be consumed in the safety of our homes versus the anxiety of a public bathroom. The system is designed to make sure addictions are as commonplace and debilitating as possible.

ONE MORE QUICK rat experiment might bring this point home. If you put the original rat back into the morphine cage and remove the toys and friends, the rat will indeed be likely to consume drugs in large doses, often to the point of death. But let's consider a slightly altered version of the experiment where instead of a water bottle filled with unlimited morphine, the rat has to push a lever for each dose. We could now measure how many times the rat will push the button in a given period of time. Keeping our evil-scientist-hat on, we could then alter various parts of the experiment to find out which environmental factors make the rat most likely to push the button most often. If our goal is still the maximization of addiction potential, perhaps we will discover some clever method for tricking the rat into pushing the button over and over, possibly even after the reward it entirely withdrawn.

The above experiment was conducted by famous behavioralist B.F. Skinner in 1956, although he used rat food pellets instead of morphine. But the results apply regardless of the reward offered.[318] If you give the rat a consistent dose of food pellets (or morphine) every time it pushes the button, and if you take away all of its stimulation to make sure it consumes the reward (food or drug) out of boredom, then the rat will push the button at a consistent level. But when you stop providing the reward with every single button-push, the rat responds in an odd way. It doesn't press the button less; it presses it *more*.

You can tinker with the percentage to dial in the maximum button-pushing ratio, and it comes down to the more random a reward, the more likely rats (and humans) are to engage in the reward-producing behavior.[319] The maximum amount of button pushing actually results from the most unpredictable rewarding. If you give the button pushers what they want almost every time, or just once out of every ten pushes, you won't get them to push the button as often as if you reward them randomly, 50% of the time, in an unpredictable pattern. And that random pattern will also get them to keep pushing the button longer than any other scenario if you decide to really get evil and take away the reward altogether.

Think about what this dusty discovery says about our current state of war, which ensures users are randomly rewarded in

varying degrees at unpredictable times by pushing the lever—
by buying and using drugs with unpredictable potency. Two
packs can look, smell and even taste exactly the same, but one
of them might barely get me high while the other results in an
overdose. You couldn't design a system more suited to make
addicted people push the button as often as possible, because
our doses are randomized, sometimes strong, other times weak,
and completely unpredictable. When we take consistent doses
at the same time every day, our risk of struggling with addiction
goes way down; we are hardwired to push the button less when
a regular dose is provided every time.[320] The desperation of not
knowing if it will be enough goes away with the predictability
that comes from consistent rewarding.

Because they are operating in a culture at war with drugs and
drug users, MAT programs (methadone and buprenorphine)
require addicted people to jump through so many hoops that
many of us do not see them as a viable option.[321] For the first
few months of these programs, we are often required to report
in person, daily, to receive our medication. And remember,
sometimes a drug test showing cocaine or even cannabis in our
systems can get us kicked out. A plant which one cannot overdose on should be the least of their concerns, but in our ongoing War on Drugs, the battles bleed into even the most demil-
itarized zones. The methadone clinic has to cover its backside
just like doctors who are now avoiding opioid prescriptions for
fear of the DEA pulling their license, or worse, pursuing criminal charges.[322] It is hard to believe at this point in our country's
history that any medical professional truly believes cutting off a
drug user from a safe supply will keep them from using drugs,
but under that faulty logic, doctors are being incentivized to
send users to the streets.

We should also remember that once-upon-a-time in the US, drug users could simply purchase our heroin, cocaine and other drugs from the grocery store. These over-the-counter remedies were clearly labeled and hygienically packaged. They were also cheap because the chemicals used to produce them were readily available and regulated. As we have seen, a kilogram of pure cocaine costs less than $1000US to produce in the jungles of South America. After being cut with poison and distributed to local street-level dealers, it might fetch upwards of $200,000 (or more) on the streets of Chicago or Detroit. Since most cocaine sold in the US is as little as 10% pure (or even less), you can imagine a not-so-far-fetched scenario where a single kilogram of cocaine, purchased for $1,000 in South America, is processed on Frank's countertop and diluted into 10 kilos, then sold gram by gram, for $100 each, netting the dealer a cool million bucks, all tax free. Those same drugs could then be cut yet further, making money for low level street dealers looking to get through the day by flipping a few packs.

I am not suggesting we go back to the pre-1900s unregulated market, not by a long shot. But while we don't want kids to have access to drugs like cocaine or heroin, we should immediately decriminalize these substances and stop sending people to prison for using them. We should stop forcing people into unregulated, illegal markets to purchase them. Drugs should be regulated, just like any other dangerous substance or device. We need gatekeepers who have something to lose in charge of dispensing our drugs, not desperate users and hustlers whose goals are survival and profit.

Although additional drugs are slowly entering the walk-in treatment market, methadone remains a favorite of both addicted people and suppliers. Alternatives like buprenorphine and Vivitrol (a drug which reduces cravings), are more available now than ever before, but all of these services need to be easier for drug users to access, and they should be subsidized by taxpayers who recognize the financial and humane benefits of providing treatment instead of funerals. As the settlements from Big Pharma make their way to the states, there will be decades of money available for grants provided to MAT participants, but only if we hold policy-makers accountable. They have repeatedly shown a willingness to divert settlement cash to things like general operations funds or frivolous purchases (a helicopter and the subsidization of a tobacco farm are two recent examples).[323]

The movement toward safe injection sites is bound to reach a tipping point sometime soon, although the stigmas surrounding use will likely prove a difficult obstacle to overcome. The next great project in the War on Drugs involves undoing the shame we have worked so hard to prop up for more than a century. Although there is much work to be done in this regard, drug war opponents have found an unlikely ally in the medical community, as doctors and therapists have opened the door to fast-track shame reduction by embracing substances once considered taboo.

The road to legalization appears to run largely through therapeutic applications, and the list of approved chemicals for loosening up prior to sitting down to chat with your mental health care provider is growing longer by the year. Instead of daily doses, sometimes for the rest of one's life, these treatments involve getting high and then talking to your therapist.[324] No tricks, no gimmicks, just a good, ol' stoned chat where you unburden yourself of things you normally don't want to talk about.

Psychedelics like psilocybin (Magic Mushrooms), amphetamines like MDMA (ecstasy or Molly), and dissociative, like Ketamine (Special K), are already being administered in therapeutic settings where patients use them to get over themselves and talk about things they otherwise struggle to discuss.[325] Users are treated to something akin to a guided trip, a deliberate journey where they access and reassess neural pathways associated with traumatic responses, or habits like smoking, gambling or drug use.[326] The results have been incredibly promising; some early studies show smokers laying down cigarettes in higher percentages than any other treatment currently offered with just 2-3 sessions.[327]

Before any of this common-sense policy can become normalized, we have to get rid of our old laws, along with our old ways of enforcing them. We have to end the war, and we have to retire the warriors. The body count has risen high enough.

Chapter 4: The Goal

"Against the dreaded outer world one can
defend oneself only by turning away. . . Pain is
but sensation. It only exists in so far as we feel
it…The crudest of methods of influencing the
body, but also the most effective, is the chemical one: that of intoxication." —Sigmund
Freud[328]

Law Enforcement

The door caved in off the hinges and flew across the room as a
dozen armed men ran into the house. No-knock warrants are
the go-to power move of police departments across the country.
What a rush it must be to charge in, guns out, yelling at the top
of your lungs:

Police! Get down! Show us your hands!

I was busted.

If you are poor and use illegal drugs, the police are probably
a regular part of your life. Sometimes it is a petty crime like
trespassing or prowling, and you can make bail the next day.
Other times it is a serious crime, like theft or drug possession.
This time was serious.

The dominos had fallen quickly once they put a name to
the face. Dozens of cameras across the state of Michigan had

captured grainy footage of a six-foot-tall, skinny, white, twenty-something man using stolen checks and credit cards to purchase electronics from a handful of big-box retailers. I had spent months tirelessly collecting gaming systems, surround sound speakers, televisions, computers, cell phones and boom boxes from every store within a hundred-mile radius. Much of the remaining evidence was stacked in a back bedroom.

I didn't have any dope. That was the reason I was stealing stuff. But as soon as they had me in handcuffs, they got to work trying to find some anyway. And they looked hard, upending drawers, flipping beds and shattering dishes as they threw them into the sink. They even emptied the fridge and unceremoniously left it opened. No dope.

There was less than $3,000 worth of stolen goods, but you would have thought I was a major player. Dozens of officers carrying assault rifles and dressed in full riot gear were involved in the raid. My guess is they expected to find enough drugs to arrest me for manufacturing and distribution. They wanted to charge me with dealing drugs so they could confiscate anything of value, especially cash, and possibly even the house, all of which they could then legally use to fund their department operations.[329]

The longer they came up empty in their search, the snottier they got. I would do time, sure. That was a win. But I would not catch the label of drug dealer, which is what they really wanted. Their jobs and their pensions depend on it.[330] And that is why the United States is currently stuck in a rut when it comes to ending drug prohibition. Every police department in the nation stands to lose a massive source of funding if the War on Drugs is ever abolished. Cops *need* drug dealers to continue amassing stacks of cash which they can periodically confiscate, because the alternative involves massive lay-offs due to losses in funding.

It is called civil forfeiture, and it's an archaic law which allows your property to be charged with a crime and confiscated, even if you are acquitted, or never even charged.[331] These laws net local police departments millions in confiscated cars, electronics, cash and toys every year, all thanks to the Comprehensive Control Act of 1984.[332] Prior to that instrumental piece of legislation, police were much less interested in drug busts.

CIVIL FORFEITURE LAWS were instituted during medieval times in a superstitious attempt to punish (the spirit of) objects used in the commission of a crime, as if the knife or gun used to carry out a murder should be held accountable instead of the wielder.[333] In an effort to combat high seas piracy and ensure the payment of import taxes, Britain amended civil asset forfeiture laws in the seventeenth century, allowing for the seizure of any ship (and its cargo) which failed to display its authentic flag of origin.[334] The law had the two-fold effect of allowing the state to charge inanimate objects (personal property) with crimes, while avoiding the pesky protections of the law which only apply to people, not stuff.

A contemporary analogy is the US Constitution. Today, the owner of property in the United States is afforded the 14th Amendment's rights of due process and equal protection under the law. But their property is not. That distinction is why civil forfeiture laws took an odd turn just over half a century ago.

In 1970, at the beginnings of what scholars now regard as the birth of the contemporary prison-industrial complex, the US amended civil asset forfeiture laws to allow the property of a suspected drug dealer to be confiscated and sold, even if the alleged "dealer" was never actually charged with a crime.[335]

The original law required that all funds be deposited into the federal treasury's general account, but it didn't take much to redirect those monies to local districts with the passage of the Comprehensive Crime Control Act of 1984. Even though drug arrests remained relatively consistent between 1970 and 1984, they increased by more than 72% between 1984 and 1989.[336] Once police officers knew that arresting someone for dope meant a possible raise and a boost to department budgets, they promptly got to work taking care of themselves: serve and protect.

Meant to incentivize arrests for drug crimes and pad agency budgets, the new law allowed local police departments to keep anything confiscated within their jurisdiction. From that point forward, our path as a country was set. We headed unflinchingly into an updated war against drugs and those who use them, and we built a massive system of local warriors to complement our already-burgeoning federal system. We incentivized cops to hit the streets and find drug users and dealers, bribing them with cushy budgets and the always-tempting offer of free stuff.

These stateside warriors are not going to give up their jobs as righteous superheroes without a fight. They are, after all, the good guys. At least that is what they are allowed to believe. Why should they be forced to resign and work a minimum wage nine-to-five when they can ramp up the War on Drugs and pay their salaries with the profits collected by drug dealers? Kicking in doors and taking anything of value has been the norm for more than 35 years, which means some of today's officers are children of the original group of profiteers who started this racket back in 1984. As Tupac Shakur said, "this country was built on gangs. This country still is run on gangs: Republicans, Democrats, the police department, the FBI, the CIA—those are gangs."[337] The police are the biggest gang in the United States, and they operate with relative impunity.

When officers arrest a murderer or a rapist, they do not get to take his property and money along with his freedom. That may be why so many murders and robberies never result in an arrest in the United States. Almost half of all homicides and aggravated assaults, and nearly two-thirds of all rapes remain unsolved.[338] We haven't incentivized these crimes in the same way as we have incentivized the waging of war against our own citizens.

It should come as no surprise that once officers understand their funding relies on drug busts, they become preoccupied with making drug busts. Now that we are living through the age of legalization, slowly-but-surely watching criminalized substances make their way to the list of decriminalized substances, we cannot expect these warriors to "go gentle into that good night."[339] Like most of us, they will be quick to protect their jobs. Unlike most of us, they have access to the inner workings of power, plus they carry a shield of cultural respectability.

Those who will suffer most are not the rookies or the desk clerks. These layoffs will start at the top, with Narcotics Units composed of career cops who have given their lives to the cause. They followed the rules and avoided reprimand. They received awards and promotions, and when it came time to create or expand their department's drug enforcement division, they were called upon to fill a role they were assured came with the perks of cultural clout: respect, notoriety, special training and a massive pension. A system this large and well-designed won't simply shut itself down.

We have long passed the tipping point of self-sustainment in the War on Drugs, and we now have a system which requires not only permanent upkeep, but also permanent expansion.[340] Without the War on Drugs, there simply will not be enough crime to rationalize the funding of outdated departments. The watershed will spread throughout the law enforcement community, as deputies, transport officers and bailiffs also experience a round of massive layoffs.

The white flag will devastate more than just law enforcement. Around 20% of all inmates at state prisons, and nearly half of those in federal joints are locked up for drugs.[341] Another large group is in jail for property crimes and strong-armed robberies, forgery and shoplifting, identity theft, petty larceny, or other crimes of desperation. Once drugs are legalized, the prisons and jails will begin to empty out, because drug users will not be criminals anymore. The wave will move quickly, rippling through food service workers and clothing manufacturers, law-enforcement training and equipment providers, transport vehicles and medical personnel, bail-bond services and commissary (jail store) workers. Many will be left jobless when the inmates who employ them are freed. The laid off work force will hit the job market at the same time as released prisoners, and if we don't get ahead of this tidal wave, it will devastate our economy.

The drug dealers will also be in big trouble. Frank will lose his job, and as much as I loved the guy and understood his motivation, you, as a reader, might not care too much for him. But what about the other people who supported my habit? What should we do with the oxycontin and fentanyl patients, whose safer products I preferred when I could afford them? These folks are not selling drugs to get rich. They are symptoms of a mismanaged and mis-incentivized system which dumps sick folks out on their own in the name of free market capitalism.

They sell their medication to make ends meet, and they don't have any cash left over at the end of the month for mansions or cruises. Putting the dope-man out of business means putting the oxy-dealing cancer patient out of business, and without intervention, we will see the streets flood with convalescing patients who have, yet again, been turned away by the system. We have built a culture which appears, at first glance, to be ethical and just, yet the margins are packed with the bodies of those who are discarded by design, abandoned as worthless and disposable.

The War on Drugs requires raids like those that targeted my residence on more than one occasion, all-out assaults on suspected dope houses that stand to net police departments a profit. There wasn't any dope in the house, so I wasn't charged with possession, a crime which might have afforded me the option of a treatment program instead of prison. Like many funneled into the prison-industrial complex, my addiction disappeared in a haze of property crimes which the court got to work prosecuting. There were dozens of felony charges by the time they all piled up. It would be a long time before I saw freedom again.

I WAS ALREADY detoxing before the cops showed up. By the time I got to jail, I was in full-blown withdrawal: sweat dripping, guts bubbling, pupils swollen, and fidgety as hell. The officer in charge of booking me in ignored my symptoms and processed me through as if I were an item on a factory line. *Spread your cheeks and cough. Put these orange scrubs on. Run your fingers through your hair. Are you thinking about hurting yourself or someone else?* The answers were becoming routine.

Mumia Abu-Jamal once said that life in prison "oscillates between the banal and the bizarre," and the factory line of intake was certainly an example of the latter.[342] As I moved from the processing area, where naked suspects are cavity searched, photographed and then forced to put on ancient, orange scrubs, I slid toward the long drag of the banal. Jail processing is a special kind of hell.

The main cell was packed with bodies, from wall to wall and everywhere in between, each having claimed a piece of the bench or the floor as their own. I dragged my mat in and wedged myself between two others, close to the back edge of the room, near the toilets. And then I waited, because that's what incarcerated people do. I waited for arraignment. I waited to see what they would charge me with and how long I would be in prison. But mostly, I waited for the detox to get worse.

I had been to jail dozens of times before, so by now that cycle was becoming quite routine. Yet each time it seemed to get worse, not better. The anxiety, the disgust, the guttural fear; I was becoming sensitized to the agony of losing one's freedom. With detox scratching at the back of my eyeballs, it was going to be a rough night.

Jails stink. If you have ever been inside one, even for a few minutes, you remember the smell for the rest of your life. It is a dank, evil stench: fear, mold, sweat, booze, blood and shit mixed with a hint of non-bleach cleaner. They always smell the same.

When you are detoxing from opioids, every sensation is painful: the taste of food, the feel of a loved-one's touch, and, especially, the dank-mold, stomach-flu stench of a holding cell. By the time the nurse came around the next morning to inquire about my medical needs, I was such a mess that she asked whether I was detoxing from alcohol, benzos or opioids. I said opioids and added a weak request for help. She responded by writing a few notes on her clipboard and promising a daily dose of Ibuprofen. Her look said more than her words ever could have. The correctional system knew what to do with a junkie like me: cold turkey detox in full display of other inmates, who would see me as a precautionary tale, the dope-sick cat in Cell One. I spent three weeks shitting and vomiting, sweating and hallucinating, all because the people in charge either got off on my suffering, or didn't care about me enough to help.

Looking back, I am as infuriated now as I was then. At the time I had no idea that treating addicted people this way increases our risk of relapse once we are released.[343] I didn't know then that a number of cheap drugs like methadone or buprenorphine would have alleviated my withdrawal symptoms without getting me high.[344] I was unaware of the benefits of cognitive behavioral therapy and psychological treatment, and without those important pieces of the puzzle, my chances of staying sober, if that's what I wanted to do, were greatly reduced. Going to jail made my addiction *worse*.[345]

I didn't realize they were torturing me, but that's exactly what happens in jails and prisons across the United States. Any time an inmate shows up with medical needs related to drug use or addiction, jail staff follows a similar script. They cut us off and use us as an example of what will happen to others if they use drugs. They turn away from our suffering, or worse, they turn towards it with a chuckle. And it only continues because the War on Drugs has us all fooled into believing that drug use is a sin, that it is criminal and dangerous, that it is a disease, yet, oxymoronically, that it should also be punished.

EVERY TWENTY SECONDS, someone in the United States is arrested for drugs, shackled, Mirandized, and branded with what Michelle Alexander calls "the badge of inferiority," a permanent felony conviction.[346] My arrests didn't leave me permanently trapped in the revolving door of criminal corrections, but 76% of those incarcerated for drugs are not as lucky as I was.[347] My young age, my white skin, my family name and my education allowed me to avoid much of what awaits the 1.5 million US citizens who are arrested for drugs *every year*.[348]

Addicted people in the United States are criminalized instead of treated, locked in cages instead of tucked into beds, and offered little treatment outside of that provided by other inmates. Meanwhile, drug users who don't struggle with addiction (the majority of all drug users) are classified as criminals and locked out of society. We are forced to contend with illegal markets and underworld characters who are incentivized to behave poorly, selling us cut dope or raising the price because we can't window shop up the street. *We* are the casualties of the War on Drugs. Dead in the streets or locked in a hole, the warriors can take credit for little more than our incapacitated bodies, and the cost to house or bury us.

That expense is exorbitant. The CDC currently claims that more than 96,000 of us are dying this way each year.[349] That's one death every ten minutes, an abysmal number, at least if it were an accurate measurement. But it is not. The CDC relies on inaccurate methods of data collection which could not be better suited to inflate already-terrifying numbers yet further without making it obvious.[350] Those inflated statistics are then consistently used to encourage further expansion of a war which is the real cause of most overdose deaths.

In the United State, war is often the only response we understand to a frightening situation.

It is telling that despite these grossly exaggerated overdose rates, the US still seems uninterested in ending drug prohibition. These statistics might not give us an accurate idea of how many people are dying from overdose, but they let us know that no amount of violence or death is enough to make us change our approach to drug control. This policy update will have to come from the bottom up, from voters and citizens who are willing to do their homework and call their Congressperson. We can't arrest or kill out way out of this mess.

CDC overdose statistics are out of whack for a number of reasons. The cause of death is decided at the local level, then pooled by the CDC, who has failed to establish consistent criteria for ensuring deaths labeled overdoses really are overdoses. Each city and state sets its own standards when it comes to the person whose job it is to decide upon the cause of death; some require medical examiners, others require coroners, and some don't require any training at all.[351] Some cause-of-death deciders are elected, others are appointed by government officials, and *none* are required by federal law to have undergone *any* training whatsoever. You or I could fill out a death certificate and decide what killed someone in many jurisdictions, and no one would double check our work, even if we are completely unexperienced in medicine and pharmacology.

The CDC tallies regional data, which might come from a local Sherriff whose annual budget relies on federal drug funding, or from a local doctor who hasn't received any specific training on how to determine cause of death, or from the mayor's friend who was trained in veterinary science. The system is designed to ensure inaccurate data informs policy. And true to form, it is set up to do much of its work in the margins, where only close inspection reveals anything is amiss.

The built-in errors are easier to spot the closer one looks. When multiple drugs are found in an autopsy, each might be counted as its own case of overdose. One death might count as five or more overdose deaths when the CDC completes its tally.[352] In some cases it is possible that there are no drugs at all in a victim's body, because many jurisdictions don't require drug testing to diagnose a cause of death as a drug overdose.[353] In fact, a full 25% of all overdose deaths are reported without any specific drug listed, largely because there is no CDC requirement to make sure drugs really were involved, nor to list which drugs caused the overdose.[354] Perhaps the worst of the CDC's blunders in data collection, and the most revealing, involves overlooking one of the most dangerous drugs of all when it comes to overdose: alcohol. If someone took one Codeine pill and then drank a gallon of Whiskey, their death might well be classified as an opioid overdose.[355]

Any statistics provided by a government in the midst of a nonstop war with the group being analyzed should be taken with a grain of salt. There has never been a time when Uncle Sam has told the truth to US citizens about drugs and those who use them.[356] But the overdose numbers have little to do with the real reason we should end the War on Drugs. Drugs should be legal because we live in a country allegedly founded on the ideals of "Life, Liberty and the Pursuit of Happiness."[357] We claim to build our lives around that last demand, the pursuit of happiness, yet we abide a war against chemicals which produce happiness in various forms.[358] The War on Drugs is contrary to what the United States claims to be.

KEEPING IN MIND that overdose deaths are consistently exaggerated in public discourse, yet believed nonetheless, let's take a look at how those data have informed our approach to the War on Drugs. Between 1999 and 2019, the US saw a massive increase in what have been labeled overdose deaths.[359] As a result, we are now in the midst of a so-called "opioid epidemic."[360] But the bodies of the dead are not representative of the society that buries them. While reported overdose deaths have increased only slightly in black and Latinx communities, they have reportedly gone way up in white communities.[361]

Between 1999 and 2015, reported white overdose deaths increased at a steady rate of 7% every year, while reported Latinx and black populations saw only a 2% per-year concurrent increase.[362] Remember, even though these statistics are not accurate, people believe them. They make their way into news reports and public debate, and they inform our cultural response to what we believe to be a crisis. And this crisis is, of late, effecting white communities more than nonwhite communities. That is the only reason it is a crisis at all.

Diseases related to addiction have also risen more in white communities than in nonwhite communities.[363] In 1999, the death rate from diseases related to addiction was nearly 30% lower for white, working class citizens than for black, working class citizens, but by 2013 it was 30% higher, and it has remained inflated.[364] The message being delivered to the average citizen via the news and government spokespeople is that white people are suddenly experiencing terrible consequences from drug use which were once limited to mostly nonwhite, impoverished communities. Sound the alarm.

Throughout the history of the United States, rich, white people have always been a privileged group. When we are threatened, that privilege provides us governmental mechanism of protection which often operate in violent fashions against those who are constructed as our enemies. It's always easiest to see in the distant past, when policies like Jim Crow and rights based on white skin were the norm, yet folks still considered themselves woke compared to their great-grandparents.[365] The same phenomenon is at work yet again, and if we don't act quickly, we will see the US respond to this threat as it does to all threats against white folks, whether real or fabricated: with more war, more promises of death to our enemies, and more torture mislabeled as punishment. These methods will be as ineffective as they have always been, and another century may well pass before our great grandchildren fix our mess and stop killing and incarcerating drug users.

My sentence was 1-5 years in prison. I was released after 13 months, but my parole lasted the entire remaining four years because the fees I had been saddled with were too substantial to repay. As a felon, it was difficult to find work that paid more than minimum wage, so I enrolled in college, certain that I was wasting my time, and that any degree I obtained would never be of any real use. After all, I was a junkie, a convicted felon, and a bad guy; those three strikes were more than most employers were willing to overlook. My future was likely resigned to long hours of manual labor, a prospect that didn't excite me. But college was fun, almost like a drug of its own, and I was compelled to learn.

My enrollment also covered parole requirements to remain employed, but since college didn't come with a salary, I couldn't pay my legal fees. I could have been released from parole years before my discharge date had I been able to afford those fines. The War on Drugs, and the entire prison-industrial complex for that matter, exist to process money, to funnel cash from "criminals" to law-abiding citizens, like parole officers and deputies, food-service workers and uniform makers, squad car mechanics and body armor manufacturers, rehab facilities and halfway houses, plus the long list of private companies who profit from un(der)-paid slave labor.[366] The list gets longer each year, as does the group of people who will be fired when this silly war is ended. The United States is indeed supporting a prison-industrial complex; some towns will fail if their detention centers ever close their doors, or even substantially reduce their population.[367] It is a precarious way to operate an economy.

Life Enhancement with Harm Reduction

Before we talk about life enhancement or harm reduction approaches to drug policy, we need to talk about what love looks like. And then we need to talk about what love *should* look like. The biggest difference between the two version comes down to one word: domination. As one of my favorite feminist scholars, bell hooks, frequently reminds us, there can be no real love in any relationship so long as domination persists.[368]

If you are scratching your head as a parent, or as someone who grew up experiencing the casual abuse called corporal punishment (spanking, shaming, hitting), you might not even understand the concept of a love that does not dominate. But it exists. There is a love that leans hard on empathy, a love that seeks to find a connection to another's suffering as well as to their triumphs. But to find this sort of empathetic love, we must first discard the poison notions of love that have invaded our cultural landscape. It is time for tough love to find its way to the dustbin of bad ideas. We must stop hitting our children, incarcerating our enemies, and dumping our friends when they struggle with addiction.

The love I encourage us to embrace as a culture trades domination for empathy. This love does not deploy shame, and it actively combats the toxic effects of stigmatization, along with other forms of oppression. Those who practice it don't make demands or offer ultimatums (aside from situations where others might be hurt). Instead, we meet people where they are at, recognizing that a few coin tosses are the only difference between that person and us. Love seeks to minimize harm and improve quality of life, and our policies and goals reflect this aim alone when we allow it to drive our decisions. Love never profits off the suffering of others.[369] It equips them for success, sometimes at one's own expense.

As the list of countries with updated drug policies grows longer each year, the United States continues to plug its ears and bury its head in the sand. That has been our typical response whenever we confront a cultural issue requiring our attention. We generally put off any real fixes as long as possible, hoping the attention fades before we actually have to do the work.[370] True to form, that has been the story of the War on Drugs. We have never managed to keep drugs off the streets no matter how hard we have tried. But as we saw in Chapter Three, that was never the real goal.

The social benefits of halting the War on Drugs and embracing alternative policies of intervention and therapy are well-researched: overdose deaths diminish, dangerous use practices decline, disease related to drug use is reduced, and lives are saved when countries abolish legal penalties for drug possession.[371] Right now in the United States, just 10% of the money spent on drug policy goes toward treatment and prevention, while 90% goes toward policing and punishment.[372] We are getting exactly what we pay for.

In some areas of the world, these numbers are flipped. In Portugal, 90% of allocated funds go toward treatment, while just 10% are earmarked for punishment and policing.[373] In Denmark, the government funds legal injection sites where addicted people can congregate and get high without fearing arrest.[374] In Switzerland they even provide the heroin, free of charge.[375] Medical professionals are always on the clock in case of overdose or other treatment needs, and just like the illegal injection sites operating in the United States, not a single overdose death has occurred in any of these facilities.[376]

In cultures where decriminalization has been embraced, users are not stigmatized or locked up for their own good. Unlike the US, these countries do not keep nearly 2% of their citizens under the thumb of state authorities.[377] Some areas of the world no longer respond to overdose deaths by incarcerating people who are in need of treatment. Instead, science informs drug policy and compassion informs the social response to addiction.

Portugal is perhaps the best available example of how easy it would be to end the opioid epidemic. Throughout the 1990s, it is estimated that a full one-percent of the Portuguese population was addicted to heroin.[378] That's probably the only reason a movement as radical as decriminalization ever got traction. Portugal had already tried everything else, including punishment, threats, and even lies about the dangers of drugs. Nothing had worked.

In desperation, politicians changed their approach and updated Portuguese laws in 2001 to prevent users from being arrested for simple possession. Now a ten-day supply of any drug won't get you charged with a crime.[379] Instead, you will be scheduled to appear before a three-person committee, members of a larger unit known as The Dissuasion Commission who are charged with evaluating whether or not users ought to be ordered to attend drug treatment.[380] If your use is not problematic and your life is going just fine, they will send you on your way with the government's stamp of approval. If they feel like you should spend some time in a treatment program, they will make sure you know where to go, and they will even foot part of the bill. To be sure, the forced appearances are a drag for users who do not need treatment, but the policy is still a huge step in the right direction. The ultimate goal is to cut incarceration out of the equation completely, and in Portugal, nobody goes to jail for getting high.

The results of the policy surprised everyone, including many who voted for it. Within just a couple years, addiction rates dropped by around 75% across the country, and drug injection rates dropped by more than half.[381] Allowing people to use drugs *reduced* the amount of people using drugs. Portugal now has the lowest overdose rate in Western Europe, with just six deaths per million people.[382] In contrast, the US currently reports 312 deaths per million, a number which, although inflated, is still certainly much higher than Portugal's new norm.[383] Decriminalization works so well that it is no longer controversial in Portugal.[384] It saves far too much money and far too many lives to go back to the way things used to be. Before Portugal decriminalized drugs, one out of every two people infected with HIV contracted it from sharing contaminated needles to inject drugs. Since drug regulation laws passed, that number has dropped to just one in five HIV cases (are contracted from drug use).[385]

Oddly, in the United States, we still tend to view Portugal's policy as progressive, even though it has been more than twenty years since it went into effect. Portugal wasn't even the first country to buck the trend of permanent war against its own citizens. Spain decriminalized all drugs in the 1970s, and some countries never criminalized drugs in the first place, or they did, but they never enforced the laws.[386] Even some US states are beginning to work from the inside out to change the law at the local level. In 2020, Oregon became the first state to effectively decriminalize personal possession of all drugs.[387]

The new systems certainly aren't perfect. For example, even though a ten-day supply of any drug is decriminalized in Portugal, and to some degree, in areas of the United States, there is no market where one can legally purchase (or sell) drugs. That means suppliers are still working through the same old underground network that winds up contributing to overdoses, drug contamination, and violence, not to mention arrest and imprisonment for anyone who can be pegged with the label of dealer. And as always, since the supply is still illegal, all drug users *are* drug dealers.

THIS CATASTROPHE WILL not halt itself. The current path of US imperialism leads only to a permanent war which becomes more expensive and less effective each year. Yet science and technology are threatening the drug war from a new angle, eroding its legitimacy yet further. Some doctors are already 3D printing some drugs in-office, and it is only a matter of time before molecular printing techniques are affordable for consumer use.[388] Imagine programing your printer to produce a morphine dose from scratch. Imagine the length the government might go to prevent such a reality if the War on Drugs is not concluded before this technology becomes mainstream. As the bodies continue to pile up, both in prison and the morgue, one thing is clear: there is a better way.

The USA's longstanding attitude about drugs has placed them high on a shelf, just out of reach, so long as our guardians are nearby. There is no preparation, no real drug education, and no socially narrated paternal role in modeling responsible drug use for our children. We teach them how to drive, how to navigate love, and how to believe (or not) in religious deities because we feel these things are important, and because failing to do so would leave them unprepared for the real world. But since most of us have never learned how to talk to our kids about drugs, we make the mistake of simply telling them they shouldn't use drugs: "Just Say No."[389] This strategy is effective when it comes to alleviating our parental anxiety about the conversation, but it leaves our kids completely unprepared.

Telling kids not to use drugs is never effective, unless one's real goal is to convince kids to keep their drug use to themselves. We have traded our children's preparedness for our own personal comfort. As a result, our youngsters seldom learn healthy habits surrounding drug use from role models. Instead, they learn from friends, or worse, from dealers. The taboo becomes the object of desire, the prohibited becomes commodity, and the disallowed is longed-for in the society that denies it. Our cultural imaginations have run amok.

There is much to be said about the romance of the forbidden. As author Johann Hari has shown, "the sexiness of drugs is very much in their prohibition, not their regulation."[390] Drug legalization proponents do not want to make drugs more attractive or romantic; we want to make them boring and commonplace.[391] The existence of safe injection sites reduces the romantic allure of drugs. In regulated cultures, the drug user and the space of drug use are no longer restricted to films and books. The spaces of sanctioned use work to destroy the romance of the unknown. (Mis)Conceptions of heroin use as exciting, glamourous or tempting give way to the real bodies which represent drug addiction in flesh and blood: we are people, we are patients, we are human. We are you.

Addiction is palliative, to be sure. But it is also cold, desperate, lonely, and at times, incredibly scary. It is not a sexy Hollywood whirlwind of excitement or a poster on a teen's wall. The romance of the forbidden becomes the doorway to vice in a species like *homo sapien*. We want what we are told we cannot have. Regulation will not eliminate that romance, but like alcohol, visibility disables the allure, especially when there is a date after which one is allowed to partake.

We have to learn to talk to our kids about drugs. That means telling them the truth, even when, as guardians, we would prefer to lie (or simplify). Most drugs are a blast, and they work great to treat things teenagers struggle with during maturation: boredom, anxiety, depression or social phobias, for example. Remember, during this period of our lives, a large portion of our neural connections to happiness, excitement, surprise and satisfaction vanish, and it can feel like drugs, sex, gambling, driving fast or shoplifting are logical choices.[392] Lying to our kids, or simply refusing to talk to them about drugs will not prevent them from using drugs; it will only prevent us from having to hear about it. And during the confusing time we call adolescence, we *need* our guardians to *want* to hear about it. We do our children no favors in protecting ourselves from their truth.

Honest conversation allows us to address the negative effects and potential consequences of irresponsible use, balancing out the current allure of drugs. And here we are in luck, even if we prefer our kids abstain, because the science is in our favor; we don't have to lie. Those who manage to make it to adulthood without developing addictions are likely to remain addiction-free throughout the remainder of their lives.[393] If you can navigate the tumultuous years of neural pruning without developing addictive coping mechanisms, you will have a wicked practice run under your belt for any other struggles you encounter later in life, no matter how miserable they might feel.[394] The onus is once again back on the parent to do whatever they can to make those years bearable. When our conversations about drugs include the good along with bad, our children are more likely to listen, and we are more likely to succeed. We have to care enough to fully prepare them for the real world, because if we don't, someone else will. The one nagging question throughout this entire story is *where were all of your people when you needed them?*

PERHAPS THE MOST common retort to the call to end drug prohibition is that appeal to child welfare: *but the kids will be able to get drugs!* This is yet another misunderstanding of the argument for legalizing and regulating drugs. Regulation would not only destroy the romantic image attached to drugs, but it would also provide additional safeguards to prevent access by minors.

The local liquor store risks its business license if a clerk sells alcohol to underaged consumers. Colorado's Sweet Leaf Marijuana Dispensary had its state license to distribute cannabis suspended in December of 2017 for allegedly failing to follow guidelines regarding cannabis sales.[395] The pharmacist is the state-sanctioned gatekeeper of legal supplies, ensuring children do not have easy access to the controlled substances behind the counter. The street level dealer has no license to protect, no FDA inspections to pass, no coveted A+ rating from the Better Business Bureau. Legalization would not only de-romanticize narcotics, but it would also make it *more* difficult for youngsters to get their hands on them without consulting a doctor.

It has been nearly a century since Freud opined, "Life as we find it is too hard for us; it entails too much pain, too many disappointments, impossible tasks. We cannot do without palliative remedies . . . intoxicating substances."[396] A stack of pancakes, a sunny vacation, a taxing workout, a sexual rendezvous, a deep tissue massage, a good book by the fire; there are countless methods for scratching the itch of human vice. As Freud goes on to note, "The crudest of these methods of influencing the body, but also the most effective, is the chemical one: that of intoxication."[397] We do ourselves no collective favors in regurgitating the lies our parents fed us about drugs and drug users, the same platitudes which have been used for hundreds of years to stigmatize addicted people, lock up poor people of color, and criminalize anyone who uses or possesses a chemical on the no-no list.

As for negative consequences related to legalization, most researchers (myself included) agree there will be a slight increase in use on the heels of legalization. It turns out that when people are not forced to purchase polluted drugs from illegal dealers in shady markets at the risk of incarceration, people sometimes choose to use them.[398] But the slight increase in use will come with a massive decrease in the harm caused by use. Skin infections and contaminated drugs will become a thing of the past, and mislabeled or unlabeled products, which contribute to the majority of opioid overdose deaths, will no longer be a concern. Our cultural beliefs about drugs will change, and along with them, the ability of users to succeed without encountering systemic barriers at every turn.

The world of drug users and dealers will also see a cultural shift. Right now, if I ask my drug dealer for heroin, he will likely give me heroin (if he has any). He will not attempt to talk me out of buying it because his livelihood would be at stake. He will not attempt to explain the effects in objective language without romanticizing his product. He is a salesman, and I am a customer.

He might, on the other hand, attempt to talk me into purchasing some additional drugs, possibly cocaine or methamphetamine in addition to my heroin. I can be certain that the drugs he is selling are cut, possibly with fentanyl(s), leaving me prone to overdose or complications related to using multiple substances together. There aren't many checks in place to prevent any of this from occurring, but there are plenty of incentives ensuring it will.

Doctors are the flipside of this coin. They get into medicine to *help* people, and when they meet someone who believes they want to try the strongest drug on the market, they can attempt to start them with something a bit lighter, and then work their way up, if necessary. They would also encourage patients to use the smallest dose possible to produce the desired effect. This is what responsible drug use looks like, and it is completely absent from our current doctor-patient relationships when it comes to intoxicants. But imagine a world where a curious consumer could inquire about heroin without fearing the judgement of their physician. And imagine a physician who would willingly write the prescription, knowing that a refusal to do so would force their patient to purchase polluted heroin on the streets. Things would look a lot different.

Doctors are taught to discuss dangerous drug combinations with patients. They don't pitch substances you aren't interested in, offering you some cocaine to go with your morphine. And they don't give patients drugs packed with unknown and unknowable substances. A doctor could not cut pharmaceutical drugs on Frank's countertop even if they wanted to. Unlike drug dealers, doctors focus on patients' overall quality of life.

In the event someone has an issue with drugs (remember, more than 80% of those who try them never will), a system of regulation ensures medical professionals are always nearby to offer harm reduction and therapeutic advice.

As anyone who has used the services of budtenders in states where cannabis is now legal can tell you, salespeople are impressively prepared to offer advice as to dosage, potency and effects. It is just good business in a legal economy. The number of drug users will rise slightly on the heels of legalization, but the number of heavy drug users will decrease.[399] A few more people might use opioids, but far less will use heroin, especially via mainline injection.

For those like myself who do become addicted at some point, there will be no street scene to contend with, no underground market to navigate, no daily visits to the crack house to purchase polluted products, no injecting fake drugs or blood, and not a single shit-covered baggy to be found. We will no longer have to scrounge up enough cash to pay for a pack or two. Addicted people will naturally opt for free and uncut chemicals administered by professionals who can offer medical help in case of addiction or overdose. Treatment can be offered during every visit, in multiple forms, free of charge and without threat of criminal sanctions. And with all the cash we save on prosecution, incarceration, correctional employee salaries and burying uninsured dead people, we can afford to take care of drug users, like we should have been doing all along.

Police officers who were once foot soldiers will be reassigned to investigating real crimes, and perhaps the smallest foundations of trust might begin to be built between law enforcement and those communities which the War on Drugs has historically worked to destroy and divide. As it stands, there is little space for that project to begin, because, as Michelle Alexander has said, "when police go looking for drugs, they look in the hood," they naturally head to communities where there are plenty of people and few walls, fences or private spaces.[400] Illegal activity is easier to spot in these areas, and suspects are less likely to be able to afford effective counsel. The system is designed to ensure poor people and people of color are easier to prosecute and arrest, and it is all unspoken, hidden in the margins, where it can be written off as business as usual.

In the United States, there has never been a time when black folks were less likely than white folks to live below the poverty level.[401] That means any system which negatively impacts poor people more than rich people will automatically, yet invisibly, perpetuate racial discrimination. White supremacy has been incredibly successful in that regard. When cops head to poor communities, they are frequently heading for communities that are disproportionally made up of people of color.[402]

Things are not getting any better when it comes to upward mobility in black communities. According to research recently published in the *Quarterly Journal of Economics*, "black Americans have substantially lower rates of upward mobility and higher rates of downward mobility than whites, leading to large income disparities that persist across generations."[403] Much like the original prohibitions against drugs at the state level, police officers can arrest poor people (of color) for doing things rich (white) people get away with doing all the time. The system is self-sustaining.

In the months following legalization, murder rates will likely plummet the same way they did at the end of alcohol prohibition.[404] Crime will decrease like it did in Portugal, since addicted people will no longer have to scramble to come up with a few bucks for a fix.[405] Trust in law enforcement will increase as bogus drug arrests and pretext traffic stops become a thing of the past.[406] Addicted folks will begin to get better instead of worse. Drug-related violence will plummet; there won't be anything to fight over since cocaine, heroin, and other drugs will be far too cheap for underworld dealers to sell profitably. And most importantly, the prison-industrial complex will quickly shrink to a size that is no longer (such) a national embarrassment.

The end of the War on Drugs, which is now more than a century in coming, will bring all of these changes and more. My people will stop dying without funerals, and instead begin to receive the services and support they need. The choice this generation has is the same choice the last generation had, and the one before them. We must choose whether or not to continue a counter-productive war, or to accept the unavoidable truth of human nature and help one another through tough times. We must choose whether to pass this legacy of oppression on to yet another generation through stereotypes and misinformation, or to end the war.

This project can begin with our language, one of the easiest ways to show love. This section was titled "Life Enhancement and Harm Reduction," two ideas that often get presented in reverse order, to the detriment of drug users. Carl Hart said this best in his book, *Drug Use for Grown Ups;* the term harm reduction, "...doesn't capture the complexity associated with grown-up activities such as love or war or drug use. Instead, it preoccupies us with drug-related harms. And the connection between harms and drug use is reinforced repeatedly through our speech."[407] Harm reduction unavoidably focuses first and foremost on the *dangers* of drug use, even though the vast majority of use is not only harmless, but positive.

It is unfortunate that we don't have a better term for public policy initiatives, but for now, harm reduction seems to be catching on more than any other paradigm, possibly because it reinforces the shame that undergirds the entire War on Drugs.[408] We need to legalize safe use sites and heroin clinics, and we need to continue working toward outright decriminalization and regulation. Not only will these policies reduce harm to some people, but they will also greatly improve the quality of many more lives than they will save.

NEEDLE EXCHANGES WERE illegal throughout the United States until 1991, when a group of eight activists in New York City announced their intent to hand out clean needles anyway. They even called the local police and the media, telling them when and where. And predictably, they were arrested and charged with violating New York law.[409] The resulting court case, which they won, paved the way for Harm Reduction efforts across the state, and eventually across the country, saving countless lives at a time when HIV was ravaging drug-using communities. That was the only reason the case had merit at all. The defendants argued the necessity of breaking the law to save lives during an unprecedented HIV outbreak amongst drug using communities. And the judge agreed, ruling that the HIV epidemic was such a pressing emergency that the group's actions were justified.[410]

Perhaps there is an opportunity here to hoist the CDC with its own petard.[411]

Given the noteworthy overreporting of overdose deaths and the current situation with fentanyl(s), this legal challenge framework will likely be used again in the near future to force the courts to reconsider the Constitutional rights of drug users. We are, after all, in the midst of an unprecedented explosion in overdose deaths that could, like HIV transmission in 1991, be halted with a single act which is currently illegal. The CDC's exaggerated death rates might actually pave the way for safe use sites to open despite their illegality, and to remain open under the same sort of necessity clause which was used to legalize needle exchanges.[412]

According to some scholars, we don't even need to challenge the Controlled Substance Act to open safe use sites. Within the federal law which forbids the operation of any premises where illegal drugs are knowingly used, also known as the "Crack House Statute," there is a provision which exempts local law enforcement agencies during "the enforcement of any law or municipal ordinance relating to controlled substances."[413] Although the original intent of this clause was likely to allow cops to possess drugs during undercover deals or drug busts without fearing prosecution, its wording and its lack of precedent might pave the way for the country's first safe use sites. With 96,000 deaths blamed on overdose last year alone, the tipping point may already be here, just waiting for someone to force the issue.

Chapter 5: A Doctor, a Criminal and a Junkie Walk into a Bar

"I don't see why everybody feels as though
they gotta tell me how to live my life. Let me
live, baby. Let me live."   —Tupac Shakur[414]

We have all been lied to, sold a bill of goods penned with innocent blood. Believing those lies, we have supported a system which seeks to incarcerate, infect and kill our loved ones, and sometimes us. But we can stop this ongoing atrocity any time we wish. We can end the war and begin a new era of reconstruction.

Life will not be perfect. Unlike the drug warriors, I will not promise the impossible. We can't wave a magic wand and stop addiction, nor the trauma which undergirds it. But we can maximize the benefits of drug use, while minimizing the dangers. And we can free up a ton of cash for dealing with any unforeseen issues that might arise in the process.

But we have a big problem. Right now, many have no interest in solving the opioid epidemic or in shutting down the prison-industrial complex. As it stands, many feel that those who wind up in prison or the morgue deserve to be there. Hollywood has only made matters worse. Study after study has shown that people who watch television shows, movies or even news pro-grams in which crime and punishment are represented are more likely to support a permanently expanding prison system, along with increased penalties for crimes.[415]

Our lust for vengeance is a direct result of our mislabeling of motives; we have convinced ourselves that people are respon-sible for actions which are beyond their control. The criminal justice system is built on the cornerstone of free will. It is time to find a better design.

Advice from a Doctor

Professor Timothy Leary loved LSD.[416] He frequently encouraged students and faculty alike to take the drug without preparing them for what to expect. Few were surprised when he was fired from Harvard for, among other things, what amounted to unsanctioned experiments wherein he gave LSD to his stu-dents.[417] Leary's gusto for psychedelic experiences became his calling card, but his advice to casually consume was lacking one important component of responsible use: preparation.

Set and setting are always important.[418] The location where you are hanging out and who you are with when you take a drug constitutes the setting, and it can have a profound effect on your experience, your reaction, and even how hard the drug hits you. Like humans, rats given daily doses of heroin until they develop tolerance can endure higher doses in the future without suffering an overdose, but only if their setting remains constant.[419] Move them to a new space, and things get weird.

Scientists believe tolerance relies on setting. Like Pavlov's salivating dogs, it appears the sights, smells, thoughts and move-ments which normally show up before a dose instigate a series of biological adjustments, preparing our bodies to tolerate the drugs we are about to consume.[420] But the effects of tolerance fade when the rats are moved to a new cage, because the context cues don't stand out like they do in the regular dose settings. These rats don't recognize the normal clues that they are about to consume a drug, so they don't activate their tolerance mechanisms prior to use. Many of them die when given the same dose of heroin they have taken dozens of times before without overdosing, the result of a simple change in setting.

Drugs affect us differently depending on where they are taken; setting is vital to tolerance. The clues and stimuli which stand out in our familiar spaces fade into the backdrop when we are elsewhere. The smell of heroin, the feel of having paraphernalia in hand, the click of the television always turned on before getting high—they all become more difficult to spot (or entirely absent) when we use outside our normal setting, so our bodies are not able to fully prepare for the incoming dose.

Setting is important for user safety, but just like with everything else in the War on Drugs, the US has created the most dangerous environment imaginable. Users are forced to shoot up in parking lots, bathrooms and backseats, wherever we can sneak away after obtaining our dope. Predictably (and avoidably), overdoses occur, not because of the drugs, but because of the environment in which we are forced to use them.

Setting is only half of the recipe. Everything going on in your life and in your body constitutes set. Psychedelic drugs (like LSD and Psilocybin) are often described from an experiential perspective as opening the channels of thought and amplifying the emotions or concerns one is already experiencing.[421] From a scientific perspective, psychedelics generate connections between areas of the brain which normally don't communicate, instigating creativity and an ability to rethink things we normally take for granted.[422] When we are struggling to find inspiration, or when we are wandering around the woods taking in nature's beauty, this effect can be enthralling. But when we are in a bad mood, a depressed state, an angry fury, or a self-destructive spin, psychedelics will amplify the thoughts and emotions associated with *those* states of mind. My set always includes my Asperger's, which is why drugs like cocaine and psychedelics provide a different experience for me than they do for most users. Opioids, too, are known for their varying effects; they put some people to sleep, while others experience energy and alertness, and some people don't enjoy them at all because of differences in genetics, biology and experience, or what drug experts call set.[423]

Set and setting are both important every time we use a drug. Leary's failure to emphasize this aspect of responsible drug use led generations of unsuspecting psychonauts to experience unnecessary challenging trips.[424] It is hard to estimate the number of people who might have benefited from psychedelics had Leary not turned them off by encouraging them to take too much, or to take them at the wrong time. Psychedelic therapy is currently showing tremendous potential in countries where it is permitted.[425] There is nothing (aside from laws) preventing the rest of us from using the same techniques to work through our own issues in the privacy of our homes. Those of us who have been doing this sort of therapy for years can attest to the value of trusting friends who help us drudge through personal hang-ups and traumas from our past. They are sometimes more valuable than therapists.

Leary wasn't the only cultural icon to hype irresponsible drug use. Sigmund Freud, too, was wrong in his insistence that cocaine was a panacea capable of curing nearly anything ailing a patient. His original writings about the drug claimed that it produced,

> "...exhilaration and lasting euphoria, which in no way differs from the normal euphoria of the healthy person...You perceive an increase of self-control and possess more vitality and capacity for work....In other words, you are simply normal, and it is soon hard to believe you are under the influence of any drug.... Long intensive physical work is performed without any fatigue...This result is enjoyed without any of the unpleasant after-effects that follow exhilaration brought about by alcohol....Absolutely no craving for the further use of cocaine appears after the first, or even after repeated taking of the drug."[426]

Freud changed his tune before his death and quit endorsing cocaine quite so vocally. But his change of heart only came after publishing numerous studies encouraging doctors to prescribe it, and after nearly killing more than one of his friends by suggesting they take huge, intravenous doses as treatment for opioid addictions.[427] Freud and Leary both discredited their own research by offering dangerous and inaccurate advice about drugs.

But when they were right, they were right.

FREUD REALIZED THE metaphors he used to describe things like neurosis and chemical imbalances would eventually be replaced with more accurate descriptions of what was going on in the body: "We must remember that all of our provisional ideas about psychology will one day be explained on the basis of organic substrates."[428] Nonetheless, he felt like he had to try and make sense of his world even if he didn't have as much physical evidence at his disposal as those who would come after him. Leary, too, was thrust into the spotlight and chose to use it as a platform to change opinions about drugs and those who use them.[429] Both men should have been a bit more cautious, but much of what they believed has survived the test of time.

Freud argued that when we are very young, we form a number of important memories which create drives for things like food, sex and fun.[430] His infamous take on the Oedipus complex suggests we all want to kill one of our parents so we can claim the other as our sex partner, an urge rooted in our earliest memories of safety and attraction to another.[431] He believed this desire arises early in life, and that it never totally goes away. Bizarre as this notion was at the time, it would become well accepted by the turn of the century. Today it is taken for granted.[432] The theory applies *not* in its original inception, where we all want to sleep with one parent and kill the other, but in the sense that hidden motives and shadowy desires are always informing our behavior at the subconscious level, all the result of specific events from our childhood. We are the stuff of our memories, the final fruit of ongoing life experiences which shape our expectations for the future.

Free will is a handy illusion, and not even a very good one. As neuroscientist Sam Harris summarizes, "Thoughts and intentions emerge from background causes of which we are unaware and over which we exert no conscious control."[433] Our actions and desires are the result of prior causes, which are themselves the result of prior causes. We do not choose our parents, who we befriend in our childhood, or what religious perspective we are taught to accept as truth. These things just happen, but they form the foundation for the rest of our lives, becoming a lens for viewing the world and a toolkit from which we make decisions. Where is the freedom in that?

To make his foresight clearer, consider a less-debated topic which Freud studied: trauma. He believed that distress experienced at a young age informs our perspective for the rest of our lives.[434] His brand of therapy varied greatly from the norm of his day. Most psychoanalysis involved observing patients while they babbled on about whatever popped into their heads when looking at a picture of a horse, or when directed to think about the color red. Therapists would listen for words or sounds made by the patient, then analyze them for hidden meanings.[435] Words like "ma" and "god" might be pulled out of a five-minute babble session and used to diagnose a patient with neurosis or narcissism.

Freud had a better idea. To be sure, he was not the first person to exploit the human need to unload on someone, to unburden fears and anxieties in an effort to process unsettled conflicts. But he was the first to turn his brand of psychoanalysis into a science, shifty as it sometimes proved to play out in application. When it came to traumatic experiences from early in one's life, Freud discovered that we never fully recover unless we examine what is going on and actively attempt to change the thoughts and reactions which appear whenever we access a particular memory, whether that memory is deliberately retrieved, or it pops into our minds unexpectedly.[436]

Freud focused on *how* we avoid those nasty feelings that show up when we are exposed to situations or people that make us feel anxious or frustrated.[437] We were bullied as a child and never dealt with the shame and fear inflicted, so now whenever we encounter a stressful situation, we clam up, shut down, and try to escape. We were robbed at gunpoint years ago and now we always carry a gun, or we struggle to leave the house at night. We were passed over for promotions and raises in the past, so now we stay in our shell and keep our head down, punching the clock and getting through the day. Our life is the stuff of daily decision based on past traumas, but few of these links remain visible in our conscious perception of the world. We don't exactly think to ourselves, *you know, being bullied 40 years ago in elementary school was tough, so I think I am going to have a panic attack today.* It all happens in the dark, in the recesses of our mind, where what Freud called neurosis lives.[438]

Think about all of the things your brain does without forcing you to notice, the unconscious, never-ending work required to make sense of the world in real time. I am writing these words as I sit in my office. A fan is running behind me because I prefer the white noise. There is a shelf full of books to my right, and, without looking closely, I can assure you that I have read many of them. I can even recall various titles on demand: Gladwell's *The Tipping Point*, Harris's *Free Will*, Freud's *The Interpretation of Dreams*, hooks's *Outlaw Culture*, and many more. The window is closed, but the door is opened, and noises from outside my office sometimes interrupt my train of thought whether I want them to or not. My son just walked down the stairs across the hall and, without looking, I knew it was him, and that the creaking I heard was the staircase (I had better turn up the white noise).

Incredibly, I didn't have to think about any of it. I could double check the books on the shelf to make sure they are all there, and that they are all indeed books and not facsimiles made by a clever book thief. I could look up from my work to verify the creaking stairs were indeed the result of my son walking down them. But I don't need to double check those things, because my brain did all of that work for me the second I walked into my office this morning, and it continues to do that work right now. That is what being a human is. We are constantly forming updated models of the world based on our past experiences.[439] From an attention-saving point of view, this is incredibly convenient, even though it comes with a massive downside.

Imagine how tedious life would be if every time we walked into a space we had to examine and identify items consciously, classifying them one at a time using our database of memories. Daily existence would become a drag. Each moment would take an hour of conscious, deliberate labeling: doorknob, door, chair, desk, drawer, pen, floor, carpet. You can attempt this yourself, if you are feeling sadistic. You can *try* to turn your autopilot off and deliberately examine everything each time you enter a space, but you won't have much luck. We tend to snap right back into autopilot.

Here's what such an experiment would look like.

I walk up to my office door to get to work, but it is not a door, not yet. First, I have to look and consider…flat surface, large rectangle, small knob…this is a portal, and that little round thing, it turns. Some clever engineer has attached the knob to a latch which opens the door. How cool is that. I figured out how a door works, and now I can enter my office. It only took 10 seconds.[440]

I open the door and look around, but I can't just walk in because I have to consciously label what I am looking at: carpet, walls, ceiling, light switch, desk, chair, pens and open space. Each must be actively observed and identified. And before proceeding, it is worth considering if I can remember the door I just walked through, or if I will need to reassess and label it once more as soon as I look away. If we decide, at this point in the experiment, to extend ourselves the luxury of short-term memory, allowing us to locate and label each item just once-per-visit, then we are already playing along with the process by which we automatically classify and label things without consciously thinking about it. These mental shortcuts minimize the work required of our brains when it comes to performing what we see as unimportant, peripheral jobs. We cut corners and make snap judgements because the payout is huge: we can focus more of our attention on the project at hand.

We do this every minute of every day, everywhere we go. We open doors without thinking. We follow sidewalks and traffic signals unconsciously. We navigate our world on autopilot, saving our attention for the things we consider more important, like social interactions and unexpected threats. On occasion we find ourselves arriving home after work and wondering, "how did I get here? I hardly remember the drive." We mow the lawn, tie our shoes, shower and shave in a haze, barely thinking about any of it consciously, allowing our minds to focus on things we consider more important, like that meeting later today, that argument last week, or that important due date around the corner.

All of our unconscious behaviors and reactions are rooted in our memories, and we have learned so well what to expect that we can now carry out complicated processes like driving or shaving without paying much attention. Our ability to *do* without realizing we are *doing* is built into our blueprints. It is yet another trait so beneficial once-upon-a-time in evolutionary history that it spread throughout the entire population.[441]

We wouldn't want it any other way. The energy necessary to do what I just described is unsustainable, and I could not teach, write, cook, or build meaningful relationships if I had to process everything in my environment all the time. I would need a nap halfway to my desk.

EVOLUTIONARY BIOLOGIST AND philosopher Richard Dawkins has described, "In nature, the usual selecting agent is direct, stark and simple. It is the grim reaper."[442] The selection process he refers to is the natural selection of evolution, the way some creatures disappear into extinction while others survive into the future. Humans live on a planet where more than 99% of all species which have ever existed are already extinct.[443] Dawkins is interested in the process through which typical causes of extinction in a population of organisms, like natural disasters or food shortages, spare some creatures while decimating others. Anything that gives one creature a chance of surviving when another dies will likely make its way through the population.

Freud's work largely focused on the human ability to tune out much of the stimuli from our environment and our own body, and to divert that attention to survival, particularly to social concerns. For Freud, our traumatic experiences and sexual desires push and pull our behavioral choices unconsciously, and unless we deliberately press past that self-imposed veil of hidden motives, we will struggle with things like anxiety or depression without recognizing the source of our discomfort.[444] Humans are largely products of unconscious decisions; our wills are not our own.

Leary toyed with the same idea. He called it the Great Neurological Robbery because he saw it as a huge loss in our ability to self-reflect and practice mindfulness.[445] Leary's infamous

"Turn on, tune in and drop out" slogan applied Freud's ideas concerning unconscious desires and anxieties to the methods we use to satiate those desires and anxieties. In capitalist societies, one of the easiest ways to scratch that itch is to consume; we buy a shiny toy and distract ourselves for a few minutes instead of heading to the therapist. Leary further claimed that only by dropping out of *all* systems of power, including school, work, protest movements, and the economy, could one ever regain a sense of connection with one's mind and body, as well as with the real world outside of capitalism.[446]

Leary's philosophies were often so radical that they were impossible to envision. What would a culture without culture look like? How could we all drop out and still eat, have homes, or enjoy life? It was a bit of an oxymoron: you have to let the system burn around you if you ever want to truly enjoy life. Given Leary's habit of keeping a head full of acid, it isn't all that surprising that his theories often landed far outside the box. Yet there is something to this idea of a Great Neurological Robbery. The concept invites Freud, Dawkins and Leary into the same conversation.

FROM AN EVOLUTIONARY perspective, humans have only survived this long because we cannot detect what's going on in our pancreas or our kidneys. We can't make our stomachs move faster or our blood vessels constrict. We often don't even realize when these things happen. What an incredible benefit to survival, or at least it was tens of thousands of years ago, in a world much different than the one most of us inhabit today. The evolutionary advantage is obvious if we rewind the clock to a setting where predators might kill a human who is busy trying to figure out how a door works for the hundredth time today, or preoccupied tinkering with their digestion speed. Anyone who could do these things unconsciously would be able to devote more attention to detecting and evading the predator at their heels just a little bit faster than their confused friend. As Colorado hikers are apt to repeat, you don't have to be able to outrun a bear. You only have to be able to outrun your friend when the bear begins chasing you both.

It is the same story with our bodily functions. Without the Great Neurological Robbery, humans might find ourselves so preoccupied with running the controls of our body that we lose track of our environment, allowing a predator to sneak up and eat us. Or we might forget to beat our heart, digest our food, or activate our pancreas. We can only pay attention to a small bit of our world at any given time.[447] What a benefit to have autopilot always engaged, thereby allowing our focus to aim outward, at the world around us. What a loss, a robbery even, to be unable to turn that autopilot completely off. We can never truly experience what is going on in our own bodies, because we wouldn't have survived this long if we could.

When Freud was discussing neurosis caused by untreated trauma from childhood, he was pointing to the brain's tendency to defer to past experiences as a shortcut for future success. When we find ourselves in a similar situation to one where we were traumatized, our *be on alert* circuits engage, and we start looking for a way to escape. But it happens automatically, often without any conscious, deliberate identification of a verified danger, and without any conscious thought given to the effectiveness of our escape strategy.[448] If you try cocaine after an argument and it works to level you out and improve your mood, you will be drawn to it the next time those same emotions and frustrations become bothersome. If you have been through an abusive relationship which comes to mind every time you interact with your boss (or anyone else for that matter), you will return to the tools which have been most effective in the past to avoid or manage those troublesome feelings.[449] You might minimize contact, or maybe you yell and insult, or you could just leave and never come back. Each of these reactions is a response to how we learned to be in the world, and it all happens outside of our conscious thought.

Some of us would never dream of cussing someone out and leaving, or resorting to physical violence, while others frequently do just that without remorse or active planning. Our urges and our responses to them are largely outside our conscious control. There is no free will in whatever pops into our minds when it is time to solve a problem, and there is no free will in the process through which we either follow that urge or resist it. It all just happens, instantaneously, and we are, at best, a witness to the process.

From the outside looking in, human responses often appear illogical. But when we are asked to explain why we did what we did, it is seldom difficult to come up with a story that makes sense to us, no matter how bizarre it sounds to everyone else.[450] We are stuck on autopilot, and that autopilot does more than just run our real time actions. It also tells us a story about the past, about why we did what we did. And what it tells us is often incredibly inaccurate, tailored to protect our personal interest.

Remember that the processes of sensitization and tolerance from Chapter Three are not unique to drug use. Our lives are the stuff of sensitization and tolerance. Without them, we wouldn't know the difference between safe, beneficial stimuli, and dangerous, exciting stimuli. When trauma comes to inform someone's worldview, they naturally view the original event as dangerous. Like anything viewed by the body as risky or exciting, we become sensitized to cues or reminders of the original traumatic experience, because that is the fastest way to react in case it happens again. We want to outrun our friend if the bear shows up.

When something is viewed as positive, safe or satisfying, our bodies develop tolerance. We make adjustments to ensure that more of the substance or behavior can be tolerated without risking overdose. Unfortunately, that means it also takes more to provide the same effects that once appeared with minimal doses. The bathroom at the dope spot was filthy, and today I would gag the second I entered such a space. But I could tolerate it then because my unconscious mind had come to view it as necessary to my safety. The edginess and paranoia from slamming cocaine, on the other hand, showed up faster each time I used, because my body viewed those reactions to the drug as dangerous, exciting and somewhat unpleasant.

There was no off switch within my field of vision, no edginess-reduction valve, no "turn on, tune in and drop out" button. Even though my conscious mind recognized the drugs as a good thing, my unconscious mind was hard at work tinkering with the dials to make sure the next time cocaine showed up, I would notice the paranoia and anxiety sooner through the process of sensitization. But my brain was also working to tolerate the good parts of the drug, to make sure I would *not* feel medicated without taking a larger dose each time through the process of tolerance. It was almost like two competing worldviews were playing out in my head simultaneously, arriving at different decisions which often contradicted one another. More on that shortly.

Our failure to notice our daily experience is also a product of tolerance. Our bodies have long recognized the benefits associated with freeing up mental energy that might otherwise be devoted to growing toenails, activating white blood cells, or labeling doors, chairs and desks every time we enter an office. We tolerate our mental state of obliviousness so much that we are oblivious to *it*, and unless something goes terribly wrong, we tend to lose track of the connection between mind and body.

The first step in mindfulness is recognizing just how unmindful humans are of our surroundings, and even our own bodies, for most of our lives. We usually don't think much about our mind/body link until things aren't working right. The importance of mindfulness when navigating drug use cannot be overstated. If something is producing anxiety, you should take the time to identify what it is before pouring booze or heroin onto it. And you should expect a difficult search for the problem, because, like everything else, your brain is more likely to spit out a lie than the truth. If you don't pay close attention, you might wind up thinking you are mad at your friend when you are actually annoyed at one of your own quirks, or you might think you couldn't sleep because of acid indigestion, when you were actually tossing and turning because of an argument you can't stop replaying.[451] Of all the tools on my shelf of self-care, mindful meditation is the most valuable and all-purpose.[452]

Sam Harris wrapped up his discussion of free will and mindfulness in a recent lecture by reminding listeners, "once we recognize that even the most terrible people are, in a very real sense, unlucky to be who they are, the logic of hating them as opposed to fearing them and restraining them begins to unravel...anyone born with the soul of a psychopath is profoundly unlucky."[453] The body you are born into and the experiences which shape you are never your choice, and the illusion that our decisions are freely made isn't even a convincing one.

As we shall see, when we look for free will, or even something we might call the illusion of free will, it is like grasping at water. The mirage disappears the second you try to snatch it up to take a good look.

Advice from a Criminal

The dope was in my right hand, an eight-ball of cocaine that stunk so bad my mouth was watering. I couldn't wait to get home and shoot up. And I was almost there, three blocks away, when the police car drove past, slowed, then turned around. The car accelerated up to my bumper as the driver activated the overheads, then honked the siren the way only cool cops do: *bwoop, BWOOOP!*

Luckily, I was prepared. I had cut the extra plastic off the baggie and rolled down the passenger window before leaving the dope spot, just in case. My palms were sweaty and my heartbeat heavy as I clicked on my right blinker, drifted toward the right curb, then turned sharply left at the next intersection. I flipped the bag of dope out the passenger window into a disserted lot, then accelerated halfway up the block before pulling to the curb. My only chance was that my toss was low enough, and that the dope traveled fast and far enough for the officers behind me to miss it.

The performance began with the customary commands: "Hands where we can see them. Get out of the car. Where is the dope?" We spent thirty minutes there, playing that game. I deliberately eyed my own car suspiciously; I acted ashamed that they had caught me; I feigned concern that they would search my vehicle. It was a performance of misdirected terror. But beneath the facade, I was ecstatic. It appeared they had missed my toss. There was nothing illegal in the car.

I was forced to walk home after the officers finished their search. Since the license plates were expired and the car was not insured, it was impounded. None of that matter. I had been pulled over with a felony charge in my car, but I had managed to walk away. Later that day, I even went back and found the dope. What a rush.

Despite my eagerness to take pride in what I saw as a victory, I didn't have a choice regarding how I felt. A million other scenarios might also have played out and caused me to experience all sorts of emotional states; horror, fear, contentment, exhilaration or disappointment were all distinct possibilities. Much of *my* reaction depended on the reaction of the officers, and try as I might, I had little control over that. Had they both consumed a fulfilling breakfast and had enough sleep the night before? Were they coming off a call where they were treated poorly by a suspect, and were they in a bad mood because of that? Were they buying my performance of misdirection? Had they both looked away at the right moment, as I tossed the dope? Were they the sort of cops who would plant evidence if they could not find any? All of these concerns were beyond my control, yet they all played a huge part in how I ultimately felt and behaved following the encounter.

Stranger still, not only was I choiceless in which emotions showed up, but I couldn't have guessed before the encounter how I would feel even if I had known the ultimate outcome. Plenty of past confrontations with police had ended without arrest. Sometimes I felt great. Other times I felt creeped out and anxious, like I was paying a group of armed warriors to rough me up and pat me down any time they wished. I never had any conscious control over which emotions showed up. I just felt the way I felt. Even if I had wanted to feel differently, it was beyond my power. Sure, I could have *lied* about how I felt and *pretended* to feel differently. But I could not have simply snapped my fingers and changed my reaction. Emotions don't work like that.

Emotions *do* work as instigators. The decisions one makes about what to do next are always based on how one feels in the moment. Did I walk home, slouch down on the couch and start complaining? Or did I barge in cheerfully with a tale of victorious dope throwing? My emotional state was the only difference, and that was entirely out of my control, based loosely on the outcome of the police encounter, along with a million other things over which I was powerless.

The feeling of confusion mixed with elation was not unusual. As an Aspie, I experience it all the time. But from where did this emotion spring? Why then? It is certainly not something I chose to experience.

Maybe it was linked to the drugs I had in the car. But then, why did I decide to use cocaine in the first place? Why was I so tempted to shoot it up when most drug users are not interested? Our entire punishment system and the War on Drugs which sustains it are built upon a foundational premise of free will which is impossible to demonstrate. The closer you look, the foggier it gets. When we punish someone in the United States, we begin with the axiom that they had the same choices as everyone else, yet they chose differently (and wrongly); that's why jury trials are a foundational right. But our decisions and beliefs, along with the emotional states which drive them, are not the result of free choices made by evaluating facts and then deciding on a course of action. We are poetry in motion, self-guided but never self-penned.

Your choice to avoid many of the things I have discussed thus far in this book has more to do with opportunity and programming than anything else. We didn't both find ourselves facing the same options with the same tool bag for navigating the same body in the same world. On the contrary, we are all different movements in different keys, directed at different tempos by forces set in motion before we existed. Free will is a farce.

We can make decisions in the moment, but we can never know nor reign in the motives which drive those decisions in real time. Yet we stubbornly maintain the illusion of control in the face of evidence to the contrary because, much like traumatic responses and unconscious auto-labeling (door, chair, etc.), it allows us to move on with our day instead of wasting time contemplating things better handled behind the scenes. Leary's Great Neurological Robbery doesn't just ignore the gaping holes in our self-perception. It provides a patchwork of stories and habits which cleverly camouflage the gaps well enough that we can pretend we don't notice them. Our inability to spot our own ignorance, or rather, our ability to *not* spot it, is yet another shortcut for life which allows us to devote attention outward, toward possible threats, instead of inward, toward the riddle of who in the world is controlling my mind and body, since it is clearly not me.

THE REASON SOME of us are drawn to heroin or cocaine while others are not even tempted comes down to chance in the form of genetics, biology and experience. There are plenty of situations which make addiction more likely, including childhood trauma, parental addictions and poverty.[454] But nothing *guarantees* someone will wind up addicted to a drug or a behavior. It takes a lot of consecutive events for that to happen, and they all have to come at the right time, in the right context.

As Maia Szalavitz has shown, "Addiction doesn't just appear; it unfolds."[455]

First, we have to encounter the drug or the behavior, and we must experience positive effects which we believe result from its use. That's not as common as you might think. Half of opioid users report they both like and dislike the effects at different times, and nearly 15% of those who try drugs like heroin or codeine don't enjoy them at all.[456] These folks can't get addicted to opioids because they don't experience the positive effects which might lead to repeated use in the face of ongoing consequences. Our use patterns cannot become automatic unless we consciously associate the drug or the behavior with positive feelings. There is no choice in whether or not one enjoys something; you either enjoy it or you do not.

Addiction also requires a belief that one *needs* whatever one is addicted to, another "decision" made behind the scenes, where free will isn't even thought to exist. The first time I detoxed from opioids, I did not know what was happening to me. I spent a restless vacation barely sleeping and sweating profusely because I left my hydrocodone at home after taking heavy doses steadily for around six months. I thought I had stomach flu, until it promptly went away as soon as I got home and took a pill. Since I had no idea at the time that the drugs were the problem, I was not tempted to cut the vacation short and head home, or to risk my safety and freedom trying to track down an underworld dealer. It was impossible for me to continue using the drug in the face of ongoing consequences because I didn't recognize the connection between the detox and the chemical.

If you don't consciously believe that something is bringing you irreplaceable comfort, you can't become addicted to it. While babies can be born *dependent* on drugs, they cannot be born *addicted* to drugs, because they lack the ability to seek them out. Plus, like me on that vacation, even when they go through the torment of detox, they don't know why they are sick.

In the United States, newborns are often separated from their mothers if they are born with drugs in their system, a cold-hearted policy which greatly increases the likelihood of the baby experiencing neonatal abstinence syndrome (drug detox).[457] When babies born with methadone or heroin in their bloodstream are allowed to stay with their mothers, only 20% of them experience detox symptoms severe enough to require controlled doses of morphine. When those same babies are removed from their mothers, nearly 80% of them experience detox symptoms requiring morphine.[458] Yet, like everything in the War on Drugs, we have settled for a set of rules and norms which assures the greatest level of suffering possible is delivered to babies who have no idea what is wrong with them. We force newborns to suffer opioid withdrawal, and we blame their mothers for their pain, knowing we could greatly reduce the suffering of both by simply allowing them to stay together. And it is all because of our cultural misunderstanding of addiction.

Once we know we enjoy a drug or a behavior, or that it relieves some sort of negative state, we still have a long way to go before meeting the criteria for addiction. The drug or behavior must be available. Continued use must become problematic and disrupt other areas of our life. And throughout the process, we must "learn" how irreplaceable the drug or behavior is, so when it becomes obvious to those around us that we should stop, we don't see it that way.

We do not choose any of it. Our insistence of starting the clock after years of life experience are already at play, then pretending we are all on a level playing field is yielding predictable results. We all make constant decisions based on a set of values, morals and concerns unique to each of us. If you do not struggle with drug use, or if you do but you have managed to overcome those struggles, you are profoundly lucky, not strong or blessed. Your feelings and responses to the world around you combined to give you a different set of desires and emotional responses, and for all sorts of reasons beyond your control, your life course played out differently than that of others. At this period in US history, you are lucky to have drawn that hand.

IRONICALLY, THE 12-STEP model both acknowledges our lack of free will and ignores it at the same time. The first three "steps" involve admitting you are powerlessness yet accepting that there are still ways for you to make changes (a "higher power").[459] This is a clever way to say free will is not real, and to constantly remind members they will have an easier go at life if they force that truth to remain in conscious thought, since it always wants to disappear into a haze of self-authored pride.

But 12-steppers forget this epiphany the second they have something to be proud of, as if the mistakes ought not count, but the successes always should. It is one thing to admit we didn't freely choose to do something awful; it is quite another to admit our achievements are no more prideworthy than our failures. It is one thing to claim my addiction and my crimes were not examples of traditional free will, but quite another to admit my PhD, my research, and even this book are not the result of buckling down and working harder than everyone else. But there is no other story that makes sense.

My successes as well as my failures were all the result of luck in the form of genetics, biology, experience and opportunity. I did not freely choose to write this book any more than I freely chose to shoot dope for half a decade. Those desires and my responses to them emerged out of the same mysterious mist as every other choice in my life. I was not invited to the meeting where these things were decided.

If 12-step programs work for you, you should keep using them. If, like me, you feel that they do more damage than good, you should be given the same opportunities as everyone else to find your most successful way of being in the world. Your reaction to the religious mentality of 12-step programing is outside of your control as much as anything else. If you grew up in any sort of Western religious environment, 12-step programs probably feel comfortable and natural, since the framework aligns with most Christian ideology.[460] And the programs' insistence on members giving up the illusion of free will is invaluable. It is unfortunate they only go halfway.

In 12-step programs, you don't have to be responsible for mistakes you made in the past because you recognize your state of mind and the use of substances that altered it had a lot to do with your behavior. That's why you must give yourself over to a "higher power," who is (hopefully) better than you at recognizing your biological drives and urges. Once your focus moves from individual decisions to your state of mind when making those decisions, you naturally come to recognize the connection between mind and body. While you might not be able to freely choose to stop using drugs or alcohol, according to 12-step models, you can freely choose to put yourself in a better position to say no when the offer or urge arises.[461]

But these programs fail to follow through with their swing by encouraging members to embrace a prideful attitude which only arrives *after* one is successful: clean and sober for xx days.[462] As great as it feels to take credit for all of our successes in life, we are lying to ourselves and to everyone else, a habit which humans have perfected. It is yet another example of the ease with which we construct stories to explain the world in simple and usually incorrect ways. No one wants to be responsible for the terrible things they do; everyone wants to be responsible for the great things they do. We can't have it both ways.

TO BRING THIS point about free will home, do me a favor. Decide to enjoy the next two paragraphs before you read them. Make an active decision to like them, even if they personally attack you or contain a message that deeply offends you. Give this a real try. Make that decision right now and watch the mental process closely. Pay attention to how you attempt to decide such an undecidable thing. Is your brain playing along? Is it rejecting the request outright? Are you trying to construct some sort of compromise? While all of that is happening too fast for you to keep up, which thoughts are you freely choosing to think, and which are you choosing not to think? Are the thoughts which are *not* popping into your head right now effecting your ultimate decision? Are you choosing what thoughts *don't* show up?

Of course, you cannot do this. You can no more decide what you will think about this paragraph before you read it than you can decide whether or not you will suddenly be distracted by thoughts of an upcoming wedding or interrupted by a phone call. You might lose track of the message and miss what I say altogether. You might become so enraged that you chuck this book in the trash and never finish reading it. Or you might enjoy what you read. It is all happening outside of your conscious control. The paragraphs said what they said, and you felt how you felt.

If we erased your memory and traveled back in time to run this experiment again, without changing anything else, you would feel exactly the same as last time. Unless we change something, nothing would be different, and the idea of coming to a different conclusion with the rest of the universe in the same state is absurd; there is nowhere for that different decision to happen. If you want an obvious example of our lives as poetry in motion, go back and start this section over and note the different choice you make when asked to like the next two paragraphs. You can't freely choose now because you know what the paragraphs say, and you couldn't freely choose then because you didn't know what the paragraphs say.

Whether or not you are resistant to the idea of rethinking free will, whether you are furious or curious at where I am headed with this train of thought, that isn't your choice either. We all have different stakes in this game: religious, professional, financial and social. Our unique combination of experiences, genetics and community connections informs our automatic reactions to the world around us, including incredible claims like the one I am making: there is no such thing as free will. We no more control our response to a proposition that challenges us than we control our response to being punched in the face by a stranger. You are the child on the merry-go-round, grasping a steering wheel which is connected to nothing, yanking and swerving, fully convinced that you are directing your own course.

Perhaps the creepiest development in contemporary neuroscience is the ease with which researchers can seemingly read our minds, and how they can do so long before *we* even know what we are going to think.[463] If a group of doctors had the proper equipment, calibrated to detect each neurological and biological change, they could predict what I was going to do seconds before I did it, long before I actually felt like *I* had decided what to do.[464] Imagine they had neuro-imaging equipment hooked up to the officers who pulled me over, allowing them to predict the outcome of the police encounter: whether or not the officers believed me, how and when I would throw the dope, and even my subsequent emotional state, which seemed to arise from nowhere. After our encounter, if we sat down with these clever researchers and allowed them to talk us through their findings, it would become obvious that many of the choices we all felt as if we had freely made were, in fact, evident to the researchers some time before we actually made them.

What we experience as decisions are in fact caused by events in our neurological network which are beyond not only our control, but also our comprehension.[465] The stories we tell ourselves about free will work to sustain our ignorance and obliviousness about what is happening in our bodies. They reinforce the Great Neurological Robbery. As a result, we learn to just accept things as they are. It is so much easier to pretend free will exists, and that we are all walking around in a world built upon it. Rethinking free will means rethinking everything.

Not only does our cultural understanding of free will fall apart upon close inspection, but so, too, does the illusion. The closest we can get to free will is our obtuse cultural refusal to have this conversation, and so we all carry on as if we really *think* it exists, even though our personal experience betrays the absurdity of the notion all the time. As soon as you look closely for this allegedly universal human trait, it disappears, along with whatever illusion we thought we had of it. Humans are Kenneth Burke's story-telling machines, tuned to a cross between fiction and convenience.[466] The explanations we produce are useful, but seldom accurate.

THUS FAR I have picked off the easy targets, pointing to obvious examples of free will being misapplied and misunderstood. But I am willing to go the other direction and accept that free will exist if I can find even a shred of it. If it is real, it should be most obvious in situations where our choices seem limitless, unhindered by outside interference, and unrushed. So I want to head right at the most obvious example, the place where it supposedly thrives, and I want to try to find it there, because if it isn't there, well, it isn't anywhere.

If I ask you to freely choose a song, any song, and to pay attention to the process through which you choose it, the illusion of free will you expect will never show up. You can easily recognize the fact that every song in the universe is not available to you, nor even every song you know of, since many of them simply don't come to mind.[467] You can't freely select any of the songs which did not pop into consciousness, nor those you haven't heard of, so free will is not evident in the long list of songs which failed to show up at the right second. Those choices remained in the darkness of unconsciousness, where you couldn't reach them. The few songs that did come to mind just popped up, and they came from somewhere beyond the reaches of conscious control or free choice. You didn't choose which options your brain presented to you and which it kept hidden; they simply emerged (or didn't) out of nothing.

Our thoughts, beliefs, emotions and attitudes all emerge from regions far beyond our control. You can't choose the trauma you experienced as a child any more than you can choose how you reacted to it. You can't choose which songs you don't know about, nor which songs presented themselves for selection at the perfect time. Where is the free will in any of this? We certainly haven't found it yet. But perhaps this search brings us closer.

It is possible that a close examination of the song you did choose will uncover free will. Let's zoom in and try to find a free choice in the limited decision to select a song from the short list your brain provided. Go ahead and pick another song (or the same one if you prefer), and again, pay close attention to the process of choosing. Did a few songs show up? Did you choose one of them, then change your mind at the last second and choose another? Did you attempt to pinpoint the spot where you freely chose without any outside interference from past memories, emotions, recent playlists or sad thoughts from past relationships?

If your list of choices was freely offered to you (by you), maybe you at least freely selected from Bruno Mars, Jimi Hendrix or Billie Holiday. Remember, in trying to disprove free will, I am willing to find even the smallest shred of it, and to take that shred as proof of its existence. If all we can find is a free choice of one out of three available options, that's good enough for me. But we haven't found it yet, even there.

If you selected from Hendrix, Holiday and Mars, chances are you have heard their music in the past (likely by no choice of your own), and at least one of their songs stuck with you well enough for you to conjure it up in when asked to pick a song (again, by no choice of your own, since you either liked the song or you didn't). So far you are a programmed robot who spit out three options at random, all from your personal experience. And when you zoom all the way in on that final choice of just one out of the three, you won't find evidence of free will so much as that same indescribable process which you witnessed more than participated in. A choice was certainly made, but it wasn't made by you acting through conscious, deliberate free will.

Your brain responded to the request to choose a song, and then it narrowed down the few available choices to just one using processes and concepts outside of both logic and consciousness. You might have thought, "I listened to Bruno yesterday, so I won't choose him." But you might have just as easily thought, "I listened to Bruno yesterday, so I *will* choose him." And then you might have changed your mind at the last second, or not, all for reasons you do not know anything about. It doesn't even *feel* like free will when you pay close attention.

If you did change your mind, you cannot explain why that happened, nor why you experienced the urge to change your mind, nor why you "chose" to follow that urge rather than resist it. There is no free will in any of this. The world was the way it was, and the decision you made was what it was. To say it could have been otherwise is to ignore the process by which you made that decision, *and you had a front row seat.* Free will requires that, all things being exactly the same as they were, one might have made a different decision than one made; it requires that the universe could have been different than it was even if everything was exactly the same as it was.[468] The entire concept is utter nonsense.

Let us return again to the experiment where neuroscientists have us strapped into equipment calibrated to read our physiological reactions in real time. Whatever remaining hold free will might have should erode under the realization that the people watching the readout could likely report which of your three songs you were going to choose some time before you felt as if you were choosing.[469] Even though our choices might feel, in hindsight, as if they were freely made, the evidence continues to expose just how confused we remain for most of our lives in regards to our own bodies.

THE HUMAN TENDENCY to deceive ourselves becomes obvious when people have injuries or operations which effectively sever the communication between left and right brain hemispheres (the corpus callosum is the portion of the brain responsible for this communication). Following these procedures, patients can experience unconscious movements which they have a hard time comprehending as their own.[470] There are examples from medical literature of people disagreeing with themselves, taking money out of their pocket with one hand, then putting it back with the other, or using one hand to push the other away as it keeps trying to stroke their face and hair.[471] One patient described his arm as having "a will of its own."[472] While I (the author) am not a neurologist, I am a Doctor of Communication, so my focus is on the stories people tell themselves and others about their own conditions. I am interested in the ways we make sense of what happens in the world around us without admitting we are clueless.

When the transfer of information (communication) between hemispheres is disrupted, whether by a permanent severing of the corpus callosum, a disabling of one hemisphere using transcranial magnetic stimulation, or even a stroke, the resulting state of confusion can sometimes lead to what has been called "Alien Hand Syndrome," a condition in which the patient can't articulate why their hand is moving.[473] When the areas of the brain responsible for moving one's left hand can't communicate with the areas of the brain responsible for assembling coherent speech, patients are unable to explain why their left hand is moving, since the speech areas lack that information. But that doesn't mean we don't *try* to articulate a reason from the information available. And like the last person in line during a game of telephone, the demand for an answer in the face of missing information leads to some clever stories, none of which track with reality.

V.S. Ramachandran studies a similar condition called anosognosia in which patients who have limb paralyses, especially from strokes or other injuries sustained in the brain's right hemisphere, do not accept their diagnosis, instead claiming that they are in fact not paralyzed.[474] These patients are not delusional. In fact, they can coherently discuss any topic which does not involve their own paralysis. But when they are asked about their paralyzed limb, they appear to simply ignore reality and instead tell a fantastic story which seems so easy to disprove that we might find ourselves questioning their sanity.[475]

Their far-fetched stories are the manufactured product of a brain designed to make sense of the world in the fastest way possible by attempting to recognize objects from prior experience. Since they lack vital connections between areas of their brain which were once functional and key to making sense of the world, they find themselves running on outdated software, processing information with missing data. They *feel* as if they are a unified whole because what else can a human be? But they don't understand why the normal messages about movement and the location of body parts are not coming through, so they rapidly process the information they have and come to what feels like a logical conclusion.

When these patients are pushed, as happens when someone asks them to move the paralyzed limb which they claim is fully functional, they might actually *feel* as if they move it, and they sometimes even claim to *see* it move. But eventually the illusion falls apart. In one experiment, researchers ask anosognosia patients to pick up a tray full of glass dishes, and truly believing they are capable of doing so, many flip the tray over when only one side is actually lifted. In these situations, it becomes impossible to ignore the lack of movement, so patients finally amend their explanations, admitting that they might indeed be experiencing some sort of paralysis. But tellingly, even when they update their stories, they seem to not notice *the update*. They usually claim their descriptions were correct all along, conveniently forgetting the wrong answers offered just seconds earlier.[476]

Ramachandran has described patients who tell stories so bizarre they often don't make sense. When he lifted one patient's hand in front of her face, she said it was his hand, not hers.[477] Other patients claimed they were consciously refusing to move their arms because they didn't like his tone, or because they were tired of being bossed around. And they believed their own stories; they were fooling *themselves*. Like the rest of us, they were incredibly versed at self-deception. Humans have an easy time coming up with a story on the spot which fits the riddle at hand, then refusing to acknowledge the clear mistakes made during our snap judgements.

ONE MORE TOE-DIP into neurology reveals what is going on here. Generally speaking, the right and left hemispheres of the brain control (and process input from) the opposite sides of the body; the right hemisphere controls the left side of our body, and the left hemisphere controls the right side of our body.[478] That means when the left hemisphere (using the right field of vision) notices the left arm (controlled by the right hemisphere) moving, it needs the right hemisphere to also send over an accompanying message: *I am going to move our left hand now*.[479] Without that update, the movement appears foreign and unexpected to the left hemisphere. And depending on the state of mind one is in, the explanation offered might be slightly illogical or straight up ridiculous.

The right and left hemispheres of the human brain are yet another conversation that has been mismanaged for decades, and our cultural muck of confusion has simplified the myth to the point of absurdity. We have been taught that the right hemisphere is responsible for images and creativity, and that the left is responsible for speech and reason.[480] There are some scraps of truth in this generalization, since much of our speech (not all) is indeed assembled in the left hemisphere. But a better way to think of the human brain is as two fully conscious supercomputers linked by an ethernet cord (the corpus collosum).[481] You might also think of humans as having an extra brain component called the frontal lobe which inhibits our actions, allowing us to think before we act on automatic messages telling us to freak out or run away when a spider falls from the ceiling.[482]

The hemispheres develop incredibly different views of the world. I like to think of my brain hemispheres like two family members having dinner, one an avid conservative blowhard, and the other a liberal, bleeding-heart activist. They could communicate, and they could even get along once they got to know each other, so long as they avoided triggering one another with contradicting views of the world. But their perspectives are so different it is hard to imagine a point of unification.

Most of Ramachandran's patients had sustained damage to their right hemispheres, allowing the left to take over and come up with wrong answers which might have been balanced out had everything been operating normally. It takes some well-orchestrated communication to keep things running smoothly. But more importantly, it takes well-orchestrated silence.[483] Just like the political family members, knowing too much about one another can pose more of a problem than not knowing enough. Given the brain's tendency to block the majority of available information from conscious thoughts, perhaps it should come as no surprise that the brain actually blocks information from itself by strategically restricting what data passes between the hemispheres.[484]

You can look to your daily life for plenty of examples of benefitting from the two-hemisphere setup, as well as our lack of awareness that it exists at all. Eating is something we have evolved to be pretty good at. But we seldom consider what it was like before we had kitchenettes and silverware, even though most animals still live this way, in the wild.

Imagine you are a human living in a hunter gatherer society, and you find a wild grove of ripe raspberries. They look delicious, and you decide to pick some and bring them back to your tribe. But you notice right away that you have to watch closely, because raspberries bushes have thorns, and the berries are small; you don't want to pick a bunch of leaves or bleed all over your fruit. This, according to neuroscientists, is the benefit of our brain's natural division of right from left. Your left hemisphere is better suited to focus in on the specific task at hand, tuning out the rest of the world to pay attention to the small area where the berries exist, then guiding your hand between thorns and leaves.[485] Relatedly, this is why such a huge portion of the population is right handed (the left hemisphere controls the right hand). But the wild is dangerous, and if you don't pay attention to your surroundings, you might be killed by a sneaky tiger who takes advantage of your distracted state of berry-picking.

What you really need is two people, one to pick berries, and another to keep watch; one to focus in on just one thing, the other to maintain a global perspective. That is where your right hemisphere comes in. It takes a wide-angle worldview and watches for threats, allowing your left hemisphere to focus on the prickly job of picking berries.[486] The right hemisphere tends to adopt a wide-angle worldview, and it is always on the lookout for threats. [487] The left hemisphere tends to zoom-in on one thing at a time, and it is always on the lookout for rewards, like berries. Normally we don't consciously notice any of it.

It isn't just food. Our brain hemispheres have evolved to share this codependent relationship in all sorts of ways. The left hemisphere tends to see the world as unchanging and easy-to-understand. It takes a literal view of things, and it has a hard time with context and metaphor. The right hemisphere adopts a global perspective of spacetime, easily incorporating updates and contextual information into an evolving model of the world. The left hemisphere, on the other hand, is stubbornly obtuse, and its one-to-one mapping of items to words—the reason most speech is constructed there—makes it nearly impossible for the left hemisphere to recognize (or admit) its own mistakes. Neuroscientist Iain McGilchrist has gone so far as to describe our left hemispheres as avid "bullshitters," and Ramachandran's experiments make clear this is no exaggeration.[488] Whenever someone concocts a fabulous story to explain their behavior, we can be sure the left hemisphere is hard at work making sense of a situation without all of the data necessary to get it right.

This duality is convenient in all sorts of human situations. The left hemisphere handles habits, whereas the right hemisphere is activated by anything seen as novel or new.[489] The left hemisphere tends to understand things by breaking them into their constituent parts, whereas the right hemisphere considers things as part of a larger whole, and in context with the rest of the world.[490] The left hemisphere prefers to think of things as mechanical and tool-like, even if they are alive, whereas the right hemisphere classifies everything as living and changing, even machines.[491] This list could continue for pages, and the dialectical tension persist at every stop. The brain hemispheres adopt opposing worldviews which normally could not be represented in a single argument, at least not coherently. But together, they are the internal voices that make sense of the world around us.

The more we learn about how our brains work, the more we recognize just how in the dark we remain throughout most of our lives. Punishing people for choices they did not freely make is both cruel and wasteful. The sooner we acknowledge this, the sooner we can move on to approaches which favor prevention over domination, and restoration over vengeance.

None of us feels like there are two people living in our heads, avoiding one another as they construct entirely disparate models of the world. But that is exactly what is happening all the time, at least if everything is running smoothly. We are experiencing McGilchrist's "two fundamentally opposed realities, two different modes of experience . . . [each] of ultimate importance in bringing about the recognizably human world."[492] We tend to miss all of that back-and-forth, and what we *feel* is more akin to a single stream of thought emanating from the doorway where those two hemispheres work out an understanding of the world.

In cases when the hemispheres cannot communicate with one other, whether because of an accident or a clever scientist using medication or electrical simulation, each hemisphere carries on as if it knows nothing about the communication outage.[493] It doesn't short out or lose control when its live-in partner disappears; rather, each hemisphere appears to simply proceed by itself as if it never knew the other was there in the first place.[494] There is a terrifying revelation here which shatters whatever remaining hold free will might have had on one's beliefs about how the world works.

The left hemisphere has no trouble in concocting stories on the spot to explain the world, including one's own body, without the help of the right hemisphere. And the stories it tells are bananas. They make no sense at all, yet people seem to fully believe what they are saying. *An alien moved my arm. That isn't my arm; it is your arm. Someone far away moved my arm using magic or spirits.*

There is also much to discover in the answers which the left hemisphere never provides, things like, *I don't know why my hand moved,* or *I guess that hand is mine even though it doesn't feel like it is.* We are hardwired (especially in our left hemisphere) to know the answer even when we are wrong, even when our explanations for our behaviors are illogical. It is easier to spot in patients whose hemispheres are not properly communicating back and forth, but we all do it all the time.[495] We make sense of the world rapidly and thoughtlessly, rushing through the process and refusing to stop to reanalyze every item or belief we come across. That would take far too long. Best to just fabricate a story, post hoc, which makes the most sense given the available facts.

There is no free will. There is no illusion of free will. And even the experience of being a front-row witness to our decision-making process is fogged by behind-the-scenes negotiations between two parties with opposing viewpoints. Those two parties, the left and right hemisphere, seem, at times, largely unaware of one other's existence.[496] The more we learn, the less ground we have to stand on when it comes to punishing people for behaviors entirely beyond their control.

Advice from a Junkie

Enough was enough. It was time to put an end to the cycle of addiction. I was clearly hooked, covered in sweat and wide awake because I had fallen asleep without taking my nightly dose of opioids. So I got up and got high, then went back to bed, content in the illusion that I would stop using tomorrow, or maybe this weekend.

We play that game a lot when we are in the midst of an addiction. What else can we do with the cognitive dissonance of a US culture which tells us we are both diseased and arrestable, powerless and destructive. We *know* we need to stop using, that drugs are bad, that it is our own fault, and that we deserve whatever we get. It doesn't matter that none of these things are true; they provide the only story available. We believe the lies just like the rest of the world believes them.

I really wanted to stop. And I tried more than once. Yet every time I reached down deep and looked for that strength to press through, it wasn't there. Some of my friends were reaching down deep and finding that strength, and they proudly insisted it was their free will which had led to their success. Yet every time I freely chose to reach down deep and find my strength, I came up empty. What gives?

Conversely, when I finally did stop using heroin on a daily basis, I found it much easier than I would have expected, given years of failed attempts. I used methadone, and that helped, but in the past methadone hadn't worked well enough to prevent me from running back to the streets. And it is clear from the research that addiction has little to do with physical dependency, since even after long periods of abstinence, addicted people often still find ourselves struggling with urges to use. So what changed? Why did I find that strength inside myself in 2006, even though I came up empty for years prior to that?

There were certainly some obvious updates in my life which I can point to. I got married and I went back to school to finish my undergraduate degree, providing a stability which proved invaluable. I can't say enough about the support of a loving partner who, for the first time in my life, didn't treat me like a dangerous loser when I got high. The world, along with my close support group and family, had kicked me to the curb because that's what we are supposed to do with drug users in our culture. And predictably, I wound up where many abandoned people wind up. The message delivered to a drug user when supposed loved ones dump them because of drug use is that they don't matter anymore, they are bad and dangerous. It shouldn't surprise anyone that treating someone like a criminal often leads directly to them acting like a criminal. That's how identities are formed. We don't just adopt and mold them from the inside-out; we are often given them through the magic of labels, nicknames, titles and degrees. Those identities stick. Sometimes they are permanent.

But it wasn't just the marriage, the college, or the methadone that changed me. I had blown up plenty of great relationships in the past, and I had decided to go back to school more than once, only to fail out. So why did those things suddenly take? What was it that suddenly made something appear deep down inside when I reached for it, when before it had been missing?

The answer is probably too complicated to summarize, but it is *not* free will. As much as I would like to take credit for my success in life, for the degrees, the podcasts, the publications and the marriage I have co-built, I know these things, and tellingly, the drive to make them a reality, are not the result of decisions I freely made when others around me decided they just didn't want to be successful. My success is the result of luck, plain and simple. I was lucky to enjoy reading. I was lucky to have professors who helped me through the tough times when I might otherwise have quit. I was lucky to have the neurology necessary to navigate the Ivory Tower, along with the educational background necessary for success. And even in those rare moments when free will seems vital to understanding my story, like when I really wanted to drop out, but I pressed through anyway, that wasn't free will either, because the strength I found when I reached down deep wasn't there years earlier. I would have freely willed it the first time if that was all it takes. It was bad luck and tough love that got me into my addiction; it was luck and love that got me out.

We use drugs because they are enjoyable. They make us feel good about life, about who we are, and about the world around us. But we aren't all starting at the same place when we get high. Some of us find in drugs a pathway to normalcy, a route to worry-free interaction with others, a doorway to regular relationships. Or we discover a source of relief from anxiety, depression, PTSD, pain or some other condition, and the drugs work so much better than anything else that we don't want to give them up. As a result, our families and friends cut us off and send us packing, so we find new support groups who are into the same things we are: drugs. The world begins calling us diseased and devotes armed warriors to the task of locking us up. Our doctors and therapists refuse to treat us until we stop using the only thing that works. And our bank accounts rapidly empty because our drugs are more expensive than gold.

And it was built this way, from scratch. What did we expect to happen?

THERE ARE STILL plenty of anti-drug propaganda films from the 1980s floating around the internet. In one of them, a cop reaches from off screen and grabs a bad guy's collar as he tries to run away in slow motion. A voiceover reminds viewers, "nobody says, 'I wanna be a junkie when I grow up.' Don't let drugs get in the way of your dreams." It's a classic example of the mainstream messages I received about drugs as a kid.

While it is true that most kids do not want to be addicted to drugs when they grow up, the idea that drugs aren't romantic in cultures where they are prohibited is laughable. *I* kind of wanted to be a junkie when *I* grew up. I don't know where that desire came from, and it certainly wasn't freely selected, but I vividly remember that commercial striking me as a failed attempt to smear a fun activity.

Drugs were off limits and taboo in my family. Because of that silence, they became romanticized. Without any real spaces like heroin clinics or people in my life who were willing to disclose their drug use, I had those romantic images and nothing else. I didn't decide to be attracted to the picture of drug use I had been given by the media. I didn't choose to view those messages at all, and I certainly didn't decide how they would impact me. Those realities and the actions which followed emerged out of nothing; they simply appeared in my mind, seemingly from nowhere. Had the urge to fight those feeling emerged alongside the romance (it did not), that would not have been a free choice either. Yet these emotions and attractions are what ultimately forged the path my life took.

Letting go of the notion that free will informs our actions does not inevitably lead to people behaving badly without consequences. Luckily, people are not barely contained monsters who fall into passionate lusts when we disabuse ourselves of the free will lie. Accepting the truth tends to have the opposite effect. It knocks the chip off our shoulder, because without free will or something like it, none of us earns (or freely chooses) our ability to buckle down and complete that degree, nor do we earn (or freely choose) our lack of ability to do so.

If you are successful, privileged, wealthy, well known and respected, the temptation to take credit for your accomplishments is understandable; we live in a culture that encourages that sort of pride at every opportunity. Our taking credit also works to absolve us from our duty to help those around us who are struggling, for if I am responsible for my success, then others are responsible for their failures. The easiest way to turn away from the man begging for change is to remind yourself, falsely, that he probably deserves what he got. The easiest way to find compassion is to recognize how much luck is involved in your different lots in life.

None of us alive today built this system. The incentives and role models were here long before we showed up, and we had no choice in soaking up the moral norms presented to us by culture. We certainly didn't build our own bodies, nor did we program them with memories and experiences from our youth. We are all the result of (un)lucky events which unavoidably shaped our worldviews, yet we are trapped in biological bodies which evolved to lie to us about our freedom of choice.

Anything labeled free will is simply the result of our lacking knowledge about causation. If we truly understood why we chose pancakes over cereal, or why we took one route to work over another, we would be forced to accept the role of hidden motives and subconscious drives. If we truly recognized the point at which a decision is made, we would be forced to accept the lag in our recognition which allows us to pretend we have freely selected it long after the fact.

Where is the freedom in a choice *I* know about before *you* make it? If it is obvious that certain preconditions are more likely to result in someone committing a crime of desperation, might we better spend our time giving people the tools to avoid committing the crime? Disabusing ourselves of the free will riddle moves us naturally toward compassion and prevention. Once we understand why people do the things they do, the game changes. We can devote our energies to stacking the deck instead of punishing people for the hands they are dealt.

The prison-industrial complex is an outlet for our cultural lust for vengeance and retribution. In the United States, where we spend more on weapons and military programs every year than we spend on education, violence is the only way we know to respond to a threat.[497] But something strange happens when you come to the conclusion that the only difference between the cruelest sadist on earth and you is dumb luck. I can't claim to be better than someone who gave into an urge to commit murder because I don't struggle with that desire. Even if I did struggle with that desire, but I managed to subdue it before I acted on it, I still couldn't take credit for having whatever it was that allowed me to deny the urge when someone else could not. These aren't free choices.

Our morals and emotional connections are made for us, by luck, by our parents, and by those we wander around with as kids. There is no free will in a universe set to motion long before we arrived. I am abhorred by violence, but I can't take credit for that any more than a UFC fighter can take credit for enjoying bloodying strangers in the ring. And if you enjoy the spectacle from the stands or from your couch at home, you can't take credit for your bloodlust, nor for your reaction when someone like me comes along and challenges the acceptability of your pastime.

We can accept that our lives are invariably influenced by things far beyond our control, and we can use that knowledge to design a court system devoted to prevention and personal improvement. To be sure, this is a project of accountability, but not for the criminal so much as for the society which allows criminals to be mass produced. Every person convicted of a crime could have done differently, but only if the universe was different at the time they committed their crime. The erasure of free will leaves little space for sideliners. If crime is indeed preventable, then we should get to work preventing it.

Once we acknowledge our lack of control in how the universe unfolds, our cultural fear melts into compassion (by no choice of our own). But that doesn't mean criminal justice disappears. I may have been horrified to learn that Hurricane Katrina was headed toward New Orleans in 2005, but I wasn't angry at the hurricane, because I did not believe it was consciously choosing to head inland without regard for life or property.[498] It would be a waste of time and money to incarcerate a hurricane as punishment for its crimes, because there is neither intent nor conscious understanding of the harm being done. But the potential for death and destruction is there even without a hint of free will, so we would probably feel comfortable spending tons of cash to change the hurricane's path *before* it hits a populated area, if such a thing were possible. I can imagine a world where we value the project of providing the hurricane with what hurricanes need to naturally turn out to sea or to dissipate before landfall. Punishment is a waste of time and resources, but prevention is invaluable.

The feelings we experience when we hear awful stories about hurricanes or earthquakes are similar to the feelings we experience when we think about a mass shooter. But there is one vital difference. In both cases, we feel compassion and empathy for the victims. But only in the case of the mass shooter do we feel fury and indignation for the perpetrator. As soon as intent appears, along with it comes a desire to hurt the hurter, to punish them for what they did. The disease or the catastrophe, on the other hand, simply makes us sad and frustrated, emotions which do far less to hinder our preventative efforts in the future.

The goal of our current retribution-based system is to incarcerate as many people as necessary. The goal of a prevention-based system would be to incarcerate as few people as possible. If the would-be shooter has not yet committed a crime, it is easy to feel compassion instead of fury, and to offer treatment instead of torture, education instead of incarceration. The entire notion of revenge melts away once we recognize a capacity for prevention. This is the country (and the world) we could build. It just means reimagining our approach to policing and rejecting the illusion of free will.

The conversation about criminal justice doesn't require us to add intent or deliberate malice into the equation, not if we wish to prevent crimes instead of punishing people after the fact. We force free will into the design whenever we have the chance, because we tend to feel better about the ease with which we torture people in prison for things they cannot control so long as we can convince ourselves they chose to be tortured. It is expensive, counterproductive, and it ensures many of them keep coming back forever. The prison-industrial complex can be dismantled and reengineered to address commonsense goals of cultural progression and crime avoidance. Ending the War on Drugs is just the first step in a larger realignment of social goals.

> "That's what this is all about. The same principles as Harriet Tubman: reach to here and bring to here. Legit…All the people you threw away: the dope dealers, the criminals, they will be legit sitting here, thanks to your boy." —Tupac Shakur[499]

Epilogue: Quality of Life

"When I was on, I was on and nobody gave
me any trouble. No cops, no treasury agents,
nobody. I got in trouble when I tried to get
off." –Billie Holiday[500]

It has been an incredible journey to write this book. I have
heard authors lament the conclusion of a project while express-
ing surprise at all they learned during its unfolding. That is
exactly how this book came together. I thought I knew enough
to write it when I began, but much of what made the final cut
was learned or relearned along the way.

I also spent a lot of time thinking about what finally changed
in my life. While it is certainly possible that my neuro-atypical-
ity became easier to navigate with age, it is also likely regions of
my brain came online, better late than never. But I also discovered two important tools for my success, both of which I had
to seek out and maintain. Looking back, both were invaluable.

The first I mentioned already in the book. Mindful meditation was important. I had no idea so much was going on
in my mind and body, and I certainly didn't believe my pre-
occupations were in any way linked to my overall mental and
emotional health. Once you begin a routine of self-reflective
mindfulness, you quickly realize how much you were missing.

You can't regain control of the ride until you first realize you are not in control, then begin to orient yourself to the direction and velocity of the spin. Correcting before that just tends to make things worse.

Mindful meditation is not an all-purpose fix, but it is applicable in all situations, and it is one of the few drugs you can take anywhere, with just a few seconds, if necessary. Correcting the spinout you didn't realize was happening and keeping the party on track is a never ending project. Lose the horizon for but a second and you wind up right back where you started. Mindfulness at least allows you to get a grasp on where you are and how you are moving through the world. It is an anchor in any storm.

The second and equally important tool for success was therapy. And just like with mindfulness, I had no idea I needed it until I started doing it. As surprised as you might be after reading this book at the notion that I didn't realize I needed therapy, very few people (in the US) think they need therapy. We all tend to feel as if life is just life, that what it feels like to be us is unchanging, and that we ought to just make it as tolerable as possible. But that doesn't have to be the endpoint. Our cultural pride stigmatizes therapy and counseling as admissions of failure, despite nearly universal value.

Therapy and mindfulness allowed me to truly grow to love myself, yet another trick which I had been duped into thinking I had already achieved.

I mentioned it briefly in Chapter Five, but I also truly can't say enough about life setting. I spent my high school years ducking my parents and hiding my drug use, although that often wasn't possible, and they knew a lot more than I realized. I knew my drug use was seen by those around me as a sin, a weakness, and a contagious disease. I knew better than to talk to my friends or family members about it (again). It was a source of contention, and at times, of physical and emotional violence. Mine, like most in the United States, was a family trained to tough love.

Once I moved out, a few days after my 18th birthday, I rebuilt the only environment I had known, only this time without the restraints of parental supervision. Tough love set me up to spin out, and that's exactly what I did. By the time I started accumulating felony charges, I knew full well I was a bad person, a stoner, junkie loser who would never amount to anything. That's what the world had told me. Eventually I got tired of arguing.

I spent more than a decade surrounding myself with fellow criminals and drug users who were just as convinced as I was that we were all bad people. Our families wanted little to do with us. The police were after us. It was obvious the world saw us as rotten. And we acted on those beliefs. We committed smash and grabs, larcenies and auto thefts, and we didn't feel bad about any of it, because by that point we all knew we were monsters in the eyes of society.

If you are a drug user, you are not a bad person, a weak person or a sinful person. You are just a person. I am not special in my achievements. They are the predictable results of taking someone like me—someone like us—and surrounding them with support, education, therapy, and most importantly, love. You can do whatever you want to do, and your drug using status has nothing to do with your value as a human, nor your ability to succeed in life.

If you or someone you know is struggling with addiction, that's okay. It is not your fault that the culture you or they were born into hates drug users, nor that it convinced your family and friends that they should hate us (drug users) for our own good. It is a racket, and one that's so huge it will soon come crashing down under its own weight. The good news is the war is almost over, one way or another.

One last thing, for those who are wondering whether I am using drugs now. I have remained deliberately vague about that for two reasons. First, there is no magic bullet, and every addicted person must navigate the space of recovery on their own terms. I spent far too long trying to follow a successful recipe offered by others, only to realize I had the personalized formula all along. Mine wasn't abstinence, and it certainly wasn't anything close to 12-steps or religion, but yours might be. Do you.

Second, do you care? Seriously, at this point, after reading about my antics and realizing I *am* the dangerous drug user you were warned about, would you feel any less safe in your world if you thought I was using heroin or cocaine right now? It isn't about the drugs we use. It is about the set and setting in which we use them.

Endnotes

Introduction

1   Sigmund Freud, *Civilization and its Discontents*, trans. Joan Riviere, (Blacksburg, VA: Wilder Publications, 1930/2010), 14.

2   National Center for Health Statistics, "Provisional Counts of Drug Overdose Deaths, as of 8/6/2017." See also Federal Bureau of Investigation, Criminal Justice Information Services Division, "2016 Uniform Crime Report," (Washington, D.C.: 2017). See also Michelle Alexander, *The New Jim Crow: Mass Incarceration in the Age of Colorblindness* (New York, NY: The New Press, 2010/2012), 141.

3   Centers for Disease Control (CDC) "Provisional Overdose Death Counts." Although the CDC's data collection techniques result in a constant overrepresentation of overdose deaths (see Chapter 4), they have become the voice of public debate. Their numbers should not be taken at face value.

4   Deborah Dawson, et. al., "Recovery from DSM-IV Alcoholism Dependence: United States, 2001-2002," *Addiction 100*, (3), 2005.

5   National Center for Health Statistics, National Vital Statistics System, "Provisional Counts of Drug Overdose Deaths, as of 8/6/2017," published by the Center for Disease Control. See also Center for Disease Control, "Drug Overdose Deaths in the United States, 1999-2018," NCHS Data Brief No. 356, (January 2020).

6   Overdose estimates November 2019 through November 2020, from CDC "Provisional Drug Overdose Death Counts."

7   Federal Bureau of Prisons, "Monthly Offenses," updated July 29, 2017.

8   Matej Mikulic, "Methamphetamine Laboratory Incidents in the U.S. 2000-2019," *Statista*, (March 12, 2021).

9   Joshua Bamberger, et. al., "Wound Botulism Associated with Black Tar Heroin," *JAMA* 280, no. 17 (November 1998): 1479-1480. See also, Center for Disease Control, "Syringe Exchange Programs—United States, 2008," *Morbidity and Mortality Weekly Report* 59, no. 45 (November 19, 2010): 1488-1491.

10   Terry Zobeck, *"How Much Do Americans Really Spend on Drugs Each Year?"* published by the White House, Obama Administration. See also Beau Kilmer, et. al., "How Big is the U.S. Market for Illegal Drugs?" RAND Corporation, (2014). Originally requested by and published on whitehouse. gov, but pulled down by Trump administration. See also Peter Wagner, et. al., "Following the Money of Mass Incarceration," *Prison Policy Initiative*, January 25, 2017. See Also The Equal Justice Initiative, *"Mass Incarceration Costs $182 Billion Every Year without Adding Much to Public Safety,"* February 6, 2017.

11   Carl Hart, "Exaggerating Harmful Drug Effects on the Brain is Killing Black People," *Neuroview 107*, (2): July 2020.

12   U.S. population levels taken from U.S. Census Bureau on 11.23.17, *https://www.census.gov/popclock/* U.S. and world overdose rates taken from United Nations Office on Drugs and Crime, *World Drug Report 2017, Executive Summary: Conclusions and Policy Implications* (United Nations publication, 2017), 10.

13   Michelle Alexander, *The New Jim Crow: Mass Incarceration in the Age of Colorblindness* (New York, NY: The New Press, 2010/2012). See also U.S. Department of Justice, *Federal Bureau of Prisons Offenses* page.

14   From *Lady Sings the Blues* with William Dufty, (New York: Lancer Books, 1956/1972), 130.

Chapter One

15   *Nick Moustoukas, et. al.,* "Contaminated Street Heroin: Relationship to Clinical Infections," *Archives of Surgery,* (June 1983). See also Thomas Lavender and Brendan McCarron, "Acute Infections in Intravenous Drug Use," *Clinical Medicine (London) 13,* (5): October 2013.

16   Elisabeth Rook, "Population Pharmacokinetics of Heroin and its Major Metabolites," *Clinical Pharmacokinetics 45,* (4): 2006.

17   The half-life of heroin is actually far less than 30 minutes; some studies have estimated a half-life of less than 10 minutes. But heroin is metabolized by the body into other opioids which have a similar effect, and which, in turn, break down into additional intoxicating chemicals. See Elisabeth Rook,

"Population Pharmacokinetics of Heroin and its Major Metabolites," *Clinical Pharmacokinetics 45*, (4): 2006.

18   Averages updated annually by the United States Drug Enforcement Administration (DEA), "2019 Drug Enforcement Administration Drug Threat Assessment," published by the DEA (December 2019). See also DEA, "2016 National Drug Price and Purity Data," published by the DEA (July 2018).

19   Opioids work on multiple sites, but the most well-known, and most pharmacologically relevant, is the Mu site, Gavril W. Pasternak, et. al., "*Mu Opioids and Their Receptors: Evolution of a Concept,*" *Pharmacological Reviews 65*, (4): October, 2013.

20   Arul James, et. al., "Basic Opioid Pharmacology—An Update," *British Journal of Pain 14*, (2): May 2020.

21   Gavril W. Pasternak, et. al., "*Mu Opioids and Their Receptors: Evolution of a Concept,*" *Pharmacological Reviews 65*, (4): October 2013.

22   Thomas Hager, *Ten Drugs: How Plants, Powders and Pills have Shaped the History of Medicine* (New York: Abrams Press, 2019), 199.

23   "Black Tar Heroin" is heroin sold prior to the final purification required for white powder heroin. The "tar" is impurities. Black tar heroin is commonly sold west of the Mississippi River in the United States, whereas "China white" (a white powder) is typical east of the Mississippi.

24   The American Psychological Association, *The Diagnostic and Statistical Manual of Mental Disorders, 5th Edition* (Arlington, VA: 2013), "Substance Use Disorder Features."

25   Maia Szalavitz, *Unbroken Brain: A Revolutionary New Way of Understanding Addiction* (New York: St. Martin's Press, 2016), 126.

26   Addiction and dependency are not synonymous terms. Dependency has to do with physical and emotional distress which occurs with the discontinuation of a substance, whereas addiction requires a number of impairments to one's quality of life, including tolerance, disruptions to life goals and habits, negative consequences, inability to not use when you don't want to, etc. See The American Psychological Association, *The Diagnostic and Statistical Manual of Mental Disorders, 5th Edition* (Arlington, VA: 2013), "Substance Use Disorder Features."

27   The American Psychological Association, *The Diagnostic and Statistical Manual of Mental Disorders, 5th Edition* (Arlington, VA: 2013), "Substance Use Disorder Features."

28   National Institute on Drug Abuse, FAQ section: *"What is Addiction?"* from Drugabuse.org, 4/14/2021.

29   Maia Szalavitz, *Unbroken Brain: A Revolutionary New Way of Understanding Addiction* (New York: St. Martin's Press, 2016), 39.

30   American Psychiatric Association, *"Substance Related and Addictive Disorders,"* 2013.

31   Carl Hart and Malakai Hart, "Opioid Crisis: Another Mechanism Used to Perpetuate American Racism," *Cultural Diversity and Ethnic Minority Psychology 25*, (1): 2019. See also James Anthony, et. al., "Comparative Epidemiology of Dependency on Tobacco, Alcohol, Controlled Substances, and Inhalants: Basic Findings from the National Comorbidity Survey," *Experimental and Clinical Psychopharmacology 2*, (3): August 1994. See also Carl Hart, *High Price: A Neuroscientists Journal of Self-Discovery that Challenges Everything you Know about Drugs and Society* (New York: Harper Perennial, 2013), 13. For caffeine not included in substance abuse disorders, see American Psychiatric Association, *"Substance Related and Addictive Disorders,"* 2013.

32   Thomas Hager, *Ten Drugs: How Plants, Powders and Pills have Shaped the History of Medicine* (New York: Abrams Press, 2019), 2.

33   United Nations Office of Drug Control, *"World Drug Report, 2020,"* Book 3. See also Thomas Hager, *Ten Drugs: How Plants, Powders and Pills have Shaped the History of Medicine* (New York: Abrams Press, 2019).

34   Carl Hart and Malakai Hart, "Opioid Crisis: Another Mechanism Used to Perpetuate American Racism," *Cultural Diversity and Ethnic Minority Psychology 25*, (1): 2019.

35   The American Psychological Association, *The Diagnostic and Statistical Manual of Mental Disorders, 5th Edition* (Arlington, VA: 2013), "Substance Use Disorder Features."

36   Laura Juliano and Ronald Griffiths, "A Critical Review of Caffeine Withdrawal: Empirical Validation of Symptoms and Signs, Incidence, Severity, and Associated Features," *Psychopharmacology 176*, (1): October 2004.

37   Alexandra Sifferlin, "13% of Americans Take Antidepressants," *Time*, August 15, 2017.

38   Bridget Grant, et. al., "Prevalence of 12-Month Alcohol Use, High-Risk Drinking, and *DSM-IV* Alcohol Use Disorder in the United States, 2001-2001 to 2012-2013," *JAMA Psychiatry 74*, (9): September 2017.

39   Shaheen Lakhan, et. al., "Prescription Stimulants in Individuals with and without Attention Deficit Hyperactivity Disorder: Misuse, Cognitive Impact, and Adverse Effects," *Brain Behavior 2*, (5): September 2012. See also criteria for Stimulant-Related Disorders in: The American Psychological Association, *The Diagnostic and Statistical Manual of Mental Disorders, 5th Edition* (Arlington, VA:

2013), "Substance Use Disorder Features."

40 American Psychiatric Association, "*Substance Related and Addictive Disorders*," 2013.

41 J.V. Chamary, "*'Work Hard, Play Hard' Lifestyle is Real, Says Science*," *Forbes*, June 30, 2016.

42 Maia Szalavitz, *Unbroken Brain: A Revolutionary New Way of Understanding Addiction* (New York: St. Martin's Press, 2016), 152.

43 The national call to defund the police in the wake of George Floyd's murder was successful on many fronts, despite its overall failure to gather much steam. Some cities instituted pilot programs which rerouted mental health calls away from armed officers, instead sending unarmed mental health care professionals. In the first six months of Denver's pilot program, 750 calls were rerouted with zero arrests. See David Sachs, "*6-Month Experiment Replacing Denver Police with Mental Health Team Dubbed a Success*," *NPR*, March 8, 2021.

44 Upton Sinclair, "End Poverty in California," Campaign Speech for Governor, 1934.

45 Michelle Alexander, *The New Jim Crow: Mass Incarceration in the Age of Colorblindness* (New York, NY: The New Press, 2010/2012).

46 Fentanyl Patches are FDA approved devices whereby a sticker is placed on the body for up to three days while fentanyl slowly releases through the skin at a controlled rate.

47 Excitement and uncertainty increase our sensitivity to the dangerous and exciting qualities of any drug. Regular consumption of drugs with unpredictable potency increases our repetitive drug seeking behavior. See chapters Three and Four.

48 Glyn Davies, et. al., "The Role of Lifestyle in Perpetuating Substance Use Disorder: The Lifestyle Balance Model," *Substance Abuse Treatment, Prevention and Policy 10*, (2): 2015. See also Alex Stevens, et. al., "Depenalization, Diversion, and Decriminalization: A Realist Review and Programme Theory of Alternatives to Criminalization for Simple Drug Possession," *European Journal of Criminology*, November 2019.

49 *Kelly K. Dineen*, et. al., "*Between a Rock and a Hard Place: Can Physicians Prescribe Opioids to Treat Pain Adequately While Avoiding Legal Sanction?*" *American Journal of Law and Medicine 42*, (1): 2016. See also *Leonard Paulozzi, et. al. and the Centers for Disease Control and Prevention*, "*Controlled Substance Prescribing Patterns--Prescription Behavior Surveillance System, Eight States, 2013,*" *MMWR Surveillance Summaries 64*, (9): October 2016.

50 Thomas Hager, *Ten Drugs: How Plants, Powders and Pills have Shaped the History of Medicine* (New York: Abrams Press, 2019), 4. See also Jonathan Jones, "*America's Forgotten History of Supervised Opioid Injection,*" *Undark*, April 29, 2021.

51 Linder V. United States, 268 U.S. 5 (1925). Thomas Hager, *Ten Drugs: How Plants, Powders and Pills have Shaped the History of Medicine* (New York: Abrams Press, 2019), 4.

52 Marc-Antoine Crocq, "Historical and Cultural Aspects of Man's Relationship with Addictive Drugs," *Dialogues in Clinical Neuroscience 9*, (4): December 2007.

53 "Land of the Free" from *US Declaration of Independence*, 1776.

54 The 1914 Harrison Tax Act was not about restriction so much as taxation and truthful advertising, but it became the first of many federal regulations which would be used to criminalize drug users and dealers. Thomas Hager, *Ten Drugs: How Plants, Powders and Pills have Shaped the History of Medicine* (New York: Abrams Press, 2019), 94.

55 Benjamin Boyce, *Discourses of Deception: (Re)Examining America's War on Drugs*, Dissertation, ProQuest, 2018. See also Thomas Hager, *Ten Drugs: How Plants, Powders and Pills have Shaped the History of Medicine* (New York: Abrams Press, 2019), 27, 43.

56 US Department of Treasury, US Alcohol and Tobacco Tax and Trade Bureau (TTB) Industry Circular, "*Volunteer Alcohol Beverage Recall,*" 2017.

57 Victor Hugo, *Les Misérables*, (Belgium, 1862).

58 Tom Wainwright, *Narconomics: How to Run a Drug Cartel* (New York: PublicAffairs, 2016).

59 United Nations Office on Drugs and Crime, "*Opium Heroin Market,*" from *The World Drug Report*, (2009).

60 Terry Zobeck, "*How Much Do Americans Really Spend on Drugs Each Year?*" published by the White House, Obama Administration. See also Beau Kilmer, et. al., "How Big is the U.S. Market for Illegal Drugs?" RAND Corporation, (2014). Originally requested by and published on whitehouse.gov, but deleted by Trump administration.

61 Artur Domoslawski, *Drug Policy in Portugal: The Benefits of Decriminalizing Drug Use*, translated by Hanna Siemaszko (Warsaw, Poland: Open Society Foundation, 2011), 40. See also Johann Hari, *Chasing the Scream: The First and Last Days of the War on Drugs* (New York, NY: Bloomsbury), 238-239.

62 Johann Hari, *Chasing the Scream: The First and Last Days of the War on Drugs* (New York, NY: Bloomsbury). See also Maia Szalavitz, *Unbroken Brain*. See also Carl Hart, *High Price*.

63 For a detailed list of policies, see Carl Hart, *High Price: A Neuroscientist's Journey of Self-Discovery that Challenges Everything you know about Drugs and Society* (New York, Harper Perennial Press, 2013). See also Maia Szalavitz, *Undoing Drugs: The Untold Story of Harm Reduction and the Future*

of Addiction (New York: Hachette Books, 2021).

64 Regine Cabato, *"The Philippines' Drug War is Putting More Pregnant Women Behind Bars. What Happens to their Children?"* *The Washington Post*, April 9, 2021.

65 See also Alex Stevens, et. al., "Depenalization, Diversion, and Decriminalization: A Realist Review and Programme Theory of Alternatives to Criminalization for Simple Drug Possession," *European Journal of Criminology,* November 2019. See also Glyn Davies, et. al., "The Role of Lifestyle in Perpetuating Substance Use Disorder: The Lifestyle Balance Model," *Substance Abuse Treatment, Prevention and Policy 10,* (2): 2015.

66 For an overview of the Learning Disorder model of addiction, see Maia Szalavitz, *Unbroken Brain: A Revolutionary New Way of Understanding Addiction* (New York: St. Martin's Press, 2016), 3.

Chapter Two

67 From VICE Documentary, *Heroin Holiday in Czech Republic.* Downloaded from YouTube on 8.14.21.

68 Sean McCabe, et. al., "Simultaneous and Concurrent Polydrug Use of Alcohol and Prescription Drugs: Prevalence, Correlates, and Consequences," *Journal on Study of Alcohol and Drugs 67,* (4), January 2007.

69 Hunter Thompson, *Hell's Angel: The Life and Times of Sonny Barger and the Hell's Angels Motorcycle Club* (New York: Harper Collins, 1967/2000).

70 There are various forms of meditation which allow practitioners to instigate states of being similar to those produced by ingesting intoxicating substances. There are also alternative drugs which cause similar effects without the risks associated with mainlining street cocaine. I seldom encourage people to completely avoid a drug, but injecting cocaine purchased on the street is a rare exception.

71 Kent Berridge and Terry Robinson, "Liking, Wanting and the Incentive-Sensitization Theory of Addiction," *American Psychology 71,* (8), November 2016. See also Gardiner Morse, *"Decision and Desire,"* *Harvard Business Review,* January 2006.

72 Kent Berridge and Terry Robinson, "Liking, Wanting and the Incentive-Sensitization Theory of Addiction," *American Psychology 71,* (8), November 2016.

73 Ronald Kuczenski, et. al., "An Escalating Dose/Multiple High-Dose Bing Pattern of Amphetamine Administration Results in Differential Changes in the Extracellular Dopamine Response Profiles in Caudate-Putamen and Nucleus Accumben," *Journal of Neuroscience 17,* (11): June 1997. See also Maia Szalavitz, *Unbroken Brain: A Revolutionary Knew Way of Understanding Addiction* (New York: St. Martin's Press, 2016).

74 I am not the first cocaine user to note this wall we all seem to hit shortly into a binge. See Richard Pryor, "Freebase," from *The Anthology: 1968-1992* (album), Warner Brothers Inc., 1982. See also Maia Szalavitz, *Unbroken Brain: A Revolutionary Knew Way of Understanding Addiction* (New York: St. Martin's Press, 2016).

75 Richard Dawkins, *The Blind Watchmaker: Why the Evidence of Evolution Reveals a Universe Without Design* (New York/London: W. W. Norton & Company, 1996/1986).

76 Charles Darwin, *The Origin of Species by Means of Natural Selection; or, The Preservation of Favored Races in the Struggle for Life* (New York: Random House, 1859/1993).

77 Theodosius Dobzhansky, "Nothing in Biology Makes Sense Except in Light of Evolution," *The American Biology Teacher 35,* (3): 1973.

78 Richard Dawkins, *The Blind Watchmaker: Why the Evidence for Evolution Reveals a Universe without Design* (New York: W. W. Norton & Co., 1986). See also Charles Darwin, *The Origin of Species by Means of Natural Selection; or, The Preservation of Favored Races in the Struggle for Life* (New York: Random House, 1859/1993).

79 Richard Dawkins, *The Selfish Gene* (New York: Oxford University Press, 1976), 38-45.

80 For great descriptions of social versus individual traits linked to Darwinian Survival, see Richard Dawkins, *The Blind Watchmaker: Why the Evidence for Evolution Reveals a Universe without Design* (New York: W. W. Norton & Co., 1986).

81 Maia Szalavitz, *Unbroken Brain: A Revolutionary Knew Way of Understanding Addiction* (New York: St. Martin's Press, 2016), 111. See also Peter Kramer, *Listening to Prozac* (New York: Penguin Books, 1997), 231-232.

82 Sigmund Freud, *Civilization and its Discontents,* translated by Joan Riviere, (Blacksburg, VA: Wilder Publications, 1930/2010).

83 Immanuel Kant and Kenneth Joseph Addison also toyed with the idea of updated outlets for evolutionary drives, which they too called sublimation. For Freud's take, see Sigmund Freud, *Civilization and its Discontents,* translated by Joan Riviere, (Blacksburg, VA: Wilder Publications, 1930/2010).

84 Maia Szalavitz, *Unbroken Brain: A Revolutionary Knew Way of Understanding Addiction* (New York: St. Martin's Press, 2016), 106-115.

85 Maia Szalavitz, *Unbroken Brain: A Revolutionary Knew Way of Understanding Addiction* (New York: St. Martin's Press, 2016), 106-115.

86 Kent Berridge and Terry Robinson, "Liking, Wanting and the Incentive-Sensitization Theory of

Addiction," *American Psychology 71*, (8), November 2016. See also Gardiner Morse, *"Decision and Desire,"* *Harvard Business Review*, January 2006. See also Maia Szalavitz, *Unbroken Brain: A Revolutionary Knew Way of Understanding Addiction* (New York: St. Martin's Press, 2016), 106-115.

87 Carl Hart, et. al., "Is Cognitive Functioning Impaired in Methamphetamine Users? A Critical Review," *Neuropsychopharmacology 37*, (November 2011).

88 Nadia R.P.W. Hutten, et. al., "Cocaine Enhances Figural, but Impairs Verbal 'Flexible' Divergent Thinking," *European Neuropsychopharmacology 29*, (7), 2019.

89 Amy Gancarz-Kausch, et. al., "Prolonged Withdrawal Following Cocaine Self-Administration Increases Resistance to Punishment in a Cocaine Binge," *Scientific Reports 4*, (6876): 2014.

90 Brendan Kelley, et. al., "Cognitive Impairment in Acute Cocaine Withdrawal," *Cognitive Behavioral Neurology 18*, (2): June 2005.

91 R. A. Jufer, et. al., "Elimination of Cocaine and Metabolites in Plasma, Saliva, and Urine Following Repeated Oral Administration to Human Volunteers," *Journal of Analytic Toxicology 24*, (7): October 2000. For cocaethylene clearance rates, see Carl Hart, et. al., "Comparison of Intravenous Cocaethylene and Cocaine in Humans," *Psychopharmacology 149*, 2000.

92 Nadia R.P.W. Hutten, et. al., "Cocaine Enhances Figural, but Impairs Verbal 'Flexible' Divergent Thinking," *European Neuropsychopharmacology 29*, (7), 2019. Elton John, *Me* (New York: St. Martin's Publishing Group, 2019). Richard Pryor, "Cocaine," from *The Anthology: 1968-1992* (album), Warner Brothers Inc., 1982.

93 G. I. Papakostas, et. al., "Towards New Mechanisms: An Update on Therapeutics for Treatment-Resistant Major Depressive Disorder," *Molecular Psychiatry 20*, 2015. See also Loris Chahl, "Opioids—Mechanisms of Action," *Experimental and Clinical Pharmacology 3*, July 1996.

94 Nadia R.P.W. Hutten, et. al., "Cocaine Enhances Figural, but Impairs Verbal 'Flexible' Divergent Thinking," *European Neuropsychopharmacology 29*, (7), 2019.

95 Numbers taken from personal experience, verified by United Nations Office on Drugs and Crime, *"Heroin and Cocaine Prices in Europe and the USA."*

96 This line, "despicable dope pedaling vulture who preys on the weakness of his fellow man," was delivered to a senate appropriations committee in the early 1930s by Harry Anslinger, the head of the Federal Bureau of Narcotics (precursor to the DEA). Downloaded 8.15.21 from *https://www.youtube.com/watch?v=xFy8_V6aMqY*

97 Tom Wainwright, *Narco-Nomics: How to Run a Drug Cartel* (New York: Public Affairs, 2016). See also United Nations Office on Drugs and Crime, *"Heroin and Cocaine Prices in Europe and the US."*

98 Carl Hart, *High Price: A Neuroscientist's Journey of Self-Discovery that Challenges Everything you know about Drugs and Society* (New York, Harper Perennial Press, 2013). See also Carl Hart, *Drug Use for Grown Ups: Chasing Liberty in the Land of the Free* (New York: Penguin Press, 2021).

99 Carl Hart, *High Price: A Neuroscientist's Journey of Self-Discovery that Challenges Everything you know about Drugs and Society* (New York, Harper Perennial Press, 2013), 16.

100 Tom Wainwright, *Narco-Nomics: How to Run a Drug Cartel* (United States: Public Affairs books, 2016), 12-14. See also Christopher Woody, "Cocaine Prices in the US have Barely Moved: Here's How Cartels Distort the Market," *Business Insider*, October 13, 2016.

101 Tom Dillehay, et. al., "Early Holocene Coca Chewing in Northern Peru," *Antiquity 84*, (326), December 2010.

102 United Nations Office on Drugs and Crime, *"Coca/Cocaine."* See also Tom Wainwright, *Narco-Nomics.*

103 Laws vary depending on municipality, and some farmers are permitted to grow restricted quantities of coca for personal use. But US sponsored drug-interdiction efforts persist throughout most regions.

104 Tom Wainwright, *Narco-Nomics: How to Run a Drug Cartel* (United States: Public Affairs books, 2016).

105 United Nations Office on Drugs and Crime, *"Columbia: Survey of Areas Effected by Elicit Crops 2016-2017."* See also Jorge Gallego, et. al., "Manual Eradication, Aerial Spray and Coca Prices in Columbia," (2012). See also United Nations Office on Drugs and Crime, *"Fact Sheet - Bolivia Coca Cultivation Monitoring report, 2019."*

106 Scott Stewart, "From Columbia to New York City: The Narconomics of Cocaine," *Business Insider*, June 27, 2016. See also Tom Wainwright, *Narconomics: How to Run a Drug Cartel* (New York: PublicAffairs, 2016). See also Peter Green, *"The Syndicate,"* The Wall Street Journal.

107 In 2012, Colorado and Washington became the first states to legalize cannabis for recreational use despite continuing federal restrictions.

108 THCa is a precursor to THC, or tetrahydrocannabinol, the best-known active ingredient in the cannabis plant. National Institute on Drug Abuse, *"Marijuana: Research Report Series,"* available on the NIDA website.

109 M.A. El Sohly, et. al., "Changes in Cannabis Potency over the Last 2 Decades (1995-2014): Analysis of Current Data in the United States," *Biological Pshychiatry 79* (7): April 2016.

110 For typical Denver, Colorado marijuana advertisements, see rear section of the local magazine,

Westword (Denver, 2015-2021).

111 David R. Smyth, "Flower Development: Origin of the Cauliflower," *Science Direct 5*, (4): April 1995.

112 Teresa Docimo, et. al., "The First Step in the Biosynthesis of Cocaine in *Erythroxylum coca*: The Characterization of Arginine and Ornithine Decarboxylases," *Plant Molecular Biology 78*, (6), April 2012.

113 Scott Stewart, "From Columbia to New York City: The Narconomics of Cocaine," *Business Insider*, June 27, 2016. See also Tom Wainwright, *Narconomics: How to Run a Drug Cartel* (New York: PublicAffairs, 2016). See also Peter Green, "The Syndicate," *The Wall Street Journal*.

114 Tom Wainwright, *Narconomics: How to Run a Drug Cartel* (New York: PublicAffairs, 2016).

115 There are numerous clips of this process available online. For one of my favorites, see Charlet Duboc's *Viceland* documentary, *Cocaine has an Iron Grip on Columbia*, (January 2020).

116 Numbers from the DEA, *"2018 National Drug Threat Assessment,"* and Tom Wainwright, *Narconomics: How to Run a Drug Cartel*. See also Christopher Woody, *"Cocaine prices in the US have barely moved in decades — here's how cartels distort the market,"* *Business Insider*, October 16, 2013.

117 Christopher Woody, "Cocaine Prices in the US have Barely Moved," *Business Insider*, October 16, 2013.

118 Christopher Woody, *"Cocaine prices in the US have barely moved in decades —* here's how cartels distort the market," *Business Insider*, October 16, 2013.

119 Tom Wainwright, *Narconomics: How to Run a Drug Cartel* (New York: PublicAffairs, 2016).

120 Common cutting agents list from *The American Addiction Centers website*, "What is Heroin Cut With?"

121 Averages updated annually by the United States Drug Enforcement Administration (DEA), "2019 Drug Enforcement Administration Drug Threat Assessment," (December 2019). See also DEA, "2016 National Drug Price and Purity Data," (July 2018).

122 John Hopkins University, *"Heroin Fact Sheet,"* downloaded June 18, 2021.

123 Kristina Davis, "Potency, Purity of Drugs Reaching Even Higher and Deadlier Levels," *The San Diego Tribune*, November 20, 2017.

124 United Nations Office on drugs and Crime, *"Heroin and Cocaine Prices in Europe and the USA 2017."*

125 United Nations Office on Drugs and Crime, *"Opium Heroin Market."*

126 All heroin prices taken from: United Nations Office on Drugs and Crime, *"Heroin and Cocaine Prices in Europe and the USA 2017."* See also United Nations Office on Drugs and Crime, *World Drug Report 2010*, published by the United Nations (New York, NY: 2010), 150. Price-per-gram of heroin taken from Lenny Bernstein, "Why a Bag of Heroin Costs Less than a Pack of Cigarettes," *The Washington Post*, August 27, 2015.

127 Denise Winterman, *"How Cutting Drugs Became Big Business,"* BBC News, (September 7, 2020).

128 The pluralized term (fentanyls) is deliberate. There are now numerous forms of fentanyl drugs which have increasingly shorter half-lives and increasingly potent pharmacological profiles. Carfentanil is estimated to be 100 time stronger than fentanyl, which means dealers can receive smaller shipments with the same quantity of doses.

129 The label Opioid Epidemic relies on overdose death numbers from the CDC, and the collection methods ensure overrepresentation, resulting in a permanent exaggeration of overdose deaths.

130 Johann Hari, *Chasing the Scream: The First and Last Days of the War on Drugs* (New York, NY: Bloomsbury, 2015), 230-231.

131 Jay Zagorsky, *"How Prohibition Changed the Way American's Drink, 100 Years Ago,"* The Conversation, January 17, 2020.

132 Philip Peng, et. al., *"A Review of the Use of Fentanyl Analgesia in the Management of Acute Pain in Adults,"* Anesthesiology 90, (February 1999).

133 Philip Peng, et. al., *"A Review of the Use of Fentanyl Analgesia in the Management of Acute Pain in Adults,"* Anesthesiology 90, (February 1999). See also PubChem website, *"Compound Summary: Carfentanil."*

134 PubChem website, *"Compound Summary: Carfentanil."*

135 US Drug Enforcement Administration (DEA), *"DEA Issues Carfentanil Warning to Police and Public: Dangerous Opioid 10,000 Times more Potent than Morphine and 100 Times more Potent than Fentanyl,"* issues September 22, 2016, (National Media Affairs Office).

136 Evelyn Hearne, et. al., "Home Manufacture of Drugs: An Online Investigation and a Toxicological Reality Check of Online Discussions on Drug Chemistry," *Journal of Psychoactive Drugs 49*, (4): March 2017.

137 Xiao Zhu, et. al, "3D Printing Promotes the Development of Drugs," *Biomedicine & Pharmacology 131*, November, 2020. See also Oliver A. H. Jones, et. al., "A Simplified Method for the 3D Printing of Molecular Models for Chemical Education," *Journal of Chemical Education 95*, (1): 2018.

138 Emily Feng, "'We are Shipping to the US': Inside China's Online Synthetic Drug Networks," *NPR*

(article & podcast), November 17, 2020.

139 Gold spot prices $1742.44/oz on 3.28.2021, while cocaine and heroin are both sold for thousands of dollars per oz. once they are cut (1 oz. becomes 5).

140 See also Caroline Jean Acker, *Creating the American Junkie: Addiction Research in the Classic Era of Narcotics Control* (Baltimore, MA: John Hopkins University Press, 2002), 140. See also Johann Hari, *Chasing the Scream: The First and Last Days of the War on Drugs* (New York, NY: Blooms-bury, 2015), 36.

141 Rufus King, *The Drug Hang Up: America's Fifty-Year Folly* (New York, NY: W. W. Norton Company & Inc., 1972), 16. See also James A. Inciardi, "America's Drug Policy: The Continuing Debate," in *The Drug Legalization Debate Second Edition,* ed. James A. Inciardi (Thousand Oaks, CA: Sage Publications, Inc., 1999), 3.

142 Linder V. United States, 268 U.S. 5 (1925). This policy was consistently revised and eroded until the practice of allowing doctors to prescribe drugs for the "comfort" of addicted patients was eventually disallowed.

143 The first morphine clinic opened in Jacksonville, Florida in 1912, followed by hundreds of others across the country. David F. Musto, *The American Disease: Origins of Narcotic Control* (New York: Oxford University Press, 1973/1999).

144 Richard DeGrandpre, *The Cult of Pharmacology: How America Became the World's Most Troubled Drug Culture* (Durham, NC: Duke University Press, 2006). See also Hari, *Chasing the Scream.*

145 Richard DeGrandpre, *The Cult of Pharmacology,* 126. See also Rufus King, *The Drug Hang Up: America's Fifty-Year Folly* (New York, NY: W. W. Norton Company & Inc., 1972), 18.

146 Caroline Jean Acker, *Creating the American Junkie: Addiction Research in the Classic Era of Narcot-ics Control* (Baltimore, MA: John Hopkins University Press, 2002), 140.

147 Carl Hart, "Exaggerating Harmful Drug Effects on the Brain is Killing Black People," *Neuroview 107,* (2): July 2020.

148 Tim Rhodes, "Risk Environments and Drug Harms: A Social Science for Harm Reduction Approach," *International Journal of Drug Policy 20* (2009): 196. See also John Strang, et. al., "Computerized Tomography and Neuropsychological Assessment in Long-Term High-Dose Heroin Addicts," *British Journal of Addiction 84,* (1989): 1011.

149 Tim Rhodes, "The 'Risk Environment': A Framework for Understanding and Reducing Drug Related Harm," *International Journal of Drug Policy 13,* (2): June 2002.

150 Karishma S. Kaushik, et. al., "Shooting Up: The Interface of Microbial Infections and Drug Abuse," *Journal of Medical Microbiology 60,* (2011): 408-422.

151 Merrill Singer, *Something Dangerous: Emergent and Changing Illicit Drug Use and Community Health* (Long Grove, IL: Waveland Press, Inc., 2006), 30.

152 Tim Rhodes, "Risk Environments and Drug Harms: A Social Science for Harm Reduction Approach," *International Journal of Drug Policy 20* (2009).

153 Phil Nicholas, et. al., "The Federal Bureau of Narcotics, the States, and the Origin of Modern Drug Enforcement in the United States, 1950-1962," *Contemporary Drug Problems 32* (2012): 595-640.

154 Johann Hari makes a similar point in his book, *Chasing the Scream: The First and Last Days of the War on Drugs* (New York, NY: Bloomsbury, 2015).

155 Vincze Milkós, "*Gorgeous Vintage Advertisements for Heroin, Cannabis and Cocaine,*" on Gizmodo.com, May 30, 2013.

156 Vincze Milkós, "Gorgeous Vintage Advertisements for Heroin, Cannabis and Cocaine" on Gizmodo.com, May 30, 2013.

157 Thomas Hager, *Ten Drugs: How Plants, Powders and Pills have Shaped the History of Medicine* (New York: Abrams Press, 2019), 90. Original advertisement images public domain, available online at *Gizmodo.*

158 Thomas Hager, *Ten Drugs: How Plants, Powders and Pills have Shaped the History of Medicine* (New York: Abrams Press, 2019), 90.

159 Rufus King, *The Drug Hang Up: America's Fifty-Year Folly* (New York, NY: W. W. Norton Company & Inc., 1972), 19. Sigmund Freud, *Cocaine Papers,* ed. Robert Byck (Massachusetts: The Stonehill Publishing Company, 1974). See also Inciardi, "America's Drug Policy," 1-7.

160 King, *The Drug Hang Up: America's Fifty-Year Folly* (New York, NY: W. W. Norton Company & Inc., 1972), 18.

161 Tim Rhodes, "The 'Risk Environment': A Framework for Understanding and Reducing Drug Related Harm," *International Journal of Drug Policy 13,* (2): June 2002.

162 US Census Bureau, Online Database, "*Fast Facts: Populations Statistics*"

163 Jonathan Sidhu, "*Exploring the APA's History of Discrimination,*" ProPublica (July 2008).

164 Thomas Hager, *Ten Drugs: How Plants, Powders and Pills have Shaped the History of Medicine* (New York: Abrams Press, 2019), 16, 76.

165 David Wootton, *Bad Medicine: Doctors Doing Harm since Hippocrates* (New York: Oxford Univer-sity Press, 2006).

166 Thomas Hager, *Ten Drugs: How Plants, Powders and Pills have Shaped the History of Medicine* (New York: Abrams Press, 2019), 16.

167 Jonathan Sidhu, *"Exploring the APA's History of Discrimination," ProPublica* (July 2008).

168 Benjamin Boyce, "Racist Compared to What? The Myth of White Wokeness," *Whiteness and Education,* (June, 2021). See also Benjamin Boyce, *Discourses of Deception: (Re)Examining America's War on Drugs,* Dissertation, ProQuest, 2018.

169 Robert Takaki, *A Different Mirror: A History of Multicultural America* (New York: Little, Brown & Company: 1993).

170 Tim Wise, *White Like Me: Reflections on Race from a Privileged Son* (New York: Soft Skull Press, 2008), 148-153. See also *Understanding White Privilege: Creating Pathways to Authentic Relationships Across Race* (New York: Routledge, 2006), 42-50.

171 Benjamin Boyce, *Discourses of Deception: (Re)Examining America's War on Drugs,* Dissertation, ProQuest, 2018.

172 For a great description of borderlands as spaces of invisible power, see Gloria Anzaldúa, *Borderlands La Frontera: The New Mestiza* (San Francisco, CA: Aunt Lute Books, 1987).

173 Frederick Douglas, "West Indies Emancipation Speech," August 3, 1857, Live Speech in Canandaigua, New York.

174 Abby Goodnough, *"Finding Good Pain Treatment is Hard. If you are Nonwhite, it is even Harder," The New York Times,* August 9, 2016.

175 Rudolph Matas, *The Surgical Peculiarities of the American Negro: A Statistical Inquiry* (USA: American Surgical Association, 1896), 25. P. R. Lockhart, *"What Serena's Scary Childbirth Story Says about Medical Treatment of Black Women," VOX,* January 11, 2018.

176 Benjamin Boyce, *Discourses of Deception: (Re)Examining America's War on Drugs,* Dissertation, ProQuest, 2018. See also Carl Hart, *The Joe Rogan Experience,* "Dr. Carl Hart," Episode 1593: (January 12, 2021).

177 Gerald Posner, *Pharma: Greed, Lies and the Poisoning of America* (New York: Avid Reader Press, 2020).

178 Thomas Hager, *Ten Drugs: How Plants, Powders and Pills have Shaped the History of Medicine* (New York: Abrams Press, 2019). Benjamin Boyce, *Discourses of Deception: (Re)Examining America's War on Drugs,* Dissertation, ProQuest, 2018. Johann Hari, *Chasing the Scream.*

179 Benjamin Boyce, *Discourses of Deception: (Re)Examining America's War on Drugs,* Dissertation, ProQuest, 2018.

180 Benjamin Boyce, *Discourses of Deception: (Re)Examining America's War on Drugs,* Dissertation, ProQuest, 2018. See also Johann Hari, *Chasing the Scream.*

181 Johann Hari, *Chasing the Scream: The First and Last Days of the War on Drugs* (New York, NY: Bloomsbury, 2015).

182 Newspaper articles compiled in Larry Sloman, *Reefer Madness: A History of Marijuana* (New York: St. Martin's Press, 1979: 60-65.

183 Donald Trump, "Presidential Campaign Announcement Speech," Trump Towers, New York, (June 15, 2015).

184 Thomas Hager, *Ten Drugs: How Plants, Powders and Pills have Shaped the History of Medicine* (New York: Abrams Press, 2019), 35, 92. See also Benjamin Boyce, *Discourses of Deception: (Re) Examining America's War on Drugs,* Dissertation, ProQuest, 2018.

185 Timothy Hickman, "Drugs and Race in American Culture: Orientalism in the Turn of the Century Discourse of Narcotic Addiction," *American Studies 41,* (1): Spring 2000.

186 Johann Hari, *Chasing the Scream: The First and Last Days of the War on Drugs* (New York, NY: Bloomsbury, 2015).

187 Johann Hari, *Chasing the Scream: The First and Last Days of the War on Drugs* (New York, NY: Bloomsbury, 2015).

188 Johann Hari, *Chasing the Scream: The First and Last Days of the War on Drugs* (New York, NY: Bloomsbury, 2015), 11.

189 Anslinger's cruelty, like many others', was directly related to traumatic experiences from his childhood from which he never fully recovered. See Johann Hari, *Chasing the Scream: The First and Last Days of the War on Drugs* (New York, NY: Bloomsbury, 2015), 10-15.

190 Johann Hari, *Chasing the Scream: The First and Last Days of the War on Drugs* (New York, NY: Bloomsbury, 2015), 10-15.

191 Michael Schaller, "The Federal Prohibition of Marihuana," *Journal of Social History 4,* (1), 1970.

192 Edward Huntington Williams, *"Negro Cocaine 'Fiends' are a New Southern Menace: Murder and Insanity Increasing Among Lower Class Blacks because they have Taken to 'Sniffing" Since Deprived of Whiskey During Prohibition," The New York Times,* Feb 8, 1914.

193 Edward Huntington Williams, *"Negro Cocaine 'Fiends' are a New Southern Menace: Murder and Insanity Increasing Among Lower Class Blacks because they have Taken to 'Sniffing" Since Deprived of Whiskey During Prohibition," The New York Times,* Feb 8, 1914.

194 There are numerous images online of Harry Anslinger and his men posing for photographs with piles of drugs and paraphernalia. See Johann Hari, *Chasing the Scream: The First and Last Days of the War on Drugs* (New York, NY: Bloomsbury, 2015). See also Larry Sloman, *Reefer Madness: A History of Marijuana* (New York: St. Martin's Press, 1979).

195 Carl Hart, "Exaggerating Harmful Drug Effects on the Brain is Killing Black People," *Neoroview 107*, (2): July, 2020. See also Edward Huntington Williams, *"Negro Cocaine 'Fiends' are a New Southern Menace: Murder and Insanity Increasing Among Lower Class Blacks because they have Taken to 'Sniffing" Since Deprived of Whiskey During Prohibition," The New York Times*, Feb 8, 1914. See also Johann Hari, *Chasing the Scream*. See also Maia Szalavitz, *Unbroken Brain*. See also Carl Hart, *High Price*.

196 Carl Hart, "Exaggerating Harmful Drug Effects on the Brain is Killing Black People," *Neoroview 107*, (2): July 2020. See also Claire Spiegel, "Effects of PCP: *Myth Vs. Reality : Stories Abound about the Drug Imbuing People with Superhuman Strength. But Some Researchers Say Those Claims are Overrated," Los Angeles Times*, June 17, 1991.

197 The *This is your Brain on Drugs* series featured numerous commercials with different actors describing a hot frying pan as drugs, and an egg as your brain. The actor would crack the egg into the pan and portray the sizzling as your brain on drugs.

198 *Reefer Madness*, also released as *Tell Your Children*, was a 1936 propaganda film originally produced by a Church to scare children into abstaining from drug use, then re-cut for use in theatres as an anti-drug propaganda piece. For examples of misleading research about drugs, see Robert Mathias, "'Ecstasy' Damages the Brain and Impairs Memory in Humans," *National Institute on Drug Abuse*, (November 1999). See also *Dr. Phil*, "A Look Inside the Brain of a Drug User," downloaded from DrPhil.com June 9, 2021.

199 For a history of Harm Reduction, see Maia Szalavitz, *Undoing Drugs: The Untold Story of Harm Reduction and the Future of Addiction* (New York: Hachette Books, 2021).

200 Malcolm Gladwell, *The Tipping Point: How Little Things can Make a Big Difference* (New York: Black Bay Books, 2000).

201 Matt MacNabb, *A Secret History of Brands: The Dark and Twisted Beginnings of the Brand Names we Know and Love* (South Yorkshire: Pen & Sword Books, 2017).

202 Coca-Cola stories taken from *corporate website*, and Matt MacNabb, *A Secret History of Brands: The Dark and Twisted Beginnings of the Brand Names we Know and Love* (South Yorkshire: Pen & Sword Books, 2017).

203 The 13th Amendment codified slavery in the United States for at least another 160 years, so long as the enslaved is convicted of a crime.

204 Kathy Forde, et. al., "Exploiting Black Labor after the Abolition of Slavery," *The Conversation*, February 6, 2017.

205 Michelle Alexander, *The New Jim Crow: Mass Incarceration in the Age of Colorblindness* (New York, NY: The New Press, 2010/2012).

206 Lisa Wada, *"How Prohibition put the Cocaine in Coca-Cola," Pacific Standard*, January 28, 2015.

207 See Supreme Court Case, "United States V. Forty Barrels and Twenty Kegs of Coca-Cola," 241 U.S. 265 (1916).

208 Drug arrests from Federal Bureau of Investigation, Criminal Justice Information Services Division, *"2019 Crime in the United States: Estimated Number of Arrests,"* (Washington, D.C.: 2020).

209 For a description of the learning disorder model, see Maia Szalavitz, *Unbroken Brain: A Revolutionary New Way of Understanding Addiction* (New York: St. Martin's Press, 2016), 36.

210 Carl Hart, *Drug Use for Grown Ups: Chasing Liberty in the Land of Fear* (New York: Penguin Press, 2021), 64-65. See also Chapter Four for an in-depth explanation of collection issues which ensure overdose deaths from illegal drugs are grossly exaggerated every year.

211 Carl Hart, "Viewing Addiction as a Brain Disease Promotes Social Injustice," *Natural Human Behavior 1*, (55): 2017.

Chapter Three

212 Arthur Conan Doyle, *A Sign of the Four,* Public Source.

213 Depending on the cutting agents and the level of heat applied, boiling cocaine in water begins the process of converting it (back to) crack cocaine (cocaine base).

214 Maia Szalavitz describes this process of a speedball kicking in at various times in her book, *Unbroken Brain: A Revolutionary New Way of Understanding Addiction* (New York: St. Martin's Press, 2016), 156.

215 Hunter Thompson, *Fear and Loathing in Las Vegas: A Savage Journey to the Heart of the American Dream* (Toronto, Canada: Vintage Books, 1971), 4.

216 This is an Alcoholics Anonymous (12-step) slogan often recited at meetings across the United States.

217 We have long recognized the similarities between states of consciousness produced by chemicals, and states produced by things like exercise or meditation. See L. Schwarz, et. al., "Changes in Beta-Endorphin Levels in Response to Aerobic and Anaerobic Exercise," *Sports Medicine 13*, (1): January,

1992. See also Stephanie Ortigue, et. al., "Neuroimaging of Love: fMRI Meta-Analysis Evidence Towards New Perspectives in Sexual Medicine," *Journal of Sexual Medicine 7*, (11): November 2010.

218 Shepard Siegel, "Drug Tolerance, Drug Addiction, and Drug Anticipation," *Current Directions in Psychological Science 14*, (6), 2005.

219 Shepard Siegel, "Drug Tolerance, Drug Addiction, and Drug Anticipation," *Current Directions in Psychological Science 14*, (6), 2005.

220 Jeffery Steketee, et. al., "Drug Wanting: Behavioral Sensitization and Relapse to Drug-Seeking Behavior," *Pharmacological Reviews 63*, (2): June, 2011. See also Maia Szalavitz, *Unbroken Brain: A Revolutionary New Way of Understanding Addiction* (New York: St. Martin's Press, 2016), 117-120.

221 Richard Dawkins, *The Extended Phenotype: The Long Reach of the Gene* (New York: Oxford University Press, 1982). Granted, there are some exceptions to this rule, as Dawkins discusses in *The Selfish Gene* (New York: Oxford University Press, 1976).

222 Jennifer Perusini, et. al., "Induction and Expression of Fear Sensitization Caused by Acute Traumatic Stress," *Neuropsychopharmacology 41*, (1): January 2016.

223 Yuval Neria, et. al., "*Posttraumatic Stress Disorder Following the September 11, 2001, Terrorist Attacks: A Review of the Literature Among Highly Exposed Populations,*" *American Psychology 66*, (6): September 2011.

224 Richard Dawkins, *The Selfish Gene* (New York: Oxford University Press, 1976).

225 Jennifer Perusini, et. al., "Induction and Expression of Fear Sensitization Caused by Acute Traumatic Stress," *Neuropsychopharmacology 41*, (1): January 2016.

226 Maia Szalavitz, *Unbroken Brain: A Revolutionary New Way of Understanding Addiction* (New York: St. Martin's Press, 2016), 118.

227 G. I. Papapkostas, et. al., "Towards New Mechanisms: An Update on Therapeutics for Treatment-Resistant Major Depressive Disorder," *Molecular Psychiatry 20*, 2015. See also Loris Chahl, "Opioids—Mechanisms of Action," *Experimental and Clinical Pharmacology 3*, July 1996.

228 Nadia R.P.W. Hutten, et. al., "Cocaine Enhances Figural, but Impairs Verbal 'Flexible' Divergent Thinking," *European Neuropsychopharmacology 29*, (7), 2019. There is no shortage of claims concerning cocaine producing self-confidence which was vital to the artistic success of many famous characters. See Elton John, *Me* (New York: St. Martin's Publishing Group, 2019).

229 Carl Hart, et. al., "Is Cognitive Functioning Impaired in Methamphetamine Users? A Critical Review," *Neuropsychopharmacology 37*, (November 2011).

230 MDMA is 3, 4-methylenedioxymethamphetamine, also known as ecstasy. See Erwin Krediet, et. al., "Reviewing the Potential of Psychedelics for the Treatment of PTSD," *International Journal of Neuropsychopharmacology 23*, (6): June 2020.

231 Lihi Bar-Lev Schleider, et. al., "Real Life Experience of Medial Cannabis Treatment in Autism: Analysis of Safety and Efficacy," *Scientific Reports 9*, 2019. See also Linda Parker, et. al., "Regulation of Nausea and Vomiting by Cannabinoids," *British Journal of Pharmacology 163*, (7), 2011.

232 Maia Szalavitz, *Unbroken Brain: A Revolutionary New Way of Understanding Addiction* (New York: St. Martin's Press, 2016), 3, 36-37.

233 Numerous researchers have been discussing the link between addiction and learning, some as early as 1968: Alfred Lindlesmith, *Addiction and Opiates* (New York: Transaction Publishers, 1968). Many others have continued the conversation, including Lee Robins, Norman Zinberg, Kent Berridge, Terry Robinson, Nora Volkow, Gene Heyman, David Duncan, and Maia Szalavitz, just to name a few.

234 The first reference I know of in literature is Alfred Lindesmith, *Addiction & Opiates* (New York: Routledge, 1968). See also Maia Szalavitz, *Unbroken Brain: A Revolutionary New Way of Understanding Addiction* (New York: St. Martin's Press, 2016), 36-37.

235 Maia Szalavitz, *Unbroken Brain: A Revolutionary New Way of Understanding Addiction* (New York: St. Martin's Press, 2016), 35-38.

236 Chuan-Yu Chen, et. al., "*Early-Onset Drug Use and Risk for Drug Dependence Problems,*" *Addictive Behaviors 34*, (3): 2009.

237 Jill Sakaki, "*Core Concept: How Synaptic Pruning Shapes Neural Wiring During Development and, Possibly, in Disease,*" *Proceedings of the National Academy of Sciences in the United States of America 117*, (28): July 14, 2020.

238 Jill Sakai, "Core Concept: How Synaptic Pruning Shapes Neural Wiring during Development and, Possibly, in Disease," *PNAS 117*, (28), July 2020.

239 Terry Robinson and Kent Berridge, "The Neural Basis of Drug Craving: An Incentive Sensitization Theory of Addiction," *Brain Research Reviews 18*, (3): 1993. Kent Berridge and Terry Robinson, "Liking, Wanting and the Incentive-Sensitization Theory of Addiction," *American Psychology 71*, (8), November 2016.

240 Jennifer Wisdom, et. al., "What Teens Want: Barriers to Seeking Care for Depression," *Administration and Policy in Mental Health 33*, (2): March 2006.

241 Maia Szalavitz, *Unbroken Brain: A Revolutionary New Way of Understanding Addiction* (New York:

St. Martin's Press, 2016), 98.

242 If you want to hear about some of these adventures, see "Free Will" and "Addiction," episodes of *The Dr. Junkie Show* podcast.

243 Ralph Hingson, et. al., *"Age at Drinking Onset and Alcohol Dependence: Age at Onset, Duration, and Severity,"* Archives of Adolescent and Pediatric Medicine 160, (7): July 2006.

244 John Salamone, et. al., "The Mysterious Motivational Functions of Mesolimbic Dopamine," *Neuron 76*, (3): November 2012.

245 *Ethan Bromberg-Martin, et. al.,* "Dopamine in Motivational Control: Rewarding, Aversive, and Alerting," *Neuron 68*, (5): December 2010.

246 Salim Megat, et. al., "A Critical Role for Dopamine D5 Receptors in Pain Chronicity in Male Mice," *Journal of Neuroscience 38*, (2): January 2018. See also Henry Chase, et. al., "Gambling Severity Predicts Midbrain Response to Near-Miss Outcomes," *Journal of Neuroscience 30*, (18): May 2010.

247 Carl Hart, *"People are Dying because of Ignorance, not because of Drugs,"* Scientific American, November 1, 2017. See also Tim Rhodes, "Risk Environments and Drug Harms: A Social Science for Harm Reduction Approach," *International Journal of Drug Policy 20* (2009).

248 Paul Cumming, *Imaging Dopamine* (UK: Cambridge University Press, 2009).

249 Maia Szalavitz, *Unbroken Brain: A Revolutionary New Way of Understanding Addiction* (New.York: St. Martin's Press, 2016).

250 Sam Harris, *Free Will* (New York: Free Press, 2012).

251 For an example of dopamine conflated with pleasure, see Hilary Bruek, et. al., "This is why our Phones are Making us Miserable: Happiness isn't the same thing as Pleasure, and our Brain knows it," *Business Insider,* March 24, 2018. For a larger examination of the media's misleading messages and how they come to effect consumers, see Carl Hart, "Exaggerating Harmful Drug Effects on the Brain is Killing Black People," *Neuroview 107*, (2): July 22, 2020. See also Carl Hart, *High Price,* 16.

252 Andrew Westbrook and Todd Braver, "Dopamine Does Double-Duty in Motivating Cognitive Effort," *Neuron 89*, (4): February 2016. See also Roshan Cools, et. al., Hofmans, *Handbook of Clinical Neurology,* "Chapter 7: Dopamine and the Motivation of Cognitive Control," (Volume 163: 2019). See also Ben Boyce, "Addiction," *The Dr. Junkie Show* (podcast).

253 Roy Wise, "Dopamine and Reward: The Anhedonia Hypothesis 30 years on," *Neurotoxicity Research 14*, (2-3). See also Peter Kramer, *Listening to Prozac* (New York: Penguin Books, 1997),

254 Jaime Kulisevsky, "Role of Dopamine in Learning and Memory: Implications for the Treatment of Cognitive Dysfunction in Patients with Parkinson's Disease," *Drugs & Aging 16,* August 2012.

255 Peter Kramer, *Listening to Prozac* (New York: Penguin Books, 1997), 231-232.

256 Maia Szalavitz, *Unbroken Brain: A Revolutionary New Way of Understanding Addiction* (New York: St. Martin's Press, 2016), 98.

257 Jaime Kulisevsky, "Role of Dopamine in Learning and Memory: Implications for the Treatment of Cognitive Dysfunction in Patients with Parkinson's Disease," *Drugs & Aging 16,* August 2012.

258 Jaime Kulisevsky, "Role of Dopamine in Learning and Memory: Implications for the Treatment of Cognitive Dysfunction in Patients with Parkinson's Disease," *Drugs & Aging 16,* August 2012.

259 Patrick Anselme, et. al., "What Motivates Gambling Behavior? Insight into Dopamine's Role," *Frontiers in Behavioral Neuroscience 7*, (182): December 2013. See also Henry Chase, et. al., "Gambling Severity Predicts Midbrain Response to Near-Miss Outcomes," *Journal of Neuroscience 30*, (18): May 2010. See also *Ethan Bromberg-Martin, et. al.,* "Dopamine in Motivational Control: Rewarding, Aversive, and Alerting," *Neuron 68*, (5): December 2010.

260 Kent Berridge and Terry Robinson, "Liking, Wanting and the Incentive-Sensitization Theory of Addiction," *American Psychology 71*, (8), November 2016. See also Maia Szalavitz, *Unbroken Brain: A Revolutionary New Way of Understanding Addiction* (New York: St. Martin's Press, 2016).

261 Masayuki Matsumoto, et. al., *"How do Dopamine Neurons Represent Positive and Negative Motivational Events?"* Nature 459, (7248): June 2009.

262 Kent Berridge and Terry Robinson, "Liking, Wanting and the Incentive-Sensitization Theory of Addiction," *American Psychology 71*, (8), November 2016.

263 Kent Berridge and Terry Robinson, "Liking, Wanting and the Incentive-Sensitization Theory of Addiction," *American Psychology 71*, (8), November 2016. See also Maia Szalavitz, *Unbroken Brain: A Revolutionary New Way of Understanding Addiction* (New York: St. Martin's Press, 2016).

264 Kent Berridge and Terry Robinson, "Liking, Wanting and the Incentive-Sensitization Theory of Addiction," *American Psychology 71*, (8), November 2016.

265 Kent Berridge and Terry Robinson, "Liking, Wanting and the Incentive-Sensitization Theory of Addiction," *American Psychology 71*, (8), November 2016.

266 Terry Robinson and Kent Berridge, "The Incentive Sensitization Theory of Addiction: Some Current Issues," *Philosophical Transactions of the Royal Society B: Biological Sciences 363*, (1507): July 2018.

267 Peter Kramer, *Listening to Prozac* (New York: Penguin Books, 1997), 231-232. See also Maia Szalavitz, *Unbroken Brain,* 111.

268 Maia Szalavitz, "Genetics: No More Addictive Personality," *Nature 522*, (7557), 2015. See also Carl Hart, *High Price: A Neuroscientist's Journey of Self-Discovery that Challenges Everything you know about Drugs and Society* (New York, Harper Perennial Press, 2013).

269 This narrative is common in people diagnoses with Asperger's. See Maia Szalavitz, *Unbroken Brain: A Revolutionary New Way of Understanding Addiction* (New York: St. Martin's Press, 2016).

270 Lihi Bar-Lev Schleider, et. al., "Real Life Experience of Medial Cannabis Treatment in Autism: Analysis of Safety and Efficacy," *Scientific Reports 9*, 2019.

271 Chad Sallaberry, et. al., "*The Endocannabinoid System, Our Universal Regulator*," *Journal of Young Investigators 34*, (6): June 2018. See also Bradley Alger, "Getting High on the Endocannabinoid System," *Cerebrum 14*, December 2013.

272 Shenglong Zou, et. al., "Cannabinoid Receptors and the Endocannabinoid System: Signaling and Function in the Central Nervous System," *International Journal of Molecular Sciences 19*, (3): March 2018.

273 Chad Sallaberry, et. al., "*The Endocannabinoid System, Our Universal Regulator*," *Journal of Young Investigators 34*, (6): June 2018.

274 Bradley Alger, "Getting High on the Endocannabinoid System," *Cerebrum 14*, December 2013.

275 Farnaz Faridi, et. al., "Behavioral, Cognitive and Neural Markers of Asperger Syndrome," *Basic and Clinical Neuroscience 8*, (5): October 2017.

276 For an impressive historical examination of safe use sites, and the harm reduction movement which made them a reality, see Maia Szalavitz, *Undoing Drugs: The Untold Story of Harm Reduction and the Future of Addiction* (New York: Hachette Books, 2021).

277 Elana Gordon, "*What's the Evidence that Supervised Drug Injection Sites Save Lives?*" *NPR,* September 7, 2018.

278 Mike Stobbe, "*An Underground Injection Site for Heroin Users has been Operating in the US for Years,*" Business Insider, August 8, 2017. See also Meryl Kornfield, et. al., "*America Needs to Reduce Soaring Overdoses. A Secret Supervised Injection Site may Show us How,*" The Washington Post, July 10, 2020.

279 Rachael Rzasa Lynn, et. al., "Naloxone Dosage for Opioid Reversal: Current Evidence and Clinical Implications," *Therapeutic Advances in Drug Safety,* December 2017.

280 For Naloxone's history, see Maia Szalavitz, *Undoing Drugs: The Untold Story of Harm Reduction and the Future of Addiction* (New York: Hachette Books, 2021). For Sheriffs who brag about disallowing their deputies to carry Naloxone, see Butler County, OH sheriff Richard Jones interviews.

281 Rick Sobey, "Zero Deaths at Underground Supervised Injection Site Helps Massachusetts Effort to Open Facilities," *Boston Herald,* July 9, 2020.

282 Jennifer Brown, et. al., "*Denver Heroin Users could use Legal Supervised Injection Site if Proposed Plan Passes Multiple Hurdles,*" *The Denver Post,* November 5, 2017.

283 Carl Hart, *High Price: A Neuroscientist's Journal of Self-Discovery that Challenges Everything you Know about Drugs and Society* (New York: Harper Perennial, 2013), 16. See also Benjamin Boyce, *Discourses of Deception: (Re)Examining America's War on Drugs,* Dissertation, ProQuest, 2018.

284 For research into how fictionalized representations cause us to learn things even when we know they are fictionalized, see Michel de Certeau, "Believing and Making People Believe, " in *The Practice of Everyday Life,* translated by Steven Rendall. See also Bill Yousman, "Challenging the Media-Incarceration Complex through Media Education," in *Working for Justice: A Handbook of Prison Education and Activism,* ed. Stephen J. Hartnett, et. al., (Urbana, IL: University of Illinois Press, 2013).

285 Benjamin Boyce, *Discourses of Deception: (Re)Examining America's War on Drugs,* Dissertation, ProQuest, 2018. See also Carl Hart, *High Price: A Neuroscientist's Journal of Self-Discovery that Challenges Everything you Know about Drugs and Society* (New York: Harper Perennial, 2013), 16

286 bell hooks, "Seeing and Making Culture: Representing the Poor," in *Outlaw Culture: Resisting Representations,* by bell hooks (New York: Routledge, 1994).

287 Bill Yousman, "Challenging the Media-Incarceration Complex through Media Education," in *Working for Justice: A Handbook of Prison Education and Activism,* ed. Stephen J. Hartnett, Eleanor Novek, and Jennifer K. Wood (Urbana, IL: University of Illinois Press, 2013), 142.

288 Benjamin Boyce, "Should Colorado Open Safe Injection Sites?" *Westword,* February 7, 2021. Safe injection sites, like liquor stores, provide a check on underage use which is entirely absent from the underworld drug market.

289 Maia Szalavitz, *Unbroken Brain: A Revolutionary New Way of Understanding Addiction* (New York: St. Martin's Press, 2016).

290 Maia Szalavitz, *Undoing Drugs: The Untold Story of Harm Reduction and the Future of Addiction* (New York: Hachette Books, 2021).

291 John Strang, et. al., "Heroin on Trial: Systematic Review and Meta-Analysis of Randomised Trials of Diamorphine-Prescribed as Treatment for Refractory Heroin Addiction," *British Journal of Psychology 207*, (1): January 2008.

292 Toby Seddon, "Prescribing Heroin: John Marks, the Merseyside Heroin Clinics, and Lessons from

History," *International Journal of Drug Policy 78*, March 2020.

293 Jeffrey Miron et. al., *The Budgetary Impact of Ending Drug Prohibition* (Washington DC: CATO Institute, 2010).

294 Ali Shahid, et. al., "Methadone Treatment of Opioid Addiction: A Systemic Review of Comparative Studies," *Innovations in Clinical Neuroscience 14*, (8-9): August 2017.

295 Thomas Hager, *Ten Drugs: How Plants, Powders and Pills have Shaped the History of Medicine* (New York: Abrams Press, 2019), 187-210.

296 Kathy Breslin, et. al., "Maintaining the Viability and Safety of the Methadone Maintenance Treatment Program," *Journal of Psychoactive Drugs 38*, (2): June 2006.

297 Maia Szalavitz, *Undoing Drugs: The Untold Story of Harm Reduction and the Future of Addiction* (New York: Hachette Books, 2021).

298 For a list of federal guidelines for methadone maintenance treatment, see The Electronic Code of Federal Regulations, "Medication Assisted Treatment for Opioid Use Disorder," updated May 27, 2021.

299 No perceptible buzz: Kathy Breslin, et. al., "Maintaining the Viability and Safety of the Methadone Maintenance Treatment Program," *Journal of Psychoactive Drugs 38*, (2): June 2006. See also Alison Seymour, et. al., "The Role of Methadone in Drug-Related Deaths in the West of Scotland," *Addiction 98*, (7): July 2003.

300 See Maia Szalavitz, "The Wrong Way to Treat Opioid Addiction," *New York Times*, January 17, 2018. See also Matthias Pierce, et. al., "Impact of Treatment for Opioid Dependence on Fatal Drug-Related Poisoning: A National Cohort Study in England," *Addiction 111*, (2): February 2016.

301 Maia Szalavitz, "Genetics: No More Addictive Personality," *Nature 522*, (7557), 2015. See also Carl Hart, *High Price: A Neuroscientist's Journey of Self-Discovery that Challenges Everything you know about Drugs and Society* (New York, Harper Perennial Press, 2013).

302 For statistical evidence of our natural tendency to learn from narratives even when we know they are fictional or exaggerated, see Travis Dixon, "Teaching you to Love Fear: Television News and Racial Stereotypes in a Punishing Democracy," in *Challenging the Prison-Industrial Complex: Activism, Arts and Educational Alternative*, ed. Stephen J. Hartnett (Urbana, IL: University of Illinois Press, 2011), 105-123.

303 There are plenty of descriptions of this project and the cultural myths surrounding it. I prefer the work of Johann Hari, *Chasing the Scream: The First and Last Days of the War on Drugs* (New York, NY: Bloomsbury, 2015).

304 Bruce Alexander, et. al., "Effects of Early and Later Colony Housing on Oral Ingestion of Morphine in Rats," *Pharmacology, Biochemistry and Behavior 15*, 1981. For a detailed description of rat park experiments, see Johann Hari, *Chasing the Scream*.

305 Bruce Alexander, et. al., "Effects of Early and Later Colony Housing on Oral Ingestion of Morphine in Rats," *Pharmacology, Biochemistry and Behavior 15*, 1981.

306 Mary Jeanne Kerrk, et. al., "Pharmacotherapy in the Treatment of Addiction: Methadone," *Journal of Addictive Diseases 29*, (2): April 2011.

307 The problems referred to include high costs related to continued enrollment in some facilities, requirements to see specific therapists, limits on take-home medication, requirements to attend the program daily, termination due to having other drugs in one's system, and strict requirements as to times of the day when users can receive their medication. See Maia Szalavitz, *Unbroken Brain: A Revolutionary New Way of Understanding Addiction* (New York: St. Martin's Press, 2016).

308 Maia Szalavitz, "Genetics: No More Addictive Personality," *Nature 522*, (48-49), June 2015.

309 Kent Berridge and Terry Robinson, "Liking, Wanting and the Incentive-Sensitization Theory of Addiction," *American Psychology 71*, (8), November 2016.

310 Maia Szalavitz, *Unbroken Brain: A Revolutionary New Way of Understanding Addiction* (New York: St. Martin's Press, 2016), 274-275.

311 Random rewarding causes rats to press a button more than any other reward schedule, which may well mean that the threat of the button returning nothing is part of the cause for the repeated button-pushing. See M.D. Zeiler, "Fixed-Interval Behavior: Effects of Percentage Reinforcement," *Journal of the Experimental Analysis of Behavior 17*, (2): 1972

312 Punishment has been shown to increase use, or at least to have no effect on use, in addicted people. Antoine Bechara, et. al, "Decision-Making and Addiction (Part II): Myopia for the Future or Hyper-sensitivity to Reward?" *Neuropsychologia 40*, (10): 2002.

313 W. R. Miller et. al., "What Predicts a Relapse? Prospective Testing of Antecedent Models," *Addiction 91*, December 1996.

314 The percentage of people with college degrees classified as heavy smokers (24 or more cigarettes daily) decreased from 33% in 1980 to 7% in 2018, largely due to heightened taxes, propaganda, and the use of sanctioned smoking areas (which legitimized non-smoking areas). Statistics from The American Lung Association, *"Overall Tobacco Trends,"* and CDC Data: "NHIS 1974-2018."

315 The American Lung Association, *"Overall Tobacco Trends,"* and CDC Data: "NHIS 1974-2018."

316 John Strang, et. al., "Heroin on Trial: Systematic Review and Meta-Analysis of Randomised Trials of

Diamorphine-Prescribed as Treatment for Refractory Heroin Addiction," *British Journal of Psychology 207*, (1): January 2008.

317 W. R. Miller et. al., "What Predicts a Relapse? Prospective Testing of Antecedent Models," *Addiction 91*, December 1996.

318 M.D. Zeiler, "Fixed-Interval Behavior: Effects of Percentage Reinforcement," *Journal of the Experimental Analysis of Behavior 17*, (2): 1972. Story about B.F. Skinner's discovery is from Maia Szalavitz, *Unbroken Brain: A Revolutionary New Way of Understanding Addiction* (New York: St. Martin's Press, 2016), 127. See also Indiana University, online Psychology 101 course.

319 M.D. Zeiler, "Fixed-Interval Behavior: Effects of Percwentage Reinforcement," *Journal of the Experimental Analysis of Behavior 17*, (2): 1972

320 Maia Szalavitz, *Unbroken Brain: A Revolutionary New Way of Understanding Addiction* (New York: St. Martin's Press, 2016).

321 Maia Szalavitz, *Undoing Drugs: The Untold Story of Harm Reduction and the Future of Addiction* (New York: Hachette Books, 2021).

322 Jesse Eisinger, et. al., *"Walmart was almost Charged Criminally over Opioids. Trump Appointment Killed the Indictment,"* *ProPublic*, (March 25, 2020).

323 Ramsey Touchberry, "Joe Manchin Wanted to Buy a $3 Million Helicopter with Money Earmarked for Tackling Opioid Crisis: Report," *Newsweek*, October 12, 2018.

324 Ben Sessa, "MDMA," *The Dr. Junkie Show* (podcast), July 12, 2020. See also Ben Sessa, et. al., "Is there a Role for Psychedelics in the Treatment of Drug Dependency?" *British Journal of Psychiatry*, January 2015.

325 Ben Sessa, "MDMA," *The Dr. Junkie Show* (podcast), Season 1, Episode 9, (July 12, 2020). See also Ben Boyce and Laura Hull, "Ketamine Therapy," *The Dr. Junkie Show* (podcast), Season 2, Episode 20, (June 2021).

326 Ben Sessa, "Why MDMA Therapy for Alcohol Use Disorder and Why Now?" *Neuropharmacology 142*, (2018).

327 Matthew Johnson, et. al., *"Long-term Follow-up of Psilocybin-facilitated Smoking Cessation,"* *American Journal of Drug and Alcohol Abuse 43*, (1): January 2017.

Chapter Four

328 Sigmund Freud, *Civilization and its Discontents*, trans. Joan Riviere, (Blacksburg, VA: Wilder Publications, 1930/2010), 16.

329 Both "No-Knock" Warrants and Civil Forfeiture of personal property were popularized during Reagan's time in office. See the Comprehensive Crime Control Act of 1984. The Crack House Statutes (21 USC § 856) are used to prosecute owners of rental properties if police believe they knew their venue was likely to be used to manufacture or distribute drugs.

330 Daniel Rothschild, et. al., "Don't Steal; The Government Hates Competition: The Problem with Civil Asset Forfeiture," *Journal of Private Enterprise 31*, (1): Spring, 2016. See also See also Dee Edgeworth, *Asset Forfeiture: Practice and Procedure in State and Federal Courts, 3rd Edition* (Chicago: American Bar Association, 2002).

331 Civil Forfeiture Laws are ancient, but they were updated in 1970 to funnel money to the federal government, and again in 1984 via the Comprehensive Crime Control Act. They are now regulated under U.S. Code § 983, Title 18, Chapter 46.

332 Daniel Rothschild, et. al., "Don't Steal; The Government Hates Competition: The Problem with Civil Asset Forfeiture," *Journal of Private Enterprise 31*, (1): Spring, 2016. See also See also Dee Edgeworth, *Asset Forfeiture: Practice and Procedure in State and Federal Courts, 3rd Edition* (Chicago: American Bar Association, 2002).

333 Daniel Rothschild, et. al., "Don't Steal; The Government Hates Competition: The Problem with Civil Asset Forfeiture," *Journal of Private Enterprise 31*, (1): Spring 2016.

334 Jefferson Holcomb, et. al., "Civil Asset Forfeiture, Equitable Sharing, and Policing for Profit in the United States," *Journal of Criminal Justice 39*, (3): 2011.

335 For information regarding the birth of the prison-industrial complex, see Michelle Alexander, *The New Jim Crow: Mass Incarceration in the Age of Colorblindness* (New York, NY: The New Press, 2010/2012). See also Angela Davis, "Masked Racism: Reflections on the Prison Industrial Complex; What is the Prison Industrial Complex? Why Does It Matter?" *Oakland 1*, (2): October 1998.

336 Brent Mast, et. al., "Entrepreneurial Police and Drug Enforcement Policy," *Public Choice 104*, (28): 2000.

337 Tupac Shakur, "The Lost Prison Interview: Clinton Correctional Facility," YouTube, 1995.

338 Statistics pulled from the *FBI web page* on 11/7/2020.

339 Dylan Thomas, "Do Not go Gently into that Pale Night," in *The Collected Poems of Dylan Thomas* (United Kingdom: Weidenfeld and Nicolson, 2016).

340 Daniel Mark Larson, "Killing Democracy: How the Drug War Drives the Prison-Industrial Complex," in *Challenging the Prison-Industrial Complex: Activism, Art and Education and Educational Alternatives*, ed. Stephen Hartnett, (Urbana, IL: University of Illinois Press, 2011): 73-97.

341 Federal Bureau of Prisons, "Offenses," updated April 2021. See also US Office of Justice Programs, Bureau of Justice Statistics, "Total Correctional Populations," 2020. See also, Wendy Sawyer, et. al., "Mass Incarceration: The Whole Pie," Prison Policy Initiative, (March 24, 2020).

342 Mumia Abu-Jamal, *Live from Death Row* (New York: Avon Books, Inc., 1995), 6.

343 Since addiction is a disorder characterized by one's failure to respond to punishment by changing one's behavior, punishment will not ever work to cure an addiction. But the trauma, pain and anxiety that comes with punishment (i.e. incarceration, forced detox, etc.) is certain to increase one's chances of using. See Ingrid Binswanger, "Return to Drug Use and Overdose after Release from Prison: A Qualitative Study of Risk and Protective Factors," *Addiction Science & Clinical Practice 7*, (1): March 2012. For Detox being unlikely to prove effective in opioid addiction treatment, see Genie Bailey, et. al., "Perceived Relapse Risk and Desire for Medication Assisted Treatment among Persons Seeking Inpatient Opiate Detoxification," *Journal of Substance Abuse Treatment 45*, (3): June 2013.

344 Kathy Breslin, et. al., "Maintaining the Viability and Safety of the Methadone Maintenance Treatment Program," *Journal of Psychoactive Drugs 38*, (2): June 2006.

345 See Ingrid Binswanger, "Return to Drug Use and Overdose after Release from Prison: A Qualitative Study of Risk and Protective Factors," *Addiction Science & Clinical Practice 7*, (1): March 2012. See also Morgan Godvin, "I thought going to Jail would get me Clean; I was Dead Wrong," *The Marshall Project*, September 3, 2020.

346 Federal Bureau of Investigation, Criminal Justice Information Services Division, "*2016 Uniform Crime Report*," (Washington, D.C.: 2017). See also Michelle Alexander, *The New Jim Crow: Mass Incarceration in the Age of Colorblindness* (New York, NY: The New Press, 2010/2012), 141-142.

347 US Office of Justice Programs, Bureau of Justice Statistics, "Recidivism of Prisoners Released in 30 States in 2005: Patterns from 2005-2010," by Matthew R. Durose, et. al., (April 22, 2014).

348 Federal Bureau of Investigation, Criminal Justice Information Services Division, "*2019 Crime in the United States: Estimated Number of Arrests,* " (Washington, D.C.: 2020).

349 National Center for Health Statistics, "Provisional Counts of Drug Overdose Deaths, as of 6/1/2020."

350 Hawre Jalal, et. al., "*Changing Dynamics of the Drug Overdose Epidemic in the United States from 1979 through 2016*," *Science 361*, 2018. See also Carl Hart, *Drug Use for Grown Ups*, 64-65.

351 Hawre Jalal, et. al., "*Changing Dynamics of the Drug Overdose Epidemic in the United States from 1979 through 2016*," *Science 361*, 2018.

352 Hawre Jalal, et. al., "*Changing Dynamics of the Drug Overdose Epidemic in the United States from 1979 through 2016*," *Science 361*, 2018.

353 Carl Hart, *Drug Use for Grown Ups: Chasing Liberty in the Land of Fear* (New York: Penguin Press, 2021), 64-65.

354 Hawre Jalal, et. al., "*Changing Dynamics of the Drug Overdose Epidemic in the United States from 1979 through 2016*," *Science 361*, 2018.

355 Carl Hart, *Drug Use for Grown Ups: Chasing Liberty in the Land of Fear* (New York: Penguin Press, 2021).

356 Johann Hari, *Chasing the Scream: The First and Last Days of the War on Drugs* (New York, NY: Bloomsbury).

357 See The Declaration of Independence.

358 Carl Hart makes this point as well in his book, *Drug Use for Grown Ups: Chasing Liberty in the Land of Fear* (New York: Penguin Press, 2021).

359 National Center for Health Statistics, "Provisional Counts of Drug Overdose Deaths, as of 8/6/2017."

360 Nick Miroff, "From Teddy Roosevelt to Trump: How Drug Companies Triggered an Opioid Crisis a Century Ago," *The Washington Post*, October 17, 2017. See also Donald Trump, "Opioid Crisis a National Emergency" (speech) Washington, D.C., the White House, October 26, 2017.

361 Holly Hedegaard, et. al., "Drug Overdose Deaths in the United States, 1999-2015," NCHS Data Brief, No. 273, published by Center for Disease Control, (February 2017).

362 Holly Hedegaard, et. al., "Drug Overdose Deaths in the United States, 1999-2015," NCHS Data Brief, No. 273, published by Center for Disease Control, (February 2017).

363 Anne Case, et. al., "Rising Morbidity and Mortality in Midlife Among White Non-Hispanic Americans in the 21st Century," *PNAS 112*, (49): December 2015: 15078-15083.

364 Anne Case, et. al., "Rising Morbidity and Mortality in Midlife Among White Non-Hispanic Americans in the 21st Century." *PNAS 112*, (49): December 2015. See also Arialdi Miniño et. al., "Drug Poisoning Mortality, by State and by Race and Ethnicity," Centers for Disease Control, March 23, 2020.

365 Benjamin Boyce, "Racist Compared to What? The Myth of White Wokeness," *Whiteness and Education 6*, (2): June 2021.

366 Benjamin Boyce, *Discourses of Deception: (Re)Examining America's War on Drugs*, Dissertation, ProQuest, 2018.

367 Tracy Huling, "Building A Prison Economy in Rural America," in *Invisible Punishment: The Collateral Consequences of Mass Imprisonment* (New York: The New Press, ٢٠٠٢). See also Daniel Mark

Larson, "Killing Democracy: How the Drug War Drives the Prison-Industrial Complex," in *Challenging the Prison-Industrial Complex: Activism, Art and Education and Educational Alternatives*, ed. Stephen Hartnett, (Urbana, IL: University of Illinois Press, 2011): 73-97.

368 bell hooks, *All About Love: New Visions* (New York: William Morrow and Company, Inc., 2000), 3-12.

369 For those scratching their heads or wondering where they can learn more, check out bell hooks, *All about Love, & Feminism is for Everybody*.

370 Benjamin Boyce, "Racist Compared to What? The Myth of White Wokeness," *Whiteness and Education 6*, (2): June 2021.

371 Artur Domoslawski, *Drug Policy in Portugal: The Benefits of Decriminalizing Drug Use*, trans. Hanna Siemaszko (Warsaw, Poland: Open Society Foundation, 2011), 40. See also Hari, *Chasing the Scream*, 238-239.

372 Michael Specter, "Getting a Fix: Portugal Decriminalized Drugs a Decade Ago. What have we Learned?" *New Yorker*, October 17, 2011. See also Hari, *Chasing the Scream*, 239.

373 Michael Specter, "Getting a Fix: Portugal Decriminalized Drugs a Decade Ago. What have we Learned?" *New Yorker*, October 17, 2011.

374 Sidsel Overgaard, *"Denmark's 'Fix Rooms' Give Drug Users a Safe Haven,"* NPR (article & podcast), December 16, 2013.

375 Michael Liebrenz, et. al., "Fifteen Years of Heroin-Assisted Treatment in a Swiss Prison—A Retrospective Cohort Study," *Harm Reduction Journal 17*, (67), October 2020.

376 Tina Rosenberg, *"Injecting Drugs, Under a Watchful Eye,"* New York Times, January 18, 2017. See also Mike Stobbe, *"An Underground Injection Site for Heroin Users has been Operating in the US for Years,"* Business Insider, August 8, 2017. See also Meryl Kornfield, et. al., *"America Needs to Reduce Soaring Overdoses. A Secret Supervised Injection Site may Show us How,"* The Washington Post, July 10, 2020.

377 Incarceration and supervision numbers from US Department of Justice: Bureau of Justice Statistics.

378 Carl Hart, *Drug Use for Grown Ups*, 50-57. See also *Nicholas Kristof, "How to Win a War on Drugs: Portugal Treats Addiction as a Disease, not a Crime,"* The New York Times, September 22, 2017. See also Johann Hari, *Chasing the Scream*, 238-239.

379 Carl Hart, *Drug Use for Grown Ups: Chasing Liberty in the Land of Fear* (New York: Penguin Press, 2021).

380 Johann Hari, *Chasing the Scream*, 240.

381 *Nicholas Kristof, "How to Win a War on Drugs: Portugal Treats Addiction as a Disease, not a Crime,"* The New York Times, September 22, 2017. See also Johann Hari, *Chasing the Scream*, 238-239.

382 *Nicholas Kristof, "How to Win a War on Drugs: Portugal Treats Addiction as a Disease, not a Crime,"* The New York Times, September 22, 2017.

383 Overdose estimates from CDC *"Provisional Drug Overdose Death Counts."*

384 Johann Hari, *Chasing the Scream*, 251.

385 Artur Domoslawski, *Drug Policy in Portugal: The Benefits of Decriminalizing Drug Use*, trans. Hanna Siemaszko (Warsaw, Poland: Open Society Foundation, 2011), 40.

386 Carl Hart, *Drug Use for Grown Ups: Chasing Liberty in the Land of Fear* (New York: Penguin Press, 2021), 134.

387 Kenneth Garger, *"Oregon Law Decriminalizing All Street Drugs Goes into Effect,"* The New York Post, February 2, 2021.

388 Xiao Zhu, et. al., "3D Printing Promotes the Development of Drugs," *Biomedicine & Pharmacotherapy 131*, (November 2020).

389 First Lady Nancy Reagan popularized the "Just Say No" adage, turning it into a campaign in the 1981, shortly after Reagan took office.

390 Johann Hari, *Chasing the Scream*, 263.

391 Johann Hari, *Chasing the Scream*, 261-266.

392 Jill Sakaki, *"Core Concept: How Synaptic Pruning Shapes Neural Wiring During Development and, Possibly, in Disease,"* Proceedings of the National Academy of Sciences in the United States of America 117, (28): July 14, 2020. See also Maia Szalavitz, *Unbroken Brain: A Revolutionary New Way of Understanding Addiction* (New York: St. Martin's Press, 2016), 98.

393 Ralph Hingson, et. al., *"Age at Drinking Onset and Alcohol Dependence: Age at Onset, Duration, and Severity,"* Archives of Adolescent and Pediatric Medicine 160, (7): July 2006. See also Chuan-Yu Chen, et. al., "Early-Onset Drug Use and Risk for Drug Dependence Problems," *Addictive Behavior 34*, (3): March 2009.

394 Maia Szalavitz, *Unbroken Brain: A Revolutionary New Way of Understanding Addiction* (New York: St. Martin's Press, 2016), 38-40.

395 Thomas Mitchell, "Sweet Leaf Licenses Suspended After Denver Police Raid Dispensaries," *Westword*, December 14, 2017.

396 Sigmund Freud, *Civilization and its Discontents,* trans. Joan Riviere (Blacksburg, VA: Wilder Publications Inc., 2010), 14-17.

397 Freud, *Civilization and its Discontents,* 14-17.

398 Johann Hari, *Chasing the Scream,* 272.

399 Drug Policy Alliance, *"Approaches to Decriminalizing Drug Use & Possession,"* February, 2015.

400 Michelle Alexander, *The New Jim Crow: Mass Incarceration in the Age of Colorblindness* (New York, NY: The New Press, 2010/2012), 124.

401 Benjamin Boyce, *Discourses of Deception: (Re)Examining America's War on Drugs,* Dissertation, ProQuest, 2018.

402 Raj Chetty, et. al., "Race and Economic Opportunity in the United State: An Intergenerational Perspective," *Quarterly Journal of Economics 135,* (2): May 20202.

403 Raj Chetty, et. al., "Race and Economic Opportunity in the United State: An Intergenerational Perspective," *Quarterly Journal of Economics 135,* (2): May 2020, 711.

404 Hari, *Chasing the Scream,* 249-251. See also Hart, *High Price,* 108-113. See also Sullum, "Everything You've Heard about Crack and Meth is Wrong." See also James A. Inciardi, "Legalizing Drugs: Would it Really Reduce Violent Crime?" in *The Drug Legalization Debate, Second Edition,* ed. James A Inciardi (Thousand Oaks, CA: Sage Publications, Inc., 1999), 55-74

405 Brian Vastag, "5 Years After: Portugal's Drug Decriminalization Policy Shows Positive Results," *Scientific America,* (April 7, 2009).

406 A Pretext Traffic Stop (or Terry Pat for a pedestrian) is the process of pulling someone over for a small, real infraction which is only a pretext for investigating a different crime which an officer believes might be occurring. See Whren v US, 1996. See also Brian O'Donnell, "Whren v. United States: An Abrupt End to the Debate over Pretextual Stops," *Maine Law Review 49,* (7), 1997.

407 Carl Hart, *Drug Use for Grown Ups: Chasing Liberty in the Land of Fear* (New York: Penguin Press, 2021), 61.

408 Maia Szalavitz, *Undoing Drugs: The Untold Story of Harm Reduction and the Future of Addiction* (New York: Hachette Books, 2021).

409 Maia Szalavitz, *Undoing Drugs: The Untold Story of Harm Reduction and the Future of Addiction* (New York: Hachette Books, 2021).

410 Ronald Sullivan, "Needle-Exchangers Had Right to Break the Law, Judge Rules," *New York Times,* June 26, 1991.

411 Quote from William Shakespeare, *Hamlet* (play), 1609.

412 Samuel Maull, "Judge Acquits ACT UP Defendants on Needle Exchange Charges," *Associated Press News,* June 25, 1991.

413 Alex Kreit, "Safe Injection Sites and the Federal 'Crack House' Statute," *Boston College Law Review 60,* (2): 2019.

Chapter Five

414 Tupac Shakur, "Only God can Judge me," from *All Eyez on Me* (Las Angeles, Ca: Can-Am Studies, 1996).

415 Bill Yousman, "Challenging the Media-Incarceration Complex through Media Education," in *Working for Justice: A Handbook of Prison Education and Activism,* ed. Stephen J. Hartnett, et. al., (Urbana, IL: University of Illinois Press, 2013). See also Travis Dixon, "Teaching you to Love Fear: Television News and Racial Stereotypes in a Punishing Democracy," in *Challenging the Prison-Industrial Complex: Activism, Arts and Educational Alternative,* ed. Stephen J. Hartnett (Urbana, IL: University of Illinois Press, 2011). See also Travis Dixon, "Good Guys are Still Always White? Positive Change and Continued Misrepresentations of Race and Crime on Local Television News," *Communication Research 44,* (6), April 2015.

416 LSD is the acronym and moniker for the hallucinogenic drug Lysergic acid diethylamide. See Ed Prideaux, "Timothy Leary Turns 100: America's LSD Messiah, Remembered by Those who Knew Him," *Vice,* October 23, 2020.

417 Nathaniel Hiatt, *"A Trip Down Memory Lane: LSD at Harvard,"* The Harvard Crimson, March 23, 2016. See also Jennifer Ulrich, *The Timothy Leary Project: Inside the Great Counterculture Experiment* (New York: Elephant Book Company, 2018).

418 For a detailed description of set and setting, see Maia Szalavitz, "Set and Setting," in *Unbroken Brain: A Revolutionary New Way of Understanding Addiction* (New York: St. Martin's Press, 2016): 122-137.

419 Katharine Seip-Cammack, "Tolerance and Sensitization to Chronic Escalating-Dose Heroin Following Extended Withdrawal in Fischer Rats: Possible Role of Mu-Opioid Receptors," *Psychopharmacology 225,* (1), January 2013.

420 Shepard Siegel, et. al., "Heroin 'Overdose' Death: Contribution of Drug-Associated Environmental Cues," *Science 216,* (4544): April 1982.

421 Jennifer Ulrich, *The Timothy Leary Project: Inside the Great Counterculture Experiment* (New York: Elephant Book Company, 2018).

422 Michael Pollan, *How to Change your Mind: What the New Science of Psychedelics Teaches us about Consciousness, Dying, Addiction, Depression, and Transcendence* (New York: Penguin Press, 2018).

423 Martin Angst, et. al., "Aversive and Reinforcing Opioid Effects: A Pharmacogenomic Twin Study," *Anesthesiology 117*, (1): 2012.

424 "Psychonaut" is a combination of astronaut and psychedelic used to describe people who frequently and eagerly consume psychedelic drugs. It was first coined by German author Ernst Jünger.

425 See Ben Sessa, "MDMA," *The Dr. Junkie Show* (podcast), Episode 9: July 12, 2020.

426 Sigmund Freud, *The Cocaine Papers*, ed. Robert Byck, (New York: Stonehill Publishing, 1974), 50-58.

427 David Cohen, *Freud on Coke*, (U.K.: Cutting Edge Press, 2011), 19-28.

428 Quote from Sigmund Freud, *On Narcissism: An Introduction* (Public Source, online), 5. Sigmund Freud, "Psycho-Analysis and Psychiatry," Lecture XVI in Sigmund Freud, *Introductory Lectures on Psychoanalysis*, trans,. & ed. James Strachey, (New York: W. W. Norton & Co., 1989), 303-305. See also Sigmund Freud, *The Interpretation of Dreams*, Preface to the Third Edition.

429 Dr. Leary's Congressional Testimony is perhaps the most well-known example of his public endorsement of drug use and demands for legalization. See Timothy F. Leary v. United States, No. 65, argued December 11-12, 1968. Jennifer Ulrich, *The Timothy Leary Project: Inside the Great Counterculture Experiment* (New York: Elephant Book Company, 2018).

430 Sigmund Freud, *The Future of an Illusion*, trans. James Strachey, (W. W. Norton & Co.: New York, 1961). See also Sigmund Freud, *Totem and Taboo*, trans. A. A. Brill, (New York: Dover Publication Co., 1918/1998). See also Sigmund Freud, *Introductory Lectures on Psycho-Analysis*, trans. James Stanchey, (New York: W. W. Norton & Company, 1966, lectures "The Archaic Features and Infantilism of Dreams," (248) and "The Sexual Life of Human Beings," (385).

431 Sigmund Freud, *Totem and Taboo*, trans. A. A. Brill, (New York: Dover Publication Co., 1918/1998), 75-77.

432 Peter Muris, "Freud was Right…About the Origins of Abnormal Behavior," *Journal of Child and Family Studies 15*, (1): February 24, 2006.

433 Sam Harris, *Free Will* (New York: Free Press, 2012), 5.

434 Sigmund Freud, *Totem and Taboo*, trans. A. A. Brill, (New York: Dover Publication Co., 1918/1998), 58-62. See also Sigmund Freud, "Children's Dreams," lecture from *Introductory Lectures on Psycho-Analysis*, trans. James Strachey, (New York: W. W. Norton & Company, 1963/1989):154-166.

435 Frederick Wertz, "Qualitative Inquiry in the History of Psychology," *Qualitative Psychology 1*, 2014. See also Wilhelm Wundt, *And Introduction to Psychology* (2020/1912).

436 Sigmund Freud, "The Common Neurotic State," in *Introductory Lectures on Psycho-Analysis*, trans. James Strachey, (New York: W. W. Norton & Company, 1963/1989): 469-486.

437 Sigmund Freud, "Psycho-Analysis and Psychiatry," in *Introductory Lectures on Psycho-Analysis*, trans. James Strachey, (New York: W. W. Norton & Company, 1963/1989): 301-317.

438 Sigmund Freud, "Psycho-Analysis and Psychiatry," in *Introductory Lectures on Psycho-Analysis*, trans. James Strachey, (New York: W. W. Norton & Company, 1963/1989): 301-317.

439 Jeff Hawkins, et. al., "Why Neurons have Thousands of Synapses, a Theory of Sequence Memory in Neocortex," *Frontiers in Neural Circuits 10*, (23), 2016. See also Jeff Hawkins, et. al., "A Theory of how Columns in the Neocortex Enable Learning the Structure of the World," *Frontiers in Neural Circuits*, 2017.

440 Clever readers will note I have already violated the game's rules by calling up terms from memory in an effort to make the navigation of space easier and less time consuming (knob, latch, engineer, and open).

441 Richard Dawkins, *The Selfish Gene* (New York: Oxford University Press, 1976).

442 Richard Dawkins, *The Blind Watchmaker: Why the Evidence of Evolution Reveals a Universe Without Design* (New York/London: W. W. Norton & Company, 1996/1986), 62.

443 Daniel Simberloff, et. al., "Now you See Them, Now you Don't!—Population Crashes of Established Introduced Species," *Biological Invasions 6*: (2004).

444 Sigmund Freud, *Totem and Taboo*, trans. A. A. Brill, (New York: Dover Publication Co., 1918/1998), 58-62. See also Sigmund Freud, "Children's Dreams," lecture from *Introductory Lectures on Psycho-Analysis*, trans. James Strachey, (New York: W. W. Norton & Company, 1963/1989):154-166.

445 Leary's *"Great Neurological Robbery"* speech from UCLA, January 18, 1967.

446 Leary's *"Great Neurological Robbery"* speech from UCLA, January 18, 1967.

447 Iain McGilchrist, *The Master and His Emissary: The Divided Brain and the Making of the Western World* (London: Yale University Press, 2009/2019).

448 Orla Muldoon, et. al., "The Social Psychology of Responses to Trauma: Social Identity Pathways Associated with Divergent Traumatic Responses," *European Review of Social Psychology, 30*, (1): 2019.

449 Orla Muldoon, et. al., "The Social Psychology of Responses to Trauma: Social Identity Pathways Associated with Divergent Traumatic Responses," *European Review of Social Psychology, 30*, (1):

2019.

450 Iain McGilchrist, *The Master and His Emissary: The Divided Brain and the Making of the Western World* (London: Yale University Press, 2009/2019).

451 For a great discussion of mindfulness and our brain's tendency to mislead us, see Iain McGilchrist, *The Master and His Emissary: The Divided Brain and the Making of the Western World* (London: Yale University Press, 2009/2019).

452 If you are looking for a place to begin, check out Sam Harris's "Waking Up" Mindful Meditation app.

453 Sam Harris, *Making Sense* (podcast), episode 241, "Final Thoughts on Free Will," March 12, 2021.

454 Maia Szalavitz, *Unbroken Brain: A Revolutionary New Way of Understanding Addiction* (New York: St. Martin's Press, 2016), 80-92. See also Carles Muntaner, et. al., "Socioeconomic Position and Major Mental Disorders," *Epidemiological Reviews 26*, (1): 2004.

455 Maia Szalavitz, *Unbroken Brain: A Revolutionary New Way of Understanding Addiction* (New York: St. Martin's Press, 2016), 38.

456 Martin Angst, et. al., "Aversive and Reinforcing Opioid Effects: A Pharmacogenomic Twin Study," *Anesthesiology 117*, (1): 2012.

457 Ronald Abrahams, et. al., "Rooming-In Compared with Standard Care for Newborns of Mothers Using Methadone or Heroin," *Canadian Family Physicians 53*, (10): October 2007.

458 Ronald Abrahams, et. al., "Rooming-In Compared with Standard Care for Newborns of Mothers Using Methadone or Heroin," *Canadian Family Physicians 53*, (10): October 2007.

459 Alcoholics Anonymous goals laid out in Alcoholics Anonymous, *Twelve Steps and Twelve Traditions* (New York: Fortieth Printing, 1952/2004).

460 Maia Szalavitz, *Undoing Drugs: The Untold Story of Harm Reduction and the Future of Addiction* (New York: Hachette Books, 2021). See also Carl Hart, *Drug Use for Grown Ups: Chasing Liberty in the Land of Fear* (New York: Penguin Press, 2021).

461 12-Step Programs are the most common type of substance use treatment programs in the United States, and they all rely, to some degree, on the Alcoholics Anonymous goals laid out in Alcoholics Anonymous, *Twelve Steps and Twelve Traditions* (New York: Fortieth Printing, 1952/2004).

462 Many 12-step programs user chips, tokens or coins to commemorate various stages of sobriety, from one day to fifty years.

463 Stefan Bode, et. al., "Tracking the Unconscious Generation of Free Decisions Using Ultra-High Field fMRI," *PLoS One 6*, (6): June 27, 2011.

464 Sam Harris, *Free Will* (New York: Free Press, 2012). See also Roy Baumeister, et. al., "*Do Conscious Thoughts Cause Behavior?*" *Annual Review of Psychology 62*, (1): January 2011.

465 Roy Baumeister, et. al., "*Do Conscious Thoughts Cause Behavior?*" *Annual Review of Psychology 62*, (1): January 2011.

466 Kenneth Burke, *A Grammar of Motives* (Berkeley, CA: University of California Press, 1945).

467 Sam Harris performed a similar experiment using "pick a city…" on a crowd at the Distinguished Science Lecture Series, March 12, 2012.

468 Sam Harris, *Free Will* (New York: Free Press, 2012), 20.

469 Roy Baumeister, et. al., "*Do Conscious Thoughts Cause Behavior?*" *Annual Review of Psychology 62*, (1): January 2011. See also Lynn Paul, et. al., "*Agenesis of the Corpus Callosum: Genetic, Developmental and Functional Aspects of Connectivity*," *Nature Reviews Neuroscience 8*, 2007.

470 Ragesh Panikkath, et. al., "*The Alien Hand Syndrome*," *Baylor University Medical Center Proceedings 27*, (3): July 2014.

471 F. Aboitiz, X. Carrasco, et. al., "The Alien Hand Syndrome: Classification of Forms Reported and Discussion of a New Condition," *Neurological Sciences 24*, (2003). Ragesh Panikkath, et. al., "*The Alien Hand Syndrome*," *Baylor University Medical Center Proceedings 27*, (3): July 2014.

472 F. Aboitiz, X. Carrasco, et. al., "The Alien Hand Syndrome: Classification of Forms Reported and Discussion of a New Condition," *Neurological Sciences 24*, (2003).

473 Ragesh Panikkath, et. al., "*The Alien Hand Syndrome*," *Baylor University Medical Center Proceedings 27*, (3): July 2014.

474 Howard Rosen, "Anosognosia in Neurodegenerative Disease," *Neurocase 17*, (3): 2011.

475 V. S. Ramachandran, "The Evolutionary Biology of Self-Deception, Laughter, Dreaming and Depression: Some Clues from Anosognosia," *Medical Hypotheses 47*, (5), November 1996. See also V. S. Ramachandran, "*Anosognosia: The Interface Between Neurology, Psychiatry and Psychoanalysis,*" lecture given at The 5th Neuro-Psychoanalysis Congress, (Rome: 2004).

476 V. S. Ramachandran, "The Evolutionary Biology of Self-Deception, Laughter, Dreaming and Depression: Some Clues from Anosognosia," *Medical Hypotheses 47*, (5), November 1996. See also V. S. Ramachandran, "Anosognosia in Parietal Lobe Syndrome," *Consciousness and Cognition 4*, (1), March 1995.

477 V. S. Ramachandran, "*Anosognosia: The Interface Between Neurology, Psychiatry and Psychoanalysis,*" lecture given at The 5th Neuro-Psychoanalysis Congress, (Rome: 2004).

478 Victoria Rosen, "One Brain. Two Minds? Many Questions," *Journal of Undergraduate Neuroscience*

Education 16, (2), 2018.

479 Lynn Paul, et. al. "Agenesis of the Corpus Callosum: Genetic, Developmental and Functional Aspects of Connectivity," *Nature Reviews Neuroscience 8*, 2007.

480 Sam Harris, *Waking Up: A Guide to Spirituality without Religion* (New York: Simon & Schuster, 2014). See also Iain McGilchrist, *The Master and His Emissary: The Divided Brain and the Making of the Western World* (London: Yale University Press, 2009/2019).

481 Iain McGilchrist, *The Master and His Emissary: The Divided Brain and the Making of the Western World* (London: Yale University Press, 2009/2019). For a revealing interview, see Sam Harris and Iain McGilchrist, *Making Sense* (podcast), episode 243, "The Divided Mind."

482 Jean Séguin, "The Frontal Lobe and Aggression," *European Journal of Developmental Psychology 6*, (1): June 2014.

483 Iain McGilchrist, *The Master and His Emissary: The Divided Brain and the Making of the Western World* (London: Yale University Press, 2009/2019).

484 Marcel Kinsbourne, "The Corpus Callosum Equilibrates the Cerebral Hemispheres," in *The Parallel Brain: The Cognitive Neuroscience of the Corpus Callosum*, edited by Eran Zaidel, et. al., (Cambridge, MA: The Mit Press, 2003): 271-281.

485 Iain McGilchrist uses a similar example of a bird eating food off the ground while also paying attention to its surroundings in *The Master and His Emissary: The Divided Brain and the Making of the Western World* (London: Yale University Press, 2009/2019).

486 Iain McGilchrist, *The Master and His Emissary: The Divided Brain and the Making of the Western World* (London: Yale University Press, 2009/2019), 126.

487 Iain McGilchrist, *The Master and His Emissary: The Divided Brain and the Making of the Western World* (London: Yale University Press, 2009/2019).

488 Sam Harris and Iain McGilchrist, *Making Sense* (podcast), episode 243, "The Divided Mind."

489 Elkhonon Goldberg, "Hemisphere Differences in the Acquisition and Use of Descriptive Systems," *Brain and Language 14*, (1): September 1981.

490 Iain McGilchrist, *The Master and His Emissary: The Divided Brain and the Making of the Western World* (London: Yale University Press, 2009/2019).

491 Guido Gainotti, "The Relationship Between Anatomical and Cognitive Locus of Lesion in Category-Specific Disorders," in *Category Specificity in Brain and Mind*, edited by Emer Forde, et. al., (Londong: Psychology Press, 2002): 403-404.

492 Iain McGilchrist, *The Master and His Emissary: The Divided Brain and the Making of the Western World* (London: Yale University Press, 2009/2019), 3.

493 David Wolman, *"The Split Brain: A Tale of Two Halves,"* *Nature 483*, March 2012. See also Iain Mcgilchrist, *The Master and His Emissary.*

494 David Wolman, *"The Split Brain: A Tale of Two Halves,"* *Nature 483*, March 2012. Sam Harris and Iain McGilchrist, *Making Sense* (podcast), episode 243, "The Divided Mind."

495 Iain McGilchrist, *The Master and His Emissary: The Divided Brain and the Making of the Western World* (London: Yale University Press, 2009/2019). See also Sam Harris, *Free Will* (New York: Free Press, 2012).

496 The right hemisphere is aware of the left's existence, but the left hemisphere, where language is compiled into speech, is not aware of the right's existence. See Iain McGilchrist, *The Master and His Emissary: The Divided Brain and the Making of the Western World* (London: Yale University Press, 2009/2019).

497 US Federal Government, Datalab, *"Federal Spending by Category and Agency,"* 2019.

498 A similar argument was made by Sam Harris, in *Free Will* (New York: Free Press, 2012).

499 Tupac Shakur, *"Interview with Tanya Hart,"* (Six CINQ, 1992).

Epilogue

500 From *Lady Sings the Blues* with William Dufty, (New York: Lancer Books, 1956/1972), 114.

About the Author

Benjamin Boyce grew up in Battle Creek, Michigan. He spent his first decade as an adult running the streets, shooting dope and hustling up enough cash for his next fix. Following an arrested in 2004, he was sentenced to prison for stealing to support his habit. After being granted paroled in 2005, he enrolled in college, completed a master's degree and then a PhD in Communication, and devoted himself to the study of drugs and the war against them. He now teaches college classes in Denver, Colorado, on the University campus, and in local prisons, where incarcerated students learn the same theory as those in traditional classrooms.

Apprentice House Press

Loyola University Maryland

Apprentice House is the country's only campus-based, student-staffed book publishing company. Directed by professors and industry professionals, it is a nonprofit activity of the Communication Department at Loyola University Maryland.

Using state-of-the-art technology and an experiential learning model of education, Apprentice House publishes books in untraditional ways. This dual responsibility as publishers and educators creates an unprecedented collaborative environment among faculty and students, while teaching tomorrow's editors, designers, and marketers.

Outside of class, progress on book projects is carried forth by the AH Book Publishing Club, a co-curricular campus organization supported by Loyola University Maryland's Office of Student Activities.

Eclectic and provocative, Apprentice House titles intend to entertain as well as spark dialogue on a variety of topics. Financial contributions to sustain the press's work are welcomed. Contributions are tax deductible to the fullest extent allowed by the IRS.

To learn more about Apprentice House books or to obtain submission guidelines, please visit www.apprenticehouse.com.

Apprentice House
Communication Department
Loyola University Maryland
4501 N. Charles Street
Baltimore, MD 21210
410-617-5265
info@apprenticehouse.com • www.apprenticehouse.com